The Control
of Aggression and Violence

Cognitive and Physiological Factors

PERSONALITY AND PSYCHOPATHOLOGY

A Series of Monographs, Texts, and Treatises

The Control
of Aggression and Violence
Cognitive and Physiological Factors

Edited by *JEROME L. SINGER*

CENTER FOR RESEARCH IN COGNITION AND AFFECT
GRADUATE DIVISION
CITY UNIVERSITY OF NEW YORK
NEW YORK, NEW YORK

ACADEMIC PRESS   New York and London   1971

ACADEMIC PRESS, INC.
111 Fifth Avenue, New York, New York 10003

United Kingdom Edition published by
ACADEMIC PRESS, INC. (LONDON) LTD.
Berkeley Square House, London W1X 6BA

LIBRARY OF CONGRESS CATALOG CARD NUMBER: 75-154363

PRINTED IN THE UNITED STATES OF AMERICA

*To my parents who taught me to shun violence
and welcome reason and compassion*

Contents

Chapter III.   The Physiology of Aggression and the Implications for Aggression Control

K. E. Moyer

Chapter IV.   The Learning and Unlearning of Aggression: The Role of Anxiety, Empathy, Efficacy, and Prosocial Values

Ervin Staub

Chapter V.   The Role of Inhibition in the Assessment and Understanding of Violence

Edwin I. Megargee

Chapter VI. **The Study and Modification of Intra-Familial Violence**

Morton Bard

LIST OF CONTRIBUTORS

Numbers in parentheses indicate the pages on which the authors' contributions begin.

MORTON BARD (149), The City College, The City University of New York, New York, New York

ARNOLD H. BUSS (7), University of Texas, Austin, Texas

EDWIN I. MEGARGEE (125), Psychology Department, Florida State University, Tallahassee, Florida

K. E. MOYER (61), Carnegie-Mellon University, Pittsburgh, Pennsylvania

JEROME L. SINGER (1, 19), Center for Research in Cognition and Affect Graduate Division, City University of New York, New York, New York

ERVIN STAUB (93), Department of Social Relations, Harvard University, Cambridge, Massachusetts

PREFACE

Few topics have generated more intense discussion and argument in recent years than the subject of the nature of man's aggressive behavior toward his fellow man. There is indeed much need for discussion and evaluation of this problem at the philosophical and ethical level. At the same time it is also necessary that we scrutinize in close detail the actual scientific evidence relating to the expression, origins, and psychological ramifications of violent or aggressive behavior in children and adults. The present volume grew out of a conference on this topic held at the Center for Research in Cognition and Affect of the City University of New York. The intent in organizing the conference was to bring together a group of individuals who had engaged in personal research activity attempting to pin down more precisely the significant aspects of human aggressive behavior or of its physiological origins. The question raised was: What scientific data or formal knowledge do we have about man's cognitive or physiological functions which can help us move toward controlling or inhibiting the destructive violence of the individual?

What was felt to be especially important in organizing the conference and what is a unique feature of the volume that has grown from it is the concern with systematic analysis of the parameters of aggressive action, the formal experimental study of relevant theories related to such behavior, and the expression of the data and implications therefrom in a reasoned, relatively dispassionate manner which can permit further scientific discourse rather than fostering tendentious disputation. It is because of the very heat generated on this topic that a book is needed both for the professional in psychology, psychiatry, or social work and for the graduate or undergraduate student, and perhaps as well the intelligent layman.

By focusing the discussion primarily upon the control of cognitive and physiological aspects of violence and aggression an attempt has been made to indicate exactly how precise research can be carried out upon very fundamental human behavior. This accounts for one of the limitations of this volume, namely its minimal emphasis on sociological and economic or political aspects of the problem. On the other hand, the strength of this point of view is that it focuses directly upon the individual and his personal contribution to any particular encounter that may lead to overt aggression. A major feature of the research and theoretical discussions that go on at the Center for Research in Cognition and Affect is the close relationship between the way in which someone feels about things and his motivation toward specific actions. This relationship between the processing of information which is perhaps the single most significant task of the human organism and the experiencing of a great range of emotions from rage through surprise and joy represents a special point of view in the research of the Center. It is also an area surprisingly neglected in much discussion of the subject of aggression which has emphasized more often than not somewhat obscure "instinctual" tendencies, man's "animal nature," and other features of behavior related to presumed primordial emotional tendencies. The group of investigators here are dealing primarily with man in his more advanced stage as both a cognitive and conative or emotional creature. In this sense this volume should be of particular value to graduate students in the mental health fields and to advanced undergraduates who have the responsibility of exploring in depth what psychology's actual contribution as a scientific discipline can be toward confronting a problem of such magnitude. In these days when the word "relevance" is often bandied about rather loosely, no topic can be more relevant than this. At the same time it is especially important that the young reader first confronted with the approaches of a formal discipline such as psychology is made aware of exactly how the field is in position to approach a topic of this complexity.

This book then is not a simplified presentation of psychological approaches to controlling and understanding aggression and violence. While it is not by any means a formal detailing of research in the manner in which it appears in professional journals, it makes no pretense of being a watering down of the critical material. Rather it strives to make clear in a relatively careful fashion just what the actual problems are that confront the investigator who seeks to study a problem such as violence and just what practical and methodological means are available for addressing the questions that serious scientists can raise. The focus of the volume is not really upon controversy as it is upon a sophisticated and mature approach to scrutiny of the issues by means of the scientific method. One hope of any gathering of papers such as this is not only its value in teaching but the likelihood that it will inspire further research efforts by readers. In this sense the papers presented indicate important directions that research can take on this problem rather than addressing the issues raised by each preceding chapter. The instructor making use of this volume for graduate or undergraduate teaching can feel free to assign specific chapters in a different order than their inclusion here in order to make his own particular point concerning the research issues raised.

ACKNOWLEDGMENTS

The editor wishes to express his appreciation to members of the Center for Research in Cognition and Affect, Harold Proshansky, Dean of the Graduate Division, and Professors John Antrobus, Charles Smith, Stanley Milgram, Sydney Segal, William Ittelson, and Leonard Kogan who collaborated in various aspects of organizing the conference on aggression and violence. Valuable assistance in preparation of the manuscript came from Miss Bonnie Kamil who prepared the index and from the staff of Academic Press. Helpful clerical services were provided by Mrs. Terry Conover, Mrs. Violet Levine, and Miss Alkmini Bitsis. Some of the material presented in Chapter II was derived from research supported by National Institute of Mental Health Grant MH-10956 and by the Research Department of the National Broadcasting Company.

THE PSYCHOLOGICAL STUDY OF AGGRESSION

JEROME L. SINGER

CITY UNIVERSITY OF NEW YORK

Throughout 1969 the National Commission on the Causes and Prevention of Violence has issued a series of reports depicting in vivid detail the historical roots and political, economic, and social correlates of violence in the United States. In grim counterpoint to the documentation and scholarly objectivity of these reports have been the news reports of continued warfare in Vietnam, the sickening shock of the Songmay massacre, increased evidence of street crime, and incidents of bizarre but no less horrible violence such as the "hippy" murder cult in California. Faced with this overwhelming load of information, one may be tempted to engage in a kind of massive denial mechanism almost to maintain sanity. Indeed it might be argued that psychologists and many other behavioral scientists have for most of this century avoided research or scientific scrutiny of the most urgent human problems surrounding man's capacity to harm others.

Even though Sigmund Freud after World War I dared to look man's aggression and his destructive potential full in the face, he still found little constructive to offer for studying what he now regarded as a fundamental human drive. When Albert Einstein wrote to him as one scientist to another asking what psychoanalysis or psychology could offer to the prevention of future wars, Freud was rather pessimistic and inconclusive in response. While early in the century the psychologists like William McDougall called attention to the desirability of man's socializing his instinct for "pugnacity" and William James proposed constructive youth programs as the "moral equivalent of war," their younger colleagues turned their attention to exploring the parameters of the conditioned reflex or the maze-running of white rats. The examination of the nature of man's aggression was left to writers, a few criminologists or psychiatrists with limited data collecting resources, or to the speculations of the psychoanalysts.

Despite these early calls for attention to the problem of aggression by leading psychological theorists, surprisingly little formal research was carried out until well into the 1930's. With the publication of the studies of frustration and aggression by the brilliant Yale group of Dollard, Doob, Miller, Mowrer, & Sears (1939) a way was opened for the empirical study of the causes and concomitants of aggressive behavior. Much of the initial work was oriented towards animal studies under carefully controlled conditions but gradually the possibilities broadened. The controversy over the degree to which aggression may be regarded as a fundamental drive, pressing for discharge or a well-established response to the frustration of intentions has been reviewed recently by Berkowitz (1969). Certainly there has been a valuable increase of useful research on this problem especially in the past decade.

Indeed, most of the research on human aggression has been carried out in the past ten years. It is as if psychologists are at last willing to look at the ugliness of much human behavior. Sociologists, criminologists, psychiatrists, and political scientists have of course provided ample documentation of the gross levels of human aggression or of the extreme forms of violence in unusual human beings, but psychology has only relatively recently addressed itself through its experimental technology to the manifestations of aggression in relatively normal individuals. The present volume represents an effort to bring together investigators whose research work and scholarly activities have been especially oriented around the issue of analyzing the nature of aggressive behavior in individual adults and children and in establishing psychological bases for controlling aggressive acts or providing alternatives for it.

The setting for the conference from which the papers in this volume are drawn was the Center for Research in Cognition and Affect at the City University of New York. A major focus of the Center's activity is the exploration of how the information-processing capacities of man are intertwined with his emotional structure. The stimulus for the 1969 conference was the desire to bring together investigators who could make some contribution to the question of how aggressive behavior can be controlled, limited, or eliminated by a fuller understanding of its nature in relation to the ways in which man organizes the complex information from his environment and reacts affectively while carrying on this fundamental organismic operation. Clearly, there are many other approaches to limiting aggression through broader social programs, improved negotiation strategies (Deutsch, 1969), or gross political reorientations (Graham & Gurr, 1969). The emphasis in this series of papers is more upon the ways in which current research knowledge can be applied to controlling or limiting *individual* tendencies toward aggressive reaction.

The investigators who present their work at this conference are all deeply committed to the careful experimental study of the phenomena surrounding overt aggression. While not afraid of speculation, they are agreed that we need to carry out considerable systematic research examining the parameters of aggressive responses in reasonably controlled situations in order to provide reasonably precise data on which theories can be constructed. Even the action-oriented work of Dr. Bard (Chapter VI) on the training of police is cast within a setting that permits data collection on important manifestations of aggressive behavior in families. This empirical emphasis is a desperately needed contrast to the years of speculation and grossly emotional discussions of aggression which have often been taken as scientific fact by clinical psychologists, social workers, psychiatrists, or others working with the emotionally-disturbed or with adults or children manifesting outbursts of aggressive action.

One outgrowth of the kind of careful empiricism demonstrated by the investigators in this conference is a change in the way one formulates the origins and nature of aggression. By far the most widely accepted notion of aggression among practical workers in the field of mental health, especially, and in political science and social organization, as well, has been the view that aggression is a fundamental human drive. Designated as an instinct by McDougall in his 1908 "Social Psychology" or as a fundamental biological motive by Freud in his concept of "Thanatos" aggression emerges as an inevitable disposition of man. Freud's emphasis on hydraulic energy models led to the description of aggression as a rising pressure which had to be discharged periodically or diverted into other channels temporarily to slow the pressure for discharge. While many of Freud's strongest adherents (e.g., Otto Fenichel) could not accept this view of the pressure towards destruction in man, others such as Karl Menninger popularized the notion (Menninger, 1942) and built it into the curriculum of psychiatric training. More recently Lorenz (1966) and Ardrey (1966) have used ethological data to support views of a periodic instinctive aggression in man, and the popularity of their writings testifies to the widespread tendency to accept this hydraulic-energy model of man's destructiveness.

The contributors to the present volume represent by contrast a mainstream of careful investigators in sociology, political science, and psychology who can find no evidence to support a drive theory of aggression. Rather than viewing man as an energy system periodically discharging aggressive or sexual forces, they are inclined to view aggressive behavior as an expression of one of man's broad repertory of potential reactions to a variety of external circumstances. The social, cultural, and political forces conducive to overt aggressive expressions have been well demonstrated in the Graham and Gurr (1969) report, *Violence in America*. It is hard to attribute a fundamental drive toward violence in humans when there is evidence that murder is far more common among the two million inhabitants of Manhattan than among the forty million inhabitants of the British Isles. The far greater aggressive behavior among men than women raises questions about its instinctive role. Efforts to deal with women's lack of overt aggression by attributing masochistic intropunitive tendencies based on psychosexual dynamics are no longer convincing. The fact that the greatest personal violence (as contrasted with socially sanctioned military violence) occurs within the bosom of the family suggests that aggressive behavior is more closely tied to the emotional consequences of frustration of hopes, images, and day-to-day stresses among people who have important, complex relationships.

Recent work on the nature of brain function, on the importance of curiosity, competence, and mastery in human motivation, on the importance of rates of processing unfamiliar information in producing or reducing negative or positive emotion, and on the significance of environmental cues or adult and peer models in producing specific behaviors all lead to a more complex model of aggressive behavior than the older hydraulic energy model. If one adopts a position such as that proposed by Izard and Tomkins (1966), for example, which describes personality as a complex organization of five subsystems, homeostatic, drive, affect, cognitive, and motor, a more subtle approach to aggression is possible. While the contributors to this conference may not subscribe to the specific structure proposed by Izard and Tomkins or to the earlier analysis of the relation of drive to affect carried out by Tomkins (1962) they are all operating within a framework consistent with this view. They stress the way in which the *interpretation* of situations (a cognitive function) interacts with a limited but differentiated affect system in producing an ultimate motor reaction. Buss (Chapter I), for example, demonstrates the ways in which aggression can be "taught" or can be self-limited depending on the meaning of the target of aggression, e.g., men don't attack women. Moyer (Chapter III) analyzes the physiological bases of the emotion of anger and its relation to the information available to the organism and to the context. Staub (Chapter IV) provides examples of how training in the recognition and practice of altruism provides alternatives to overt aggression. Bard (Chapter VI) indicates how increased information available to police concerning the nature of family life in different cultures as well as training in alternative responses for intervening in family quarrels can break the chain of aggression and counteraggression so often found in the behavior of police. The manner in which one construes a situation, the available alternatives within the individual's behavioral repertoire, and the complexity rate or persistence of new information to be processed which generates specific emotions such as surprise, fear, interest, anger, or joy all operate to determine the ultimate motor response.

The advantages of a systems analysis approach (sketched here in most rudimentary form) opens the way for a more effective ultimate approach to diagnosing the likelihood of an aggressive response or to controlling the occurrence of the response. One can begin to approach the control of individual aggression by determining which personality subsystem can be most effectively altered to produce a desired reduction in the likelihood of aggressive response. Moyer deals with modifications at the physiological level in the affect system, Megargee (Chapter V) in the diagnostic determination of those people whose restricted construction of potential aggressive situations is such as to lead to suddenly extended outbursts, and Singer (Chapter II) indicates how predisposition to imaginative behavior may limit the likelihood of overt aggressive response to television violence. These approaches are just the beginnings really of what may be, in the next decade, a truly significant psychological approach to the control of aggression.

The shock and many horrors of the decade of the 1960's scarcely leave one in an optimistic mood. The cancer of racism in America, the continued warfare in Vietnam, Nigeria, and the Middle East leave little reason to feel that we can envision any massive reduction in the level of violence on this planet in the 1970's. Yet a careful reading of the research and the directions toward control suggested by papers in this volume will indicate that we may be on the threshold of more effective control of aggressive behavior in the individual. The technology for research has at last matured; psychologists are at least eager to address the questions of aggression through research and action-programs; and the investigators seem to be free of the limiting, pessimistic implications of instinctual or drive theories of aggression. This volume will have served its purpose if it generates an even greater spurt of serious research and scientifically controlled community-action programs which are oriented towards providing children and adults with techniques for controlling aggression or with alternative action-tendencies in contexts which have too often elicited only aggression or self defeating destructive behavior.

REFERENCES

Ardrey, R. *The territorial imperative,* New York: Dell, 1966.

Berkowitz, L. *Roots of aggression.* New York: Atherton, 1969.

Deutsch, M. Socially relevant science. Reflections on some studies of interpersonal conflict. *American Psychologist,* 1969, **24,** 1076–1092.

Dollard, J., Doob, L., Miller, N., Mowrer, O., & Sears, R. *Frustration and Aggression.* New Haven, Conn.: Yale Univer. Press, 1939.

Graham, H. D. & Gurr, T. R. Historical and comparative perspectives. *Violence in America.* New York: Signet, 1969.

Izard, C. & Tomkins, S. Anxiety as a negative affect. In Spielberger, C. (Ed.), *Anxiety and behavior.* New York: Academic Press, 1966.

Lorenz, K. *On aggression.* New York: Harcourt, Brace, 1966.

Menninger, K. *Love against hate.* New York: Harcourt, Brace, 1942.

Tomkins, S. *Affect, imagery, consciousness,* Vol. I. New York: Springer, 1962.

CHAPTER I

AGGRESSION PAYS

ARNOLD H. BUSS

UNIVERSITY OF TEXAS

There is a large and significant payoff for aggressing in our society. This paper spells out the assumptions underlying this statement, presents documentation for it, and finally outlines some consequences of it. Thus there are three sections: the general issues concerning human aggression, a report of an experiment, and some implications about aggression and its control.

GENERAL ISSUES

If we examine the aggression of animals, it appears at first that there are many different varieties. Closer examination reveals that animals attack each other with a rather limited arsenal of natural weapons, and the modes of aggression can be counted on the fingers of both hands: biting, clawing, hugging (bears), squeezing (constrictor snakes), hitting, stinging, kicking, butting, spraying (skunk), and "shooting" (porcupine). All these responses share the common property of harming another animal, which is the defining property of animal aggression. Animal aggression is relatively easy to define and identify because it is all physical and direct: the aggressor attacks the victim and inflicts pain or physical damage.

The aggression of humans is not limited by our natural physical equipment. Aggression need not be physical, and the "bite" of verbal aggression may be as sharp (psychologically) as the serpent's sting, as may be documented by any married couple. The victim need not even be present, the punishment being delivered indirectly, as for example when the air is let out of one's tires by an irate neighbor. Nor, in the extreme case, need the aggressor necessarily actively instigate the attack; occasionally inaction is itself a punishment, as for example, in negativism.

These examples point to three dichotomies of aggressive behavior: physical-verbal, active-passive, and direct-indirect. The interaction of the three categories yields eight different types of aggression. Examples of each are presented in Table I. The four types of active aggression are easy to recognize, for they include the majority of human aggressive responses, as well as the most prominent ones. Those listed as passive aggression are not only less common but also less intense. The essence of passive aggression is obstruction of the victim's usual sequences of behavior, and in this sense it is equivalent to frustration. If these examples of frustration are to be included as aggressive responses, they must share properties with the examples of active aggression, and these properties obviously define aggression.

TABLE I
VARIETIES OF HUMAN AGGRESSION

	Active		Passive	
	Direct	Indirect	Direct	Indirect
Physical	Punching the victim	Practical joke booby trap	Obstructing passage, sit-in	Refusing to perform a necessary task
Verbal	Insulting the victim	Malicious gossip	Refusing to speak	Refusing consent, vocal or written

Definition

Many aggressive responses occur in the context of anger, a contingency that has led some persons to equate anger with aggression. The formal definition would be: aggression is any response that occurs when the individual is angry. Further examination shows that this definition will not do. Anger may be followed by a variety of nonaggressive behaviors, including flight, anxiety, depression, or even distraction to other activities. On the other hand, aggression may occur in the total absence of anger: the soldier shooting the enemy may be as calm and unemotional as is the politician (verbally) cutting up his opponent for political office. If anger can occur without aggression and aggression can occur without anger, then anger cannot be a defining property of aggression.

All the varieties of attacking behavior in animals and the eight categories of aggressive behavior in humans share a single property: *one individual delivers noxious stimuli to another.* This definition of aggression makes it nearly equivalent to punishment. All aggression is punishment, but not all instances of punishment are aggression. We conventionally exclude punishing behavior if it occurs in the context of an accepted social role. The parent disciplining his child and the teacher criticizing his student both punish others, but we do not ordinarily classify their behavior as aggressive. Similarly, the judge sentencing a criminal to jail, a surgeon cutting open his patient, and a dentist drilling his patient's teeth are delivering noxious stimuli as part of their social roles and are therefore not called aggressive. In all these examples the punishment is delivered in the hope of achieving ultimate good for the individual or the society, and the noxious stimuli must be placed in this larger perspective.

Of course a potential aggressor can hide behind his social role. A father can beat his child unmercifully in the name of good childrearing practice, a dentist may hurt his patients excessively in the name of good dental practice, or a judge can become a "hanging judge" in the name of protection of society against criminals. There are accepted, if loose and often implicit, standards for appropriate intensities of punishment in these various situations, and when these intensities are exceeded, the behavior is accordingly labeled aggressive. This has implications for the laboratory, as we shall see below.

What about accidents? Noxious stimuli can be delivered by chance, as when one person bumps into another while the two are passing in a hallway. Accidents are easy to identify when it is possible to examine behavior over time: by definition they rarely occur. If I pass you in the hallway a number of times and jostle you once, it is clearly an accident. But if I jostle you several times, the recurrence denies the possibility of accident and it should be labeled as aggression.

More perplexing than accidents is the class of stimuli called *annoyers.* Consider the case of a crowded elevator which contains a man who has just eaten garlic. His merely standing next to me and breathing delivers noxious stimuli, but is this aggression? No, the mere presence of annoyers does not constitute aggression. The punishing stimuli have to be "aimed"; thus if he turned and blew his breath at me, this would be considered aggressive.

Intent

If there is accidental punishment that is not really aggression, there is also accidental *non*-punishment that really is aggression. If I aim a gun, pull the trigger, and the shot misses its mark, no noxious stimuli are actually delivered but this is surely an instance of aggression. Only poor marksmanship or accidental factors prevent the harm from being done, but the attempt is to deliver punishment. Thus aggression may be defined in terms of the *attempt* to deliver noxious stimuli, regardless of whether it is successful.

The issues of accidents, attempts at punishment that misfire, and special classes of social punishment that are not called aggressive—all these concern the issue of intent. How do we infer the aggressive intent of an individual? We can ask him if he means to cause harm, but he may not know, he may be wrong, or he may lie. Yet, the notion of intent, which is very old, implies something inside the head of the responding individual: some future anticipation or some purpose in forthcoming behavior. This is precisely the problem: the philosophical baggage carried along by the term *intent* over the centuries. One solution would be to abandon the term, but an earlier attempt to discard it in defining aggression (Buss, 1961) resulted in considerable muddying of the theoretical waters (Bandura & Walters, 1963; Feshbach, 1964).

An alternative solution is to specify in objective terms the meaning of intent. *Intent is inferred by examining the stimuli antecedent to the response and its consequences.* Consider the behavior sequence in which one boy taunts another, who becomes angry, fights, and hurts his tormenter. The inference of intent to do harm is simple and straightforward. In many instances of aggressive behavior the intent may not be so easy to infer, but the basis of inference remains the same: examining the cues that initiate the aggression. Seen from this perspective, aggression has two major intents: making the victim suffer or the aggressor's acquiring some reinforcer.

Angry Aggression and Instrumental Aggression

It is useful to distinguish two classes of aggression in terms of their reinforcers (Buss, 1961). The first class, *angry aggression,* is initiated by any anger-inducing stimuli: insult, attack, or the presence of annoyers. These are cues for anger, which is followed by aggression, the intent of which is to make the victim suffer. The second class, *instrumental aggression,* is initiated by either competition or a desired reinforcer's being possessed by another person. These are cues for cold-blooded (non-angry) aggression, the intent of which is to win the competition or acquire the reinforcer. The behavioral consequences for the two classes of aggression are outlined in Table II.

Angry aggression has probably been overemphasized in theoretical accounts of aggression. In psychoanalytic terms, aggression is merely the

TABLE II
ANGRY AND INSTRUMENTAL AGGRESSION

	Stimulus	Emotion	Response	Reinforcer ("Intent")
Angry aggression	Anger-inducers: → insult, attack, annoyers, etc.	Anger →	Aggression →	Discomfort of the victim: pain, suffering, embarrassment, etc.
Instrumental aggression	Competition, → a reinforcer possessed by another person	(None) →	Aggression →	Acquisition of the reinforcer: victory, food, money, status, etc.

Sequence →

surface manifestation of underlying angry affects (Fenichel, 1945), and the frustration-aggression hypothesis (Dollard *et al.*, 1939) implicitly assumes that all aggression occurs in the context of anger. Angry aggression is admittedly widespread, and a case may even be made for it on an international scale, as for example, in the attacks by the Arab nations on Israel.

But most aggression appears to be instrumental. Instrumental aggression must be ubiquitous in the usual nature of things because it is the response that tends to guarantee acquiring the reinforcer. Whenever there is competition for rewards, and this is frequent, a variety of nonaggressive responses *might* achieve the rewards. Nevertheless, it is the most powerful aggressor who will surely achieve the rewards, and this appears to hold as well for men as for animals.

The term *instrumental* has been used here to refer to the property of aggression that leads to subsequent rewards, that is, an attacking response that is instrumental in achieving the reinforcer. It shares this property with many other instrumental responses, which means that it can be manipulated by appropriate reinforcers. In everyday life there are many situations in which aggressive behavior is strongly rewarded, and several aspects of the development of masculinity favor the enhancement of aggressive behavior.

Laboratory demonstrations of the effect of rewarding aggression are rare and, with one exception, have used children as subjects. Lovaas (1961) reinforced children for verbal aggression against dolls ("bad doll," "doll should be spanked"), and the number of such responses increased sharply. In a series of experiments Walters and his colleagues reinforced children for striking a large Bobo doll, and again the frequency of this "aggression" rose markedly. Of particular interest was an experiment (Walters & Brown, 1963) which showed that the training with a Bobo doll carried over to a competitive situation, with reinforced children manifesting more aggression than controls.

The only adult experiment, also by Walters (Staples & Walters, 1964), demonstrated that adult women gave more severe electric shocks to another person when reinforced for doing so. Unfortunately, the reinforcement consisted of the experimenter's saying "good." This experimental paradigm (the experimenter's saying "good" after the subject gives one of a limited number of responses) has been challenged as not being operant conditioning. It may with equal justification be regarded as a problem-solving, hypothesis-testing situation (Dulany, 1961), and the issues of awareness and several methodological problems have rendered the technique questionable as an example of how reinforcement shapes human behavior (Holz & Azrin, 1966). So far as the writer knows, there are no published studies that unequivocally demonstrate that adult subjects will aggress more as a function of reinforcement.

AN EXPERIMENT ON REINFORCEMENT OF AGGRESSION

The instrument was an "aggression machine," which allows one person to give electric shocks of varying intensity to another person. The subjects were college men, and the reinforcement was nonverbal and of a type that minimizes awareness.

Apparatus and Procedure

The aggression machine has been described elsewhere (Buss, 1961, 1966). Briefly, the subject playing the role of an experimenter, delivers electric shock to a "subject," who is really an experimental accomplice (hereafter called *the victim*). In the bogus learning task the victim makes mistakes which are to be signaled by shock; the total number of mistakes per subject is 35, which means there are 35 opportunities to shock.

There are 10 shock buttons and intensity increases steeply from 1 to 10. The real subject is first given shock from buttons 1, 2, 3 and 5 so that he will know the painfulness of the shock he later delivers. The shock from button 1 can barely be felt; that from button 2 is mild; that from button 3 hurts; and that from button 5 is rather painful. He is told that the intensity increases at the same rate for buttons 6 through 10. By extrapolation the shock from button 10 would knock the victim out of his chair, but these circuits are not even connected. Fuses protect against any possibility of real harm, and the victim does not actually receive the electric shock.

Pain sensitivity is one determinant of the intensity of shocks administered (the greater the sensitivity, the less intense the shock given later), and it must be controlled. Each subject rates the shock from button 5 on a 70-point scale ranging from Can't Feel It to Extremely Painful. If the rating is either extremely high or extremely low, the subject is told that there has been some "drift" in the apparatus and that it must be reset. A rheostat is then adjusted, lowering voltage for pain-sensitive subjects and raising it for pain-insensitive subjects. Shock is again administered from buttons 1, 2, 3 and 5, and again the subject rates the shock from button 5. The rare subject who does not then rate it in the middle range is not used in the research. This procedure has been found to eliminate the relationship between pain sensitivity and intensity of shock (the correlation was −.01).

The delivery of electric shock to another person is certainly punishment, but why call it aggression if the subject is so instructed? It is true that the subject is instructed to give shock, but only as a signal that the victim's response is incorrect. All the subject need do is give shock from button 1 or 2 (not noxious), and he fulfills his obligation as experimenter. Shock from buttons 3 and higher deliver painful stimuli, and they are clearly more intense than is needed merely to signal an incorrect response. The situation is analogous to a parent disciplining his child or a teacher criticizing his student's work, and the delivery of punishment more intense than is warranted by the social role should be called by its proper name, aggression.

The subject is instructed to shock the victim on every one of the first 10 trials "in order to wipe out the effects of any previous learning or preconceived notions." The victim surreptitiously records these shock levels (he is separated from the subject by the bulky apparatus) and notes the highest shock given at least twice. Starting with the trial 11, the subject shocks only when the victim makes a mistake. The victim makes nothing but mistakes until the subject raises the shock level at least one button higher than the highest level of the first 10 trials. When the subject does raise the shock, the victim makes two or three correct responses in succession (the two or three are varied randomly so that the subject cannot discern any regularities of the contingency); then the victim returns to making incorrect responses. This procedure continues until the subject gives 5 consecutive higher shocks or until a total of 35 shocks have been administered. Then the victim "learns" (makes 5 consecutive correct responses), and the experiment is finished.

The subject wishes the victim to learn, although this is certainly not a very strong motivation. Thus the correct responses by the victim, although reinforcing, are probably only minimally reinforcing. Nevertheless, the victim is shaping the subject's behavior on every trial (after the first 10), and such close control might be expected to yield results.

Results

A total of 68 male subjects were run, 34 with a male victim and 34 with a female victim. The criterion of whether aggression intensity rose was 5 consecutive shocks at least one unit higher than the highest during the first 10 trials. By this criterion when the victim was a male, 24 raised their shock intensity and 10 did not; when the victim was a female, the numbers were reversed, with 10 raising and 24 not. The difference between 24/10 and 10/24 is statistically significant.

These data are better seen graphically, but to plot graphs it was first necessary to equate for total number of shocks given (some subjects reached the criterion of 5 consecutive raised shocks early, some late, and

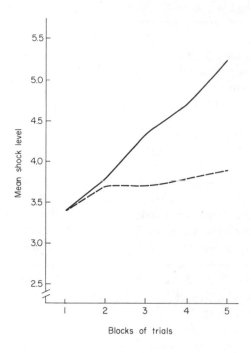

Figure 1. Reinforcing aggression, male victim. −, Raising; − −, nonraising.

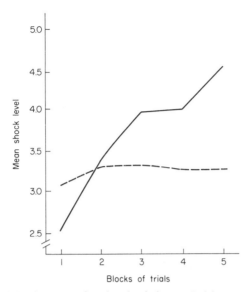

Figure 2. Reinforcing aggression, female victim. —, Raising; – –, nonraising.

some never). This was done by dividing each subject's total number c
shocks into 5 blocks of trials, a procedure which allows graphic presentation but prevents statistical comparisons. The resulting curves are
presented in Figures 1 and 2. In Figure 1 (male victim) the Raising N was
24 subjects and the Nonraising N was 10 subjects, whereas the Ns were
exactly reversed in Figure 2 (female victim). It is clear that in both figures
the Raising curve is considerably steeper than the Nonraising curve,
which merely reflects the adequacy of the criteria used to separate Raising from Nonraising subjects.

The important datum concerns the difference caused by the gender of
the victim. When the men aggressed against another man, 24 of 34 subjects raised their aggression intensity with only minimal reinforcement,
but when they aggressed against a woman, only 10 of 34 subjects raised
aggression intensity. The difference may be seen graphically in Figure 3,
in which the Ns are equal (34 for each curve). When the victim is a male,
the aggression intensity curve starts higher and climbs more steeply than
the curve for a female victim.

In brief, this experiment has yielded two facts. First, minimal reinforcement for intensified aggression does work, but by no means for all
subjects. Second, the gender of the victim determines whether the reinforcement will be generally effective in raising the level of aggression:
with a male victim, yes; with a female victim, no.

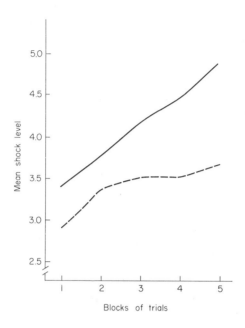

Figure 3. Reinforcing aggression, male versus female victim. −, Male victim; − −, female victim.

IMPLICATIONS ABOUT AGGRESSION AND ITS CONTROL

Human aggression is essentially a problem for men, not women. It is men who wage wars, engage in bitter competition, fight each other individually, and maintain vendettas lasting for years or even decades. That men are initially more aggressive toward men than toward women and that they more easily elevate aggressive intensity toward men than toward women as a function of minimal reinforcement—these facts agree with casual observations of everyday life, as well as with laboratory research (see Buss, 1966).

Why do men aggress less against women? The simplest assumption is that they have learned during socialization to inhibit aggression against females. One fights with other boys, not with girls. Beating a boy in a fight or in a competition is worthy; beating a girl, worthless. It is shameful and cowardly to attack girls. These lessons are well learned by most boys, and adulthood sees strong inhibitions against attacking women. These speculations suggest a possibility for controlling male aggression: teach boys that, concerning competition and aggression, there are no important differences between the two genders. Teach them that it is just as worthless and cowardly to attack a boy as it is to attack a girl. In other words, the taboo object would be broadened to include *all* humans, not just girls and women! All this would entail is a major upheaval in this society's concept of masculinity, and the reader can judge how easily this might be accomplished.

Let us return to the theme of this paper, that aggression pays. The reinforcers are money, prestige, and status. Each of these reinforcers is crucial to one area in which aggression pays very well.

The first is *organized crime.* Criminal syndicates, whether Mafia or otherwise, obtain their money by methods that are obviously aggressive: extortion, destruction of property, and murder. And their hands are only slightly less clean than those of the politicians, law officers, and businessmen who cooperate with them. The payoff for this kind of aggression varies from a living wage for those at the bottom to millions of dollars for the syndicate bosses.

The second area is that of our *national myths.* In the last century our national aggressiveness was openly stated as the "manifest destiny" that led to seizing land from Mexico and Spain, as well as from our own Indians. In this century such strident imperialism has been muted, but our schoolchildren are still taught that we never lost a war, and our legends make heroes of men who kill on a mass scale in time of war (Sergeant York of World War I, Audie Murphy of World War II) or even in time of peace (Jesse James and Dillinger were both vicious killers). Thus the royal road to prestige is via aggression. on either a national or an individual scale.

The third area, mentioned earlier, is our *masculine role:* tough, competitive, hardhitting, dominant, and in a word, *aggressive.* Status as a male is to be achieved by being aggressive, and masculinity is perhaps the most basic aspect of a man's identity.

In brief, there is a huge payoff for aggression in terms of money, prestige, and status. The scope of the problem is tremendous, but it is a small task to list the solutions. We need to realign our economy and law-enforcement procedures so that criminal aggression does not pay, alter our national myths from warloving to peaceloving attitudes, and revise our masculine role to exclude aggressiveness. Changes of this breadth and complexity could be accomplished only by means of a religious movement, and I hereby take the first step in initiating such a movement by giving it a name: Quakerism.

REFERENCES

Bandura, A. & Walters, R. H. *Social learning and personality development.* New York: Holt, Rinehart and Winston, 1963.
Buss, A. H. *The psychology of aggression.* New York: Wiley, 1961.

Buss, A. H. The effect of harm on subsequent aggression. *Journal of Experimental Research on Personality,* 1966, **1,** 249–255.

Dollard, J., Doob, N., Miller, N. E., Mowrer, O. H., & Sears, R. R. *Frustration and aggression.* New Haven, Conn.: Yale Univer. Press, 1939.

Dulany, D. E., Jr. Hypotheses and habits in verbal "operant conditioning." *Journal of Abnormal and Social Psychology,* 1961, **63,** 251–263.

Fenichel, O. *The psychoanalytic theory of neuroses.* New York: Norton, 1945.

Feshbach, S. The function of aggression and the regulation of aggressive drive. *Psychological Review,* 1964, **71,** 257–272.

Holz, W. C. & Azrin, N. H. Conditioning and human verbal behavior in W. K. Honig (Ed.) *Operant behavior. Areas of research and application.* New York: Appleton-Century-Crofts, 1966, Pp. 790–826.

Lovaas, O. I. Interaction between verbal and nonverbal behavior. *Child Development,* 1961, **32,** 329–336.

Staples, F. R. & Walters, R. H. Influence of positive reinforcement of aggression on subjects differing in initial aggression level. *Journal of Consulting Psychology,* 1964, **28,** 547–552.

Walters, R. H. & Brown, M. Studies of reinforcement of aggression: III. Transfer of responses to an interpersonal situation. *Child Development,* 1963, **34,** 563–571.

CHAPTER II

THE INFLUENCE OF VIOLENCE PORTRAYED IN TELEVISION OR MOTION PICTURES UPON OVERT AGGRESSIVE BEHAVIOR

JEROME L. SINGER

CITY UNIVERSITY OF NEW YORK

INTRODUCTION

Dramatic instances of violence have recently shocked the American public into a re-examination of the elements of our culture which may contribute to such outbreaks. Assassinations of national leaders such as President John Kennedy, Senator Robert Kennedy, and Dr. Martin Luther King have sent convulsions of fear and dismay through the country. Bizarre mass killings such as the nurses' murder in Chicago, the killings in an Arizona beauty salon, and the frightening and destructive sniping from the tower on the University of Texas campus have received nationwide attention. The widespread rioting and looting in the urban centers all over the nation, rioting of college students, the occasionally excessive counter-reactions of the law enforcement authorities, and related incidents have evoked deep concern to the point that "law and order," vaguely defined indeed, has become a more significant political issue than the persisting war in Vietnam. Interview surveys suggest that a

[1] Support for the preparation of this chapter and some of the research described herein by this author came through the National Broadcasting Company Research Department and the National Institute of Mental Health Grant MH 10956. The author wishes to acknowledge the assistance of Dr. Thomas Coffey of the National Broadcasting Company.

large percentage of the U.S. population feels less safe in the streets and in the use of public transportation.

While there is some reason to believe that a proportional degree of violence and crime in the population has not increased significantly during the century, the statistics do indicate that crimes of violence by young men, adolescents, and boys have indeed accelerated (Masotti, 1968). The riots in the cities reflect a special problem relating largely to racial unrest by Negroes and other minorities whose aspirations have been aroused without comparable opportunity for economic, education, or housing mobility. Since young people predominate in the urban riots and their middleclass counterparts have assumed a strikingly militant (but less overtly violent) pattern in the colleges, the question arises as to whether some recent significant cultural changes have engendered in today's youth a predisposition to direct violent action and a comparable disrespect for authority.

While motion pictures and radio programs have been widely available for almost fifty years, by far the most dramatic change in the daily experience of the recent generation of youth has been the availability of television in almost every home in the nation. Clearly the *percentage* of the population which is daily exposed to graphic portrayals of violence and crime through the imaginative content of the major entertainment media, as well as by depictions and news reports of actual events, far exceeds the actual increase in the population in the last two decades. Given the widespread attraction of television (and, to a lesser degree, motion pictures) can it be that the regular diet of incidents of assaultiveness and crime available in these media have indeed contributed the changing pattern of youthful involvement in crimes of violence?

The present paper proposes to examine the formal scientific evidence relevant to the question of the influence of violence portrayed in movies or TV upon direct aggressive behavior. Thoughtful consideration of the major historical developments in the almost seventy years of this century make it clear that far more potent factors than the effects of popular communication media are at work. This nation has been involved in four large-scale wars since 1917, all of which have offered American youth models of the militancy and effectiveness of our troops, once engaged in a just conflict. The consequences of the vast armament programs and military training to the point where there are approximately fifty million veterans in the present population, the increased general availability of firearms, and the "revolution of rising aspirations" of the urban poor are undoubtedly far more significant elements in providing youth with a predisposition to violence. Viewed historically, the average citizen experiences less violence or confronts dramatic illness and death less frequently than was the case fifty or more years ago. The increase in deaths by violence reflects almost certainly man's improved technology in destruction during war or the greater availability of guns for all segments of the population. Until the mid-nineteenth century men rarely walked abroad after dark for fear of attack. Accounts of life in ancient Rome describe the nocturnal dangers to the citizenry, perils from marauding bands of ruffians as well as from youthful patricians on an evening lark.

Thus, while the majority of Americans (except for the poor in urban ghettos or rural slums) experience far more freedom from thievery, robbery or direct violence, the exposure of adults and children to graphic depictions of acts of violence via the television screen or the motion pictures has increased amazingly. While most Americans including a large percentage of the U.S. armed forces probably never saw a single person badly wounded or killed during all of World War II, incidents of violence are a commonplace event as depicted in the daily television viewing of every home. And, in addition to the graphic but fictional representations of assault and killing, the news reporting of actual violence has become increasingly frequent and visually effective by the television medium. Perhaps forty million persons were witnesses of the shooting of Lee Harvey Oswald by Jack Ruby and many millions each night see newsreel film footage of violence from Vietnam or other scenes of assault photographed live in urban riots, demonstrations for various causes, etc. It is not unreasonable therefore to examine the psychological consequences for adults and children of this frequent observation of acts of violence brought right into the bosom of the family by the television screen.

The objective of the present report is a careful examination of the scientific evidence regarding the effects of observing violence as depicted on film or via television on the attitudes and especially the likelihood of assaultive behavior by child and adult viewers. The content of popular myths, legends, children's tales, drama, novels, sculpture, painting, and opera all bear a high percentage of incidents of violence. *Little Red Riding Hood* and *Hansel and Gretel, The Iliad, King Lear, Titus Andronicus, The Brothers Karamazov, For Whom the Bell Tolls,* operas like *Salome, The Love of Three Kings* or *La Tosca,* all involve vivid incidents of violence. Until the advent of movies and more especially television, no cultural media possessed the degree of penetration into the daily experience of so great a proportion of the population, however. To keep perspective we must acknowledge that popular entertainment has shown a most humanitarian evolution especially in the past century. The day of the bloody circuses for the Roman masses, of great popular turnouts to witness public torture and executions; of bear-baiting or even bare-knuckle, bloody prizefighting is past. Boxing today is far less popular, vicious, and damaging; and bull-fighting and cock-fighting persist only in limited cultural areas. The undoubtedly heavy diet of violence provided on television must be viewed against the clear evidence that most men today take far less pleasure in viewing actual physical harm inflicted upon others than was ever the case before in history.

There are serious concerns nevertheless about how the heavy fare of violence served up in movies such as the popular James Bond series or in a great many television dramatic programs as well as movie reruns influences our society. Many thoughtful parents and educators express concern about the harmful possible consequences of such presentations (Logan, 1950), yet the overall reaction of parents towards television is favorable (Coffin, 1955). Criminologists (Banay, 1955) and psychiatrists (Wertham, 1954) have proposed that the large-scale presentation of violence in popular communication media cannot help but have effects upon the impressionable youth of the country. That a heavy dose of violence is provided on television today is scarcely questionable. Various counts suggest literally thousands of such incidents on any given channel (except for educational TV) in a given week. At this writing a *one-minute* commercial for a motion picture is being run regularly on major TV channels at times when children as well as adults can watch; the commercial includes over a dozen direct acts of violence and closes with the disclaimer, "Suggested for adult audiences." Presumably the latter restriction may be imposed because sexual material is fairly openly included in the movie. In general our society operates on the myth that sexual incidents incite children while aggressive material is cathartic or merely innocuous. In Sweden, by contrast, sexual material can be openly shown to children while violence is forbidden to young audiences. Neither position can as yet be satisfactorily supported by scientific evidence.

In approaching a review of the evidence concerning the psychological effects of TV violence certain ground rules seem desirable. First of all it is necessary to review the specific proposed consequences, positive and negative, of such material. Then some agreement on a proper definition of aggression must be established. The major theoretical positions concerning the nature of human aggression must be reviewed since these imply somewhat different predictions for the effects of popular media. The criteria for evaluating specific research evidence must be spelled out since many experimental results, however clear-cut statistically, lend themselves to quite different degrees of generalization. Finally the specific studies must be examined in their own right to establish their value in relation to the issues raised here.

THE PRESUMED CONSEQUENCES OF TELEVISION AND MOVIE VIOLENCE

Let us begin by reviewing the major proposals concerning the consequences for children and adults of viewing incidents of violence on the screen. Most of the suggestions of harmful effects have come from psychiatric clinicians or educators, of whom Wertham is perhaps most vocal (Wertham, 1962, 1966). Earlier concerns relative to the impact upon children of TV in relation to eyesight, sleep loss, reading-time, educational attitudes, etc. have been extensively surveyed (Furu, 1962; Maccoby, 1964; Himmelweit *et al.*, 1958; Schramm *et al.*, 1961) and will not be reviewed further here. In general, except for consistent findings that frightening programs do indeed produce some anxieties and sleep disturbance in a minority of children or reduce reading-time for fiction somewhat, these studies provide no indications of large-scale harmful effects of the media. The limitations of the survey method in providing adequate data on some of the most significant issues has been generally recognized, however (Maccoby, 1964; Wertham, 1962), and experimental studies directed specifically to cause-effect analyses seem essential.

The major objections to violence and destructive content in movies and especially television may be summarized as follows (see also a comparable presentation by Klapper, 1960).

1. The witnessing of acts of violence or destruction is essentially frightening and can provoke anxiety both in adults and children with consequences such as persistent nightmares or sleeplessness, distracting daydreams, or the development of nervous mannerisms. Reading about such material may have similar consequences but viewing incidents of this type in a movie or on television may be very similar to actual presence at the scene and evoke comparable traumatic reactions.

2. Excessive portrayal of violence in popular media may create general misinformation in the public concerning the frequency and types of actual violence in our society.

3. Depictions of criminal activity and violence may actually provide individuals with information about clever or effective means for attempting various crimes.

4. Observers of aggressive activity on a screen may actually be impelled to direct imitation of the observed behavior through immaturity or direct suggestibility.

5. The observation of aggression may generate a predisposition to comparable activity in individuals who may be angered or emotionally

frustrated shortly after watching a movie or television portrayal. Under circumstances of great emotional arousal an individual may recall a scene from a recent movie or TV play and behave impulsively in a comparable fashion. In some instances actual "conditioned" reactions may occur, i.e., aggression towards a person who bears even a superficial resemblance to a TV character who was the object of aggression.

6. "Contagion" effects, social reactions of groups, may be occasioned by witnessing mob violence such as lootings or student sit-ins.

7. Arousal of hopes for achievement or for material success which can only be frustrated and arouse aggression may take place for urban ghetto viewers.

8. Beyond the "triggering" or imitative effects suggested above, it is possible that frequent exposure to acts of aggression whether imaginary or actual (as in news films of rioting or the fighting in Vietnam) may create a more pervasive phychological readiness to engage in aggressive behavior. That is, observers may be inured to the seriousness of violence and more inclined to take it lightly, may be inclined to regard it as a worthwhile and socially accepted means of overcoming obstacles, or may experience great personal conflict over the contradiction between the "apparent" social sanction of violence as portrayed in popular media and their own cultural, religious or ethical training. The widespread availability of information as well as direct presentation of aggression may create a general cultural atmosphere of lowered inhibitions concerning such acts in contrast with the more normal restraints most people feel about harming others directly.

Evidence in support of the first objection is extensive for very young children both from television studies as well as the earlier studies of motion pictures. Changes in programming for young children have reflected industry concern over such effects and parental control over children's viewing habits has generally been characteristic of middle class families. While there are occasional individual clinical studies that indicate onset of emotional disturbances associated with material presented on TV, there is no reason to assume that such incidents could not as well have been provoked by movies or by actual incidents in daily life.

There are some suggestions that public information on crime or that general attitudes and belief systems can be effected by the content of programs. A study by Larsen, Gray, and Fortis (1963) indicates that effects such as the induction of attitudes contrary to the social norm are achieved by a variety of TV programs, irrespective of focus on violence or presumed orientation to child or adult audiences. The question of the effect of popular media on public information and broader belief systems is outside the scope of the present review, however, and will not be dealt with further here.

The question of whether criminals or potential criminals learn methods for carrying out crimes from TV is as yet not dealt with satisfactorily in formal research. Individual instances do exist where delinquents have reported the influence of movies upon the specific types of criminal patterns (Blumer & Hauser, 1933) but there are many negative findings such as studies in Japan, England, and Canada. It seems likely, however, that members of the "culture of violence" (Wolfgang & Ferracuti, 1967) would seek out methods for criminal action from a variety of sources and would use material on thievery from movies like "Topkapi" when they seemed relevant enough.

The major available evidence based on systematic experimentation is addressed largely to the issues of imitative and "triggering" effects of film-mediated violence. It is to these that the present review will be primarily addressed, since the evidence on "contagion" or on "revolution of rising aspirations" through TV is as yet conjectural.

Some Possible Positive Effects of Television

Counterpoised against this impressive list of criticisms of the potential effects of violence on TV are a number of suggestions of possible value of such material. Generally TV has few defenders in the intellectual community but scientific concern raises some serious questions concerning its adaptive utility from a psychological standpoint.

1. Many theorists and clinicians would argue that since all of us experience frequent frustrations or periodic arousal of aggressive drives or anger, the opportunity to experience vicariously such resentments through fictional means reduces our likelihood of direct expression. This is the well-known *catharsis* hypothesis and it would argue that man's enjoyment of violent events in all art forms or in sports such as boxing is explicable on the basis of an almost universal need for safety-valve aggressive experiences that limit overt violence in the population (Feshbach, 1955, Levine, 1968).

2. A somewhat different position that also indicates some benefit in the availability of adventurous and violent content in television might be termed the *imaginative development hypothesis*. Here it would be argued that the intrinsic interest of such material aids children to obtain material for use in their imaginative play and increases the likelihood that children will enjoy such forms of activity rather than direct physical con-

tact play which is more likely to eventuate in aggression (Singer, 1966).

3. A third argument that bears on the question of possible positive value of television violence is simple enough. Time spent viewing television is time taken away from gang play or potentially delinquent behavior. In this sense if potentially aggressive, restless children could be encouraged to sit quietly watching television and enjoying it, they would be less likely to be chasing around the streets looking for violent confrontations. Studies in Japan and a finding reported by Eron (1963) do indeed suggest that viewing time may be *inversely* related to overt aggressive behavior.

4. Just as television may be expected to communicate negative beliefs or possibly harmful orientations, it also appears to encourage a variety of socially-relevant interests, desires for friendship, sports or travel and other inclinations to satisfaction that are valuable alternatives to direct aggression. Even within the context of a detective or adventure story with its attendant violence, material is presented that may encourage desires for new occupations such as newspaper reporting, police work, medicine, merchant seamanship, etc., all posing intriguing alternatives to a life of crime. Since there is evidence (Maccoby & Wilson, 1957) that children retain best material where they have made positive identification with the "hero" figure it would appear likely that if the hero or heroine has an interesting personality and line of work and is not strongly inclined to violence *himself*, the likelihood of positive identification is greater than identification with aggressive behavior.

5. A further more general benefit from television including adventure programs would bear on the issue of the general cultural enrichment and social sophistication accruing from the material. It is possible that considerable concern about man's social role, the importance of democratic process, the dignity of men of independent stature may also be conveyed despite a considerable portion of violence in a picture. Awareness of varied national norms, or of broader cultural patterns may increase the general interest and cultural level of a child and build in constraints against antisocial behavior in his own environment. General values such as the importance of education may also come through in many ways along with the excitement of adventure in the story.

The issue is joined, therefore, on the question of whether the violence which writers and producers generally feel makes for absorbing content as well as artistic effectiveness yields so negative an effect as a promoter of violence in attitude and behavior as to warrant serious self-restraint or censorship of popular media. What evidence can be considered satisfactory in deciding this question? Some tentative criteria can be established and will be briefly enumerated below.

Criteria for Scientific Evidence

1. One of the ground rules of scientific evidence in an issue of possible social, legal, and legislative significance is the reliance on operationally defined, replicable formal investigation. There is already much heat and opinion from men of distinction such as Wertham but what is needed is convincing evidence from reasonably controlled surveys or experiments. In so complex a field there can be no "experts" and even so impressive an experimental social psychologist as Berkowitz moves several steps beyond his actual findings in taking a stand that implies some regulation of movie and television content (Berkowitz, 1968).

2. A critical issue is the question of the proper definition of aggression. The term violence is not generally of scientific value but it implies direct physical action of a noxious type. The question of a definition of aggression has been carefully analyzed by Kaufmann (1965) who proposes that the term be limited to the delivery of a noxious stimulus to another person by someone who has reasonable expectation of success. This definition avoids the use of fantasy or aggression in play which involves no direct effort to harm any person. Society is concerned with direct attacks; it cannot become involved in controlling aggressive daydreams or drawings or cowboy and Indian games that hurt no one. In this sense many studies by using verbal reports or rating scales of aggressive reactions are too many steps removed from true aggression.

3. Ultimately an evaluation of the undesirable consequences of television must show a relation of viewing of specific program material to actual occurrence of crimes. Such evidence is of course difficult to obtain except in correlational forms that are likely to be misleading, e.g., a Canadian report that while fictional violence on television and radio increased tremendously in a period of years in the 1950's there was actually a decline in the crime rate among juveniles for that time (Whalen, 1959). Even if one could show dramatic associations between frequency of viewing of violent films or TV shows in a delimited sample of boys and also a greater incidence of violent crime by members of that sample, it would be necessary to tease out more precisely whether the taste for TV violence was a reflection of well-established aggressive interests or whether the heavy diet of TV violence was indeed encouraging aggressive behavior in the boys. Indeed there is evidence in Japanese studies (Furu, 1962) that more aggressively oriented children do not show a preference for violent TV shows and that more intellectual and less aggressive chil-

dren seek out the more complicated violent adventure films rather than simple comedies.

4. In following up this point care must be exercised to avoid confusing aggressive fantasy, hostility, anger, hostile wit or sarcasm, vituperation, and direct violence. Many studies fail to make clear which they are studying. There is evidence from studies of aggressive behavior that verbal and physical attacks are not on the same continuum and cannot be considered aspects of the same aggressive factor.

5. Aggression in a laboratory setting must be examined carefully before it can be assumed to be relevant to studies of direct aggression in daily life. The subject who participates in an experiment in a college setting accepts a set of premises that he will himself not be seriously harmed nor will a professor allow him to do terrible harm to another person. Within this set of assumptions about the relative benignity of the atmosphere, aggressive manifestations may at best be part of a playful game and far from typical of an $S's$ response in daily life.

6. The comparability of a laboratory viewing of a movie or of laboratory fantasy behavior to actual TV viewing in a home setting needs careful scrutiny before generalizations can be drawn. Indeed the witnessing of a direct assault on the street, of a news film or live shot of a direct assault (as in Chicago convention riots or footage from Vietnam), of a fictional representation of assault with the participants close in age or life situation to the viewer, and of a fictional representation of violence where the characters are far removed psychologically from the viewer (knights or pirates), all of these may represent a continuum of reality-unreality with differential consequences for a viewer. Almost no research has been addressed to this problem especially as regards the impact of news coverage of violence.

7. The background of the viewer, age, sex, social class, personality predisposition, family or personal viewing pattern, imaginative or aggressive tendencies are also parameters that require exploration in formal studies of the effects of TV.

8. Finally, the effects of individual exposure of specific content to long-term, cumulative viewing needs clarification. Here, too, almost no research of an experimental kind is addressed to this issue.

In the following presentation the above criteria will be employed as relevant to the specific studies to be reviewed. Before embarking upon a specific discussion of the research, however, it is necessary to review the major theoretical positions concerning aggression and fantasy to establish some baselines for evaluating the points of view and scientific significance of the work underway or completed in this field.

THEORIES OF AGGRESSION AND ITS RELATION TO FANTASY PROCESSES

Biological or Instinctive Theories of Aggression

One major group of theories concerning the nature of aggression emphasizes the fact that some type of direct assaultiveness or some destructive inclinations are inherent in man, part of his animal nature. This view would emphasize the inevitable emergence of aggressive reactions as much an instinct as reproduction for man as a biological organism.

In 1908 William McDougall in the first book on "Social Psychology" proposed that what he called "pugnacity" was a fundamental instinct in mankind. He hoped it could be harnessed into constructive channels to become what might be called "healthy assertiveness." At about the same time William James was proposing that the comparable energies of youth be channeled into some forms of national humane service, the "moral equivalent of war," an idea that was a forerunner of the CCC in the 1930's and our present Peace Corps or Vista Volunteer Programs.

Sigmund Freud (1962), the most influential psychological theorist of this century, at first rejected the notion of an instinct of aggression but his experiences in World War I led him to propose, somewhat hesitantly, a theory that all mankind was two major driving forces, an erotic or life-building force and a destructive or death-oriented force. Freud's view of aggression has often been termed a "tragic" or pessimistic theory, for it proposes that despite man's efforts to tame the instinct and redirect it into culturally useful forms, it persists in striving for discharge and must be constantly defended against. For Freud one means of dealing with aggressive impulses was through fantasy or imagination. He proposed a modern version of Aristotle's theory of catharsis, namely, that daydreaming or thinking aggressive thoughts or expressing them through art or literature or the experience of witnessing depicted violence or through humor might *partially* reduce the strength of a person's inner aggressive pressure and make it less likely that he would engage openly in a destructive act. From this point of view man's enjoyment of a sport like boxing would partially reduce his own aggressiveness.

A comparable theory has recently been proposed by the ethologist, Konrad Lorenz (1966), based upon his observations of a variety of animal species. Lorenz, too, has suggested that the aggressive instinct must find periodic outlets through "catharsis" or it builds to a tremendous explosiveness and can lead to violent activity without any external instigation.

The Frustration-Aggression Theories

Somewhat less speculative than the instinctual theories of aggression are those which propose that aggressive behavior is a fundamental response of the organism to frustration or blockage of goal-oriented efforts. This theory developed originally at Yale University in the late 1930's by John Dollard and a group of distinguished associates assumes that the tendency to aggression is a constitutional reaction to frustrating circumstances but that it can be altered considerably through learning. While there have been modifications in the technical details of the learning theory of which this position on aggression was one part, the proponents of this view would also support some features of a catharsis hypothesis. They would argue that once the aggressive drive was aroused following frustration, it could indeed be at least partially reduced by imagining events associated with satisfaction of the drive (e.g., daydreaming about punching the boss in the nose) or by observing an athletic event or dramatic production which bore some relationship to the intended aggressive act. In this sense, since we are all daily subject to many frustrations, we are likely to seek out and enjoy vicarious opportunities for aggressive expression, i.e., situations in which we symbolically kill off or beat up the "bad guys" in our lives. The popularity of movie Westerns, of TV wrestling matches, of James Bond thrillers, or of aggressive humor such as pratfalls, pie-throwing, insulting comedians all attest to the need for such outlets of aggression.

More recently Leonard Berkowitz at the University of Michigan has re-examined the frustration-aggression theory. In a series of carefully controlled experiments during the past five years (see below), he and his co-workers have demonstrated that persons thwarted in their purposes do indeed respond by becoming more aggressive and engaging in actions likely to cause harm to another person. Berkowitz points out that the essence of frustration is not so much a deprivation of food or basic necessity but rather the blocking of the wishes of individuals. A study just published by Leonard Geen, an associate of Berkowitz, supports the conclusion that the frustration of purposes is most likely to lead to aggressive action. Berkowitz differs sharply with other frustration-aggression theorists in his rejection of the catharsis theory. He argues that such a theory is too simple and that a frustrated person who has recently observed a film in which "justifiable" violence occurred is likely to increase his own aggressive actions rather than reduce them. In this sense presentation of violence in the popular media may indeed trigger overt aggression on impulse in someone highly emotionally aroused soon after exposure to the material. Specific experiments in this connection will be cited below.

While other theorists do not accept the specific frustration-aggression notion, a widely held view in psychology today is that people behave very differently depending upon how "aroused" or excited they are. A leading personality theorist, Silvan Tomkins (1962), has proposed that prolonged and intense stimulation, whether frustration, noise or recurrent fear, leads to a greater likelihood of rage and aggressive anger. Even Freud admitted that simple catharsis is not likely to occur under such conditions of prolonged, intense distress. In this sense one might argue that violence in popular media or aggressive humor has a tension-releasing effect for people not very upset but that for those extremely frustrated the opposite influence, an actual increase in aggression might be the consequence. No formal research has yet been done that is addressed to this notion, however.

Social Learning and Cultural Theories

While animal experiments of the type carried out by J. P. Scott (1958) have failed to support theories that fighting and aggression are fundamental instinct, there is considerable evidence that animals and children do learn to fight by participating in rough and tumble with peers or by observing and then imitating aggressive actions of adults. Albert Bandura of Stanford University is a representative exponent of a widely supported position in American psychology and psychiatry which emphasizes the fact that much of child's behavior is acquired in more or less direct imitation of parental or peer models. Of special importance is the issue of aggression, and Bandura and his collaborators have been able to show that children will indeed imitate the destructive behavior of an adult whether witnessed in life or in film. Indeed others have shown that such imitation can occur in adults as well.

The significance of social learning theories lies in the emphasis they place on the child's likelihood of frequent imitation. If the child is constantly experimenting with ways of talking or acting, those he observes carried out by his parents whom he admires will have special appeal. In new situations where a child is at a loss for what to do he is likely to remember what he saw his parents do and behave accordingly even occasionally to his own detriment. Indeed adults when they become parents and are faced with the novelty of their role revert to the type of behavior they saw their parents engage in when they were children — sometimes against their current adult judgment. Delinquent children are much more likely to have had parents who engaged in criminal or overtly aggressive behavior.

Bandura and others in this group would argue that observation of adult violence on television would indeed lead to comparable behavior more

often than not in children aroused to anger. They seriously question the
"catharsis" view or any related position such as Freud's or Lorenz'.

The Nature of the Fantasy Process

None of the major theorists in the field of aggression except for Freud
have devoted much attention to the nature of the fantasy response. This
is a serious deficiency since much of the violence to which objection is
made is not directly observed in real life by a child but is filtered through
the medium of some imaginative medium. The tendency to engage in
fantasy of "as-if" play is a fundamental characteristic of childhood. Much
of this "make believe" play, especially among boys, involves aggressive
material, cowboys, pirates, invaders from Mars. Such fantasy play seems
eventually to merge into enjoyment of movies, television, and literature.

An examination of the research literature by this writer, as well as a
series of studies of the nature of daydreaming, suggests that tendencies
to behave imaginatively in play or in thought are established quite early
in children.

It seems likely that an important feature largely neglected in formal
research on film — aggressive behavior — is the predisposition of the child
towards imaginative material. It seems likely that children already oriented to imaginative play might prove less likely to express in overt
behavior any aggressive impact from TV but rather to carry such activity
over into their play, or into some quasi-literary or creative activity. Children who have for some reason failed to develop the imaginative abilities
might find television a useful source of pleasure but unless they develop
a capacity to "internalize" the imaginative materials presented there,
the likelihood is that they may express the aggressive material observed
in direct action against their peers when angered. Research examining
these questions is currently underway under the direction of this writer.
Results are not yet available, however.

RESULTS OF SURVEY RESEARCH

If we address ourselves to the major questions raised in the introduction
concerning the possible harmful effects of television, as well as the possible benefits, we come first of all to the large-scale surveys carried out
by investigators such as Himmelweit (in England in the late 1950's), by
Schramm (early 1960's), Furu (1962), and Maccoby (mid 1960's). These
surveys are intended to examine a host of issues concerning the impact
of television from its effects on vision to the effect on school achievement.
Briefly the major results suggest no grossly harmful consequences of
television viewing ascertainable through the mass interviewing techniques.
Surveys of this type suggest that children do indeed show increased night-

mares and some traumatic reactions to television. Since for most middle- and lower-middle class children television-viewing has largely eliminated regular movie attendance, it is unclear whether such reports reflect an increase since television or rather a shift in the source of nightmares. At least one experimental study of nightdreaming by children has provided evidence that children have *fewer* nightmares after viewing frightening scenes of aggression than after relatively innocuous shows such as base-ball games (Foulkes *et al.,* 1967, see below).

There seems little doubt that children acquire considerable information from television. Enrichment of vocabulary, of knowledge of social studies, history, and geography take place inevitably although not always in ways especially useful for formal schoolwork. Frustrated middle class children prove more likely to watch more TV (even with restrictions from strict parents) while more satisfied children show a greater variety of activities. Children from lower socioeconomic status watch extensively but this is more likely a part of their regular family pattern since in lower socio-economic groups TV viewing is a major source of family recreation and the set may be on all day long. A number of surveys carried out in Europe and Australia, as well as early experimental studies in this country, make it clear that children's social attitudes, their imagery, the aspirations they profess and the persons they wish to emulate, as well as some of their fears, are clearly effected by viewing.

If we turn specifically to the effects of violence on television or other comparable media, the results are less clear from surveys. As summarized by J. Klapper (1960), the data show that while about 20% of children report fearful reactions to violence, the context of violence is more sig-nificant than the sheer amount (which is decidedly very heavy in all media). Westerns in general evoke less disturbance because of their familiar qual-ity, minimal attention to the reality of suffering by wounded, and high predictability. Violence by knife or other weapons closer to the actual daily experience proves more upsetting. There are suggestions but far from proven that there is more distress when film subjects of violence are closer to the viewers in age, sex, way of life, or other characteristics. Despite individual case reports concerning delinquents influenced by TV, children who watch a great deal were not shown to be more delin-quent in five separate large surveys.

Some Limitations of Survey Studies

On the whole the survey results do not argue for any clear direction in the findings which can serve as a sound basis for an overall judgment on the impact of television or movie violence on behavior. There are suggestions that some negative emotional impact is forthcoming for very young children from frightening scenes and that violence closely related to the life experiences of viewers is more disturbing.

There are serious limitations in these studies for they ignore the impact of violence in actual news reports, war films, riot scenes, and related events which have been increasingly presented in pictorially effective forms. The survey studies are also unable to answer the kinds of questions raised by experimental research – the effect of viewing violence on behavior immediately afterward. Surveys ask respondents for general estimates of typical behavior, and it is likely that many specific incidents of direct reactions to filmed aggression could have been forgotten. Indeed children or adults so influenced would probably not even recognize the connection between a family dispute or a fight between children and the preceding film. Nor, indeed, could respondents describe the so-called cathartic effects. Clearly there is a current need for a series of more extensive and differentiated surveys of reactions to real and fictional violence as witnessed on TV or in movies, to the closeness or distance of the violence depicted to the viewer's own life situation. Day-to-day studies of viewing habits of children must be compared to actual observations of the tendencies toward aggression in spontaneous play. Pending such systematic research, the present evidence is scant indeed on the effect of popular media.

A much more complex question that may elude investigation deals with the issue of whether long-term viewing of violence has established an atmosphere in the nation conducive to tolerating aggression as a means of settling disputes. In this connection it remains to be seen whether news films of semi-violent or rebellious behavior, such as manifested in some student revolts or in the various urban ghetto riots, influence viewers to direct action. The extreme rapidity with which news of such events is transmitted nationally or even internationally is far beyond any previous experience of mankind and it may prove likely (following extensive surveys of participants) that contagious effects were indeed generated.

EXPERIMENTAL STUDIES OF IMITATION AND MODELING

Review of Studies

An important new direction in the experimental study of child development has emerged from the work of Bandura and his collaborators (Bandura & Walters, 1963) on the nature of social imitation or modeling. In a careful and impressive series of experiments Bandura has been able to demonstrate that children, expecially in the three- to five-year-old age group, do indeed show a great deal of learning on the basis of direct observation of the behavior of adult models. This work has cut through the complexities of the Freudian concepts of introjection and identification to trace out systematically some of the conditions conducive to children imitating their parents or expanding their repertory of behavioral responses by observation of adults in a variety of situations.

Of special significance for this report are the studies dealing with the children's imitation of aggression manifested by adults whom they have observed. In an initial study (Bandura & Houston, 1961) children in the course of their play saw an adult engage in various play activities, some of which included aggressive reactions. Subsequently 90% of the children specifically exposed to the aggressive play were inclined to show aggressive reactions in their own play, although such reactions were incidental to the actual game itself. Control Ss, not exposed to aggressive play, failed to manifest any incidental aggressive reactions. A second study (Bandura, Ross, & Ross, 1961) involved nursery school aged children who observed an adult attacking a Bobo doll, a life-sized inflated rubber toy. A control group witnessed the same model engaged in innocuous constructive tinker-toy play. The children were then frustrated by being shown desirable toys with which, however, they were forbidden to play. Then they were taken to another room in which there were a variety of playthings, e.g., Bobo doll, mallets, etc. The spontaneous play of the children was then observed. A third control, a frustrated group not exposed to a model's aggression was also involved. The results indicated that the frustrated children exposed to the model's aggression showed significantly more aggression in their own play than the other two groups. Indeed in some instances they showed remarkably direct imitations of the actual aggressive play of the model, e.g., sitting on top of Bobo and pummeling "him."

The next study in the series attempted to compare a filmed model's effects with that of a live model (Bandura, Ross, & Ross, 1961). Here four groups were involved. One group of nursery school children saw a modeling situation similar to the previous study, a live adult aggressing against the Bobo doll, etc. The second group saw a film of the same activity projected via a TV screen. The third group saw a film of the aggressive behavior with the adult this time disguised in a cat-like costume as a cartoon-type character. A fourth group saw no model. After mild frustration the children's spontaneous play was observed. The three experimental groups showed significantly more aggressive behavior than the control group. Of special importance in this study were the fairly clear-cut indications that the film-mediated models, both the adult and cartoon-type figure, were more effective in producing aggressive responses by the children than the live adult model. In other words, the children who observed either a TV screen projection of an adult or cartoon-type character engaging in aggressive play tended to imitate the same kinds of actions in their own play by toy gun shooting, pounding the Bobo doll, etc.

Another study in this series (Bandura, Ross, & Ross, 1963a) used a similar design and examined the effect of having a film-mediated adult model punished or rewarded for the aggression he showed. The children who saw the aggressive model punished proved less likely to imitate the reaction later in their own play than those who saw the model rewarded for aggressive play, or than those who saw a nonaggressive model or had no modeling experience. Even though the children labeled the rewarded model's behavior in negative terms, they were still inclined to imitate it by verbal and physical aggressive play.

Bandura (1963) in still another study was able to demonstrate that children imitated the aggressive play of either a rewarded or neither-rewarded nor punished model more than they did the aggressiveness of a punished model. When the children were later encouraged to reproduce the behavior of the models, the children who had seen the punished model could indeed replay his aggressiveness quite accurately. In other words, the observation of punished aggression had suppressed manifestations of aggression but it had not prevented the children from taking notice of it and from being able to reproduce it later on. Comparable results were obtained in a series of studies directed by the late R. H Walters (Walters, Leat, & Mezei, 1963; Walters & Parke, 1964; Walters, Parke, & Cane, 1965).

Studies related to these may be briefly cited here too. Lovaas (1961) had children observe an aggressive cartoon. Later they were given a chance to play with one of two alternative games, a ball bouncing vs. a doll-hitting game. Those who saw the aggressive film chose the hitting game more often than did control Ss who had seen a nonaggressive film. Mussen and Rutherford (1961) used a similar design but in their case the children merely indicated desire to "pop" a balloon or not. Those who saw the aggressive cartoon were more inclined towards balloon popping. Siegel (1956), also using an aggressive film, found a trend toward increased aggressive play by children subsequently.

A final study of considerable importance in this series was carried out by Hicks (1965). This investigation showed films of children and adults engaging in aggressive play to boys and girls who were then mildly frustrated and then given an opportunity for free play. The children tended to imitate all models more than control children who saw no model with the greatest effect occurring for the aggression by the boy-model. A special feature of this study was a check on long-term effect. All children were retested six months later. Only the imitation of the male adult's aggres-

sion seemed to have persisted at all and the effect was not quite statistically significant. In other words, a single exposure to an aggressive
model may indeed be effective within an hour or so in producing imitative
aggressive play but it is not likely to have a lasting effect. The persistence
to some extent of the increased aggression imitative of the filmed adult
cannot be ignored, however.

The Critical Import of These Studies

The major import of this series of studies on the imitation of live or of
film-mediated models may be summed up in the following points:

1.   The evidence seems clear that nursery school age children do indeed imitate the aggressive behavior of adults or cartoon-type figures
whether observed live or on film.
2.   The imitation in such young children often takes the form of rather
direct imitation, down to specific movements, but more often, especially
in older children, involves expression of more general aggressive patterns, as if the observation of an aggressive model has given license to
the children for general aggressive expression.
3.   The observation by children of film-mediated aggressive play leads
to imitation subsequently especially if (a) the model is rewarded in the
film or neither rewarded nor punished, (b) if the adult model is the same
sex as the child, (c) if the child is moderately frustrated, (d) if no disapproval of the model's behavior is provided by adults in the child's presence, and (e) if the aggressive play is carried on by a boy of the same
general age group as the Ss.
4.   While observation of film-mediated aggression does not seem to
produce long-term imitative effects, there is some indication of persistence of adult male-instigated aggression.

These conclusions have led Bandura (1963) and Walters (1965) to
propose that violence presented on television can indeed lead to imitative
behavior with drastic consequences on the part of children, especially
if they are angered or frustrated. Bandura cites in a number of articles
an actual incident in which teen-agers imitating the switchblade knife-
fight scene in the movie "Rebel Without a Cause" which they had seen
the day before on TV became sufficiently embroiled to lead to a serious
wounding. Although in this specific instance an imitative effect seems
to have occurred, it should be noted, however, that most of the actual
research cited on modeling involves much younger children. Indeed
the age group in the Bandura series is least likely to observe any extended

television involving aggression by children or male adults and, indeed, might be hard put to follow programs watched by older children.

Some Criticisms of the Generalizations Drawn

The results of this series of researches on imitation seem most useful in psychology as demonstrations of significant theoretical issues in school learning. Their extension to the practical question of the actual impact of television-mediated violence upon the overt aggressive behavior of children is subject to the following limitations, however:

1. Almost all of the studies involve nursery school children of predominantly middle class backgrounds. Such children may prove compliant imitators of adults or other children in an experimental setting, but may not imitate material observed in the course of their normal TV viewing. We have almost no information about whether lower class children would manifest comparable patterns.

2. The measures of aggression employed in practically every study involve *play* situations and attacks on inanimate objects. The definition of aggression proposed by Kaufmann (1965) stresses an intent to deliver a noxious stimulus to another person (or even the property of another person) with some expectation of success. It remains an unanswered question whether aggressive play is at all the same as a direct assault upon another child. Indeed there is evidence that one of the characteristics of imaginative children is their capacity to engage in vigorous aggressive play quite comparable to the situations occurring in the Bandura-type experiments (Lesser, 1962). For many children vigorous imaginative play often involves making up interpersonal situations involving adventure and conflict. It remains to be seen whether such play bears a direct relation to overt aggression. In Lesser's (1962) study, the same imaginative children who played "aggressively," hitting Bobo, shooting a "boy's gun," etc. were given a choice of valuable games which they might keep later on. These imaginative children chose the more "creative" and much less aggressively oriented playthings while the less imaginative children who had been somewhat apathetic and hence less "aggressive" in their spontaneous play were more likely to have chosen potentially aggressive toys as their prizes.

A very recent study by Hanratty, Liebert, Morris, and Fernandez (1969) addressed itself to the question of imitation of film-mediated aggression toward live or inanimate objects. Four- and five-year-old boys observed a movie of an assault by an adult model on a human clown made up to resemble closely a plastic clown available in the playroom. The assault was by mallet or by shooting a toy gun. Subsequently the children were brought into a room with either the plastic clown or the human clown present. The children did indeed shoot at the human clown and hit her with the mallet but they showed a much greater degree of aggressive responses (e.g., punching) not demonstrated on the film towards the plastic clown. Control children who had not seen the film aggressed towards the plastic clown but never towards the human clown. The data thus suggest some modeling of film-mediated aggression shown towards the human but far less than toward the plastic clown. Since toy-gun shooting can scarcely be as aggressive as direct assault only the occasional mallet strokes can be viewed here as real violence directed toward a human in imitation of a film.

3. The "one-shot" film of an aggressive model is simply atypical of an actual television viewing experience. It is entirely possible that as a child watches many programs he is subjected to a complex series of stimuli of which the overt violence is but one feature. While it is possible that a repeated dose of violent films could have an accumulative effect in building up the potential for imitation, this has simply not been demonstrated yet in imitation or modeling experiments (see Feshbach study, below, however). It is also possible that a steady dose of television experience helps the child to define television clearly as an entertainment medium and that over the long run it will indeed be the real-life models in the child's life who will elicit imitation while television will influence chiefly the *play* patterns of the child. Eron (1963) reported more overt aggression in those children into a natural social play situation with minimal adult contact after viewing. Evidence of mutual physical assault by those who had witnessed fantasy-medium aggression would be a more telling bit of evidence against violence in TV. In all cases in these studies there is a single model and the child's behavior is observed while he is alone (or with an adult observer).

4. There is evidence that direct imitative effects are less potent or obvious in older children (Gottlieb, 1968). While observation of an adult model can yield somewhat similar behavior in adolescents as well as 9–10-year-olds, the effects are much stronger in the younger children and more subject to longstanding personality predispostion in the older ones. A critical factor may be the child's degree of imaginative development (Singer, 1966). For children who have had considerable experience and family support for engaging in fantasy play, television-viewing of aggressive behavior may simply provide interesting "story content." For less imaginative-predisposed children the exposure to aggressive models on the screen may evoke direct aggression or simply may help the child *begin* to try out aggressive content *in play*. At present there is simply no evidence from these studies on this point since predisposition in imaginative play was not studied. Predisposition to aggressive play did not in

itself prove to be related to imitation (Bandura, Ross, & Ross, 1963a). The whole issue of general background and approach to the viewing situation is largely unexplored by these investigations. The imaginative orientation of a child to play is a significant determinant of the play pattern (Singer, 1961; Gottlieb, 1968; Pulaski, 1968; Lesser, 1962) and is in turn a function of parental experience and cultural orientation (Singer, 1966).

Some evidence on the effect of imaginative predisposition is forthcoming from a recent study by Biblow (1970). Children aged 10–11 were angered by having their play disrupted by an older child. One angered group was shown a film-strip with considerable aggressive material. Another angered group was shown a film-strip with no aggressive content and a third received no film-mediated intervening stimulus. The subsequent free play of the children was observed and rated for specific acts of physical aggression toward each other as well as for expressions of various emotions such as anger, sadness, joy, etc. The results were rather complex but they indicated that children initially designated as highly imaginative behaved very differently from those with little predisposition for imaginative play. The former showed a reduction in aggressive play following exposure to the films, especially the neutral film. The less imaginative children seemed more likely to increase aggression after exposure to the aggressive film. No simple catharis theory can account for the findings. Instead it is clear that considerably more study is needed of what prior experiences or personality predisposition the child brings to the viewing situation.

5.   These studies give very few clues as to the children's perception or cognitive organization of the experimental situation. This would be more possible to investigate of course if studies were done with older age groups who could report on their interpretations. To what extent did the Ss get a feeling of what E wanted and respond accordingly?

6.   If indeed imitation does occur in children, the complexity of the TV stimulus cannot be ignored. Positive as well as negative messages are provided by TV as well as parental figures. Gordon and Cohen (1963) have shown that nursery school children's inclination to aggressive play can be sharply altered if a story involving friendship intervenes. Kaufmann and Feshbach (1963) have shown that encouragement of new responses to otherwise objectionable events may circumvent a more aggressive reaction by the individual. In this sense many of the positive features of television, the emphases on friendship, ingenuity, affection, or integrity in many films available to young children could indeed counteract the aggressive model's influence. There is ample evidence that children are especially responsive to danger to animals (Schramm et al., 1961). Clearly they have already picked up a feeling of sympathy and inhibition to

aggression that could counter direct imitation in real life while not impeding its expression *in play*.

7. Bandura (1963) and Walters (1965) themselves call attention to the counteractive influences of parental attitudes. Studies of the family backgrounds of children who develop strong antisocial and assaultive or criminal behaviors make it clear that a critical factor is the actual deviance, aggressiveness, or criminality in the parental figures themselves (Robins 1967; McCord & McCord, 1958).

Despite these limitations of the research on imitation of film-mediated violence, they pose a challenge to further research on the nature of the influence upon children of aggressive behavior by cartoon characters, children, or adults witnessed on TV. Clearly we need more careful studies taking into account the child's imaginative potential, familial orientation, and pattern of viewing habits. The modeling situation should involve some of the more natural experiences actually available in regular programming and the criteria of aggression ought to be evidence of direct aggression on others or destruction of property rather than play aggression. The issue of the degree to which an inner core of imaginative capacity and internal control plays a role cannot be minimized. There is very strong evidence from a large number of studies (summarized in Buss, 1961; Singer, 1966; Singer, 1968) which indicates that children and adults showing overt aggressive behavior show less evidence of imagination or fantasy capacity on a variety of measures and are less likely to indicate concerns about punishment or evidences of guilt or awareness of consequences in the fantasy behavior. McCasland (1961), for example, found clear support for the fact that young children prone to direct aggression with their peers did not differ in the amount of aggression shown in imaginative behavior from nonaggressive children, but showed *less* defensive content along with the fantasy than the more peaceable children. Any study of aggressive fantasy play by children must take into account not simply amount but defensiveness or complexity in aggressive play if one proposes to extrapolate to the issue real social concern, actual aggression toward others. Some of the reports from survey studies in Japan make it clear, too, that the children less inclined to aggression or antisocial behavior prefer more *complex* crime or aggression material on TV and watch more of that while their more aggressive peers prefer entertainment shows. A report by Spivack (1964) also makes clear that middle class children who show antisocial "acting out" behavior are no more interested in aggressive content than their more socialized peers but are less able to organize its expression into imaginative play.

Pending research along the lines proposed above, it seems premature to draw the conclusion from the modeling studies that aggressive content (which characterizes so much of all imaginative material available to children) evokes direct imitative behavior by children. Without minimizing the valuable heuristic influence of the work of Bandura and Walters on imitation and social learning, it remains to be seen whether more precise examination of the parameters of the problem, cast in definite relation to the actualities of TV viewing, supports their proposals concerning the dangers of much of the adventure content currently available.

INFLUENCE OF FILM-MEDIATED AGGRESSION ON AGGRESSIVE BEHAVIOR IN YOUNG ADULTS

Review of Studies

We have focused thus far on experimental studies with children. Modeling or imitation research has not been carried out with adults in the same pattern described. Instead the emphasis has been upon the more general impact of witnessing violence in a brief motion picture upon subsequent mood and inclination to deliver a noxious stimulus to another person. Almost all of these studies have involved experiments of a rather complex nature in which college students have participated as subjects. Only two film stimuli have been employed, the switchblade knife-fight scene from the movie "Rebel Without a Cause" and a seven-minute prize-fight sequence from the movie "Champion" in which Kirk Douglas experiences a vicious beating.

Although the initial research in this field was conducted by Feshbach (1961) who sought to establish evidence for a catharsis (effect), the major thrust in this field has been directed by Berkowitz. Feshbach introduced the use of the prize fight film but relied upon verbal measures as his criteria of aggression, while Berkowitz and his group developed the "delivery of electric shock" as a more direct indication of aggression.

The central issue grew out of the efforts of Feshbach to establish the basis of a cathartic effect of viewing violence. He proposed that if a subject is angered at the time he witnesses a film involving violence he is likely to experience a partial reduction of his aggressive inclinations. The significant experiment he carried out involved insulting college students, presenting them with the "Champion" film sequence, and immediately afterwards obtaining word associations (scored for aggressive content) and reactions to the insulting experimenter. There were three other conditions, an Insult-Neutral film condition, a Non-Insult-Aggressive film condition, and a Non-Insult-Neutral film. Feshbach proposed that Ss angered by insult and shown an aggressive film would show less subsequent hostility while those not angered but shown the aggressive film might actually show an *increase* in aggressive inclinations. His results clearly supported the *decrease* in aggression for the Insult–Aggressive film group—a cathartic effect—but no increase in aggression for the group exposed to the fight film.

Quite different results were obtained in a study reported by Walters and Thomas (1963) and Walters, Thomas, and Acker (1962). They exposed adolescents and male and female hospital attendants to the knife-fight scene from "Rebel Without a Cause." Control *S*s saw a film about adolescents engaging in cooperative activities. Subsequently the *S*s were tested for persisting verbal aggression but in addition were put in a situation in which they believed themselves to be delivering electric shocks to confederates as part of a learning experiment. The *S*s exposed to the aggressive film subsequently showed more verbal aggressive ratings and showed greater aggression in delivering electric shocks to their peers in the learning task. Thus these investigations obtained the findings of an increased aggressive tendency after exposure to a film involving violence. This study incidentally was the only one to use *S*s from lower socio-economic groups.

The same film was employed by Lefcourt, Barnes, Parke, and Schwartz (1966) who were interested in the effect of reactions of approval or disapproval of the aggression in the film on the subsequent aggressive reaction. They found that those *S*s who witnessed the knife-fight sequence under conditions in which a confederate expressed disapproval of the participant's conduct showed no subsequent increase in the intensity of the shocks they delivered in the simulated learning task. By contrast *S*s who heard the confederate express approval of the fighting showed an increase in subsequent aggression. Thus the social context of exposure to the aggressive film takes on more meaning and the aggression-arousal is not an automatic process.

The extensive sequence of studies by Berkowitz and his colleagues have been addressed to examining in detail the social parameters of the situation of observing violence. The studies use essentially the same design—*S*s are told that they and a confederate of the *E* are co-participants in a learning experiment. They are to provide each other with electric shocks to improve learning and to penalize errors. The shocks increase in intensity so that the button *S* pushes indicates just how much shock (the analog of aggression) he is delivering to his confederate. The *S*s observe either the "Champion" film or a scene from an exciting foot race (non-aggressive but interesting). Subsequently they are angered and given the opportunity to shock the confederate. As a protection for the confederate, the apparatus has been disconnected but *S*s presumably do not know this and presumably believe themselves to be delivering rather painful shocks.

Berkowitz' position is that aggression is indeed a significant consequence of frustration, which he defines as the thwarting of intentions. He argues that if a person has been frustrated he will be more prone to show aggression if there are indications of aggression-eliciting cues in the environment. Thus if he witnesses an aggressive film this may increase his inclination to react aggressively. This is more likely to be the case if the action in the film is justified, if the object of *S*s aggression bears some justifiable basis for attack (e.g., he is described as a college boxer, bears the same name as the recipient of aggression in the film (Kirk), or if other aggression-eliciting cues are in the room (guns lying on a nearby table).

The series of studies in which these findings emerge are impressive because they yield replicable findings. Berkowitz and Rawlings (1963) found that *S*s observing the violent prize-fight who were told that the protagonist who received the beating (Kirk Douglas) was a "heel" who deserved his fate were subsequently more aggressive than those who were told that Douglas' beating was unjustified. A similar result was obtained by Berkowitz, Corwin, and Heironimus (1962). In another series of experiments Berkowitz (1965) also obtained an increase in aggression (verbal) and in shock intensity following the aggressive film, but there were indications that the cue value of the target of the *S*'s subsequent aggression could elicit aggressive reactions whether or not the *S* actually had seen the aggressive film. That is, even if the *S* had not seen the aggressive film he was likely to direct more shocks toward a person identified as a college boxer simply because such a designation had an aggressive cue value. This was clarified in a study by Berkowitz and Geen (1966) where assigning the recipient of aggression in the "Champion" film and the ultimate object of the *S*'s aggression, the confederate to be shocked, the same name (Kirk or Bob) yielded higher aggression than when the names differed. Geen and Berkowitz (1966) replicated this result with a different set of names. Still later Berkowitz and Geen (1967) studied the cumulative effect of designating the aggression as justified and the confederate as bearing the same name as the deserving victim of aggression. Geen and Berkowitz (1967) and later Geen (1968) alone further replicated the findings of increased aggression after witnessing the violent film and showed that frustration associated with aggressive cues produced aggressive reactions. Similar results were also obtained by Hoyt and Tannenbaum (Berkowitz, 1968).

Implications

The results of almost ten separate studies employing mainly young college students as *S*s indicate that witnessing a violent film can indeed serve as one cue for evoking aggressive reactions. Berkowitz (1968) has summarized these results as suggesting that violence in public media can indeed reduce normal inhibitions to aggressions at least for a short time afterwards and increase the likelihood that an angered or frustrated person will engage in an impulsive assault. He argues that the justified beatings received by villains and the shooting down of "bad guys" by the Matt Dillons of TV create a "frontier atmosphere" which support inclinations to direct assault in young people if they are sufficiently frustrated. He questions whether violence is necessary in entertainment media to the degree that it is presently offered.

Certainly the weight of evidence of this group of studies argues against any simple catharsis theory in which observing violence in a "make-believe" medium reduces inclinations to actual aggression. The studies consistently point to the fact that exposure of young adults to an aggressive movie provides them under special circumstances with a justification or additional incentive towards noxious behavior as measured chiefly by the delivery of electric shocks. This tendency in not "built-in" but reflects to some extent the social meaning of the film for when its aggression is represented as unjustified or when overt disapproval of the fighting is expressed by a companion there is indeed no enhancement of subsequent aggression.

Some Critical Questions

The experimental studies cited in the section above represent a most convincing group of investigations. Methodologically they are sophisticated and rigorous, and statistically they are convincing in the magnitude of their effects. The question arises, however, as to whether the generalizations from these studies to the real life situation of the TV viewer or movie-goer are supportable. In this connection a number of series of criticisms can be raised.

1. The major criterion of aggression employed in most of the studies is the delivery of a shock of high intensity to another student presumably as part of a learning experiment. To the extent that the S knows how painful the shock can be and intends to hurt his fellow student by raising the intensity of the shock the criterion for aggression is met. In some studies Ss did experience the shock (in moderate fashion) beforehand so that he could realize that by pressing a button for higher intensity he would actually discomfort his fellow participant. Many of the studies do not permit S to experience the shock in advance, however. It remains a serious question whether the delivery of the shock really is analogous to an act of overt aggression. If E asked the frustrated S to slap the other participant in the face or to whack him with a paddle we might not get the same reaction. Conceivably by setting up a complex situation in which S

gets minimal feedback from his fellow player of distress and has every reason to believe that a faculty member of a college would not permit him to harm anyone seriously, the whole situation takes on a game-like atmosphere. While it has been shown in studies of obedience that some Ss do indeed become upset by the possibility they may hurt someone badly, such reports are not forthcoming in this group of studies. It remains to be demonstrated whether the shock score is more than a game-like performance on the part of S and not sufficiently analogous to an act of direct aggression.

2. A related question arises out of our increased awareness since Rosenthal's (1966) studies of experimenter-effects that Ss may seek to fathom the E's purpose in a study and respond accordingly. The authors of these investigations do not seem to have completely ruled out the possibilities that the Ss may get a "hidden message" about the meaning of the study, if not from the E then from the very nature of the procedure, and consequently show the desired effect. Despite the convincing repeatability of the findings, we hear too little about how Ss actually perceived the rather complicated experiences of jumping from one situation to another, getting insulted, seeing movies, having to shock someone, etc.

3. Two movies have been used in these studies. Both are especially aggressive and frightening, indeed more extended and vicious by far than most of the aggressive scenes in television at any rate. If an aggression-enhancing effect does occur, would it actually be as powerful under normal circumstances especially since the viewers are not as likely to be angry while watching or frustrated immediately afterwards or exposed *only* to aggressive material? Berkowitz (1968) admits that any aggression-enhancing effect might be quite temporary. The nature of the TV viewing situation (smaller screen) or the interruption by commercials may mitigate against persistence of the cue value of the film. Indeed aggressive reactions are more likely to be directed towards the sponsor of a breezy commercial which interrupts a dramatic battle scene! Actually the interruptions of commericals and of announcements certainly break the spell of the viewer and probably minimize intense reactions. This may be less true in movies and some studies do suggest increased hostility after a full scale aggressive movie (Ancona & Bertini, 1967). For television, however, absorption of the type likely to create the degree of aggressive orientation necessary seems unlikely.

4. The fact that TV viewing takes place in a social situation ordinarily with others around and with conversation mixed in with viewing needs to be considered further. A few of the studies show that the confederate's reaction to the movie influences the degree of subsequent aggression and it seems likely that in many homes where young people are involved

some negative reactions to excessive assaultiveness will be forthcoming. Of course the reverse could occur, too, and one can imagine some parents viewing the recent Chicago Democratic Convention scenes of police striking demonstrators and saying things like, "Serves that Commie right!" in the presence of their children. On the whole, however, it is likely that the home-viewing situation or even the semi-social atmosphere that prevails in movie houses or the mixture of necking and viewing in a drive-in theatre as providing more complex influences for the viewers than the direct aggression provided in these experiments. Indeed while undoubtedly conflicts aplenty arise in the bosom of the family, they are not likely to reach the intensity while people are watching TV to produce the aggression-eliciting effects which the experimentalists have so carefully set up.

5. The studies so far, except the one by Walters, employ college students and are hence geared toward middle class Ss. We have no clue really as to whether less well-educated Ss would react in a comparable fashion. To the extent that a certain degree of compliance by Ss is necessary to move through the procedures in orderly fashion, the use of middle class college students enhances the likelihood of clear-cut outcomes. We have no basis for saying how such sequences of events would effect lower socioeconomic or less well-educated students.

Perhaps the major criticism of these studies is their artificiality. They smell of the laboratory and involve complex sequences of procedures that simply seem too far removed from the ordinary course of events in real life. They give little feeling of what an actual viewer's experience would involve with a long sequence, two to three hours of watching a variety of programs, some relaxing, some tense, some involving aggression, others evoking sexual interest, social interests, affiliative tendencies, achievement motivation, etc. Clearly what is called for are studies involving actual TV programming in relatively natural settings (e.g., homes, dormitory rooms, etc.) and experimental situations that permit expression of more realistic aggressive reactions. In addition, attention must be paid to the identification patterns of the Ss (Maccoby & Wilson, 1957) their predisposition to imagination or to aggression (Meyerson, 1967) or other relative predisposing personality characteristics, thus far completely overlooked in these studies. Since we know too that the viewing of stress films calls forth rather different reactions (Lazarus & Opton, 1966), one would wonder whether such reactions operate to distort some of the reactions to the aggressive films employed.

We cannot avoid a verdict of "not proven" to the claim that this series of experiments on film-mediated aggression argues against presentation of violence on television. This should not minimize, however, the theoretical value of Berkowitz' work, his analysis of the relation of cues as incitement to aggressive response and of the conditions which leads to an aggressive reaction to frustration or anger-arousal.

THE CATHARSIS THEORY RE-EXAMINED EXPERIMENTALLY

Review of Studies

As suggested in the early section of this report, the catharsis theory appears to have serious limitations on theoretical grounds. Nevertheless there are available a sizeable number of experimental studies that relate to the phenomena of vicarious reduction of aggression or anger. Even if one questions the concept of aggression as a periodic drive reduced partially by fantasy expression, one can still consider the possibility that witnessing an aggressive film may provde some pleasure to an angry person, enough to change his mood at any rate even if it does not dispel the original anger. Or one can view the enjoyment of aggressive material as simply providing alternative behavioral patterns so that Ss are distracted from a narrow focus on direct assault.

The research on catharsis takes a number of diverse forms. There are studies which focus on the vicarious experience of a social type in which S observes someone else engaging in an aggressive action which he would ordinarily do himself (Rosenbaum & de Charms, 1960). Other studies (Bramel, Taub, & Blum, 1968) focus on Ss observing an enemy discomfited or on the communication of processes itself as a reducer of anger (Thibaut & Coules, 1952). For the purposes of this presentation the major research involves the effect of some fantasy experience such as viewing a movie, listening to humor, or engaging in imaginative play upon reduction of an inclination to aggression.

Perhaps the critical early study in this field was carried out by Feshbach (1955). Feshbach aroused anger in college students by having them insulted while taking some tests. Later some were given an opportunity for fantasy expression through writing imaginative stories while control Ss performed a non-fantasy task. The results supported the catharsis theory since there was less aggression evident on some verbal ratings for the fantasy-expression group than for the non-fantasy group. When Feshbach (1956) attempted a comparable study using the fantasy play of children as the cathartic medium, however, he found some increased tendency for aggressive play. In this latter study, however, the children were not angered just before their fantasy play. An unpublished study by Kenny (1953) also found that aggressive play increased the likelihood of further aggression in children. Lesser (1962) also failed to obtain a cathartic effect with children frustrated by their failure to solve a problem who had an opportunity to tell imaginative stories.

On the whole studies with children have not supported the catharsis theory especially when aggressive *play* or some form of rating methods were employed to evaluate the level of aggression (Siegel, 1956; Emery, 1959; Albert, 1957). One unpublished study with young children did report that frustrated boys became less aggressive after seeing a Western movie (Estess, cited in Singer, 1966). A study of movie viewing carried out by Heinrich (1961) obtained ratings on scales of aggression from over two thousand children ages 12–16 who watched aggressive, "appeasing," or ambivalent films. Subsequent ratings of aggression increased in many instances after aggressive films that were *especially realistic* and *susceptible to imitation* by children. No catharsis effect could be discerned.

Clearly the evidence from movies or imaginative aggression play in children does not support a catharsis theory, especially if the criteria of aggression are attitude scales or other forms of verbal response. Only Siegel (1956) observed direct aggression in children.

For adults the findings are somewhat different. In a well-known study Feshbach (1961) showed angered college students the "Champion" movie and found a reduction in subsequent aggression (compared with controls) as measured by self-ratings. Singer and Rowe (1962) arranged to have surprise midterm examinations administered to college students. After the tests some were given an opportunity to daydream and others performed an absorbing task. The former group showed a reduction in anger and aggression on the Feshbach scales but tended to increase their anxiety level. A complex study by Pytkowicz, Wagner, and Sarason (1967) found a reduction in aggression ratings for angered *S*s who had opportunities either for daydreaming or writing imaginative stories. The effect was obtained chiefly for those *S*s already strongly predisposed to daydreaming as a personality characteristic. A very recent unpublished study by Paton under this author's direction has also yielded evidence that persons aroused to anger show a subsequent reduction in such reactions (compared with various control *S*s) if permitted to inspect and fantasize about neutral pictures as well as aggressive pictures (such as Vietnam war scenes). The evidence seems to suggest that when persons are angered an opportunity to change their mood by becoming absorbed in interesting fantasy activity which distracts them somewhat can lead to less persistence of an aggressive inclination.

Similar results have been obtained in studies of the psychology of humor (Levine, 1968). For example, Dworkin & Efran (1967) found that angered persons showed subsequent reductions in aggression after exposure to recordings of either aggressive *or* neutral humor. Singer (1968) exposed Negro civil rights workers in the South to white racist speeches in order to arouse their anger. Then they heard aggressive or neutral humor (monologues by Dick Gregory). The general findings led to the conclusion:

> . . . . under appropriate conditions gratifying fantasy can have profound cathartic effects without in any way altering external reality. . . . These findings also support the view that symbolic processes such as fantasy and the humor response can serve as mediators; affording the possibility of delay between impulse and action, and furnishing a satisfying alternative to action on the one hand and rigid suppression on the other (Singer, 1968).

The research on humor as well as a large body of studies on the role of imaginative development as a control over overt aggressive or impulsive behavior (Singer, 1966, 1968) point up the importance for man of having available alternative response possibilities which can provide pleasure, distract one, or offer different avenues of reaction in the face of frustration and aroused anger. Many studies with the Rorschach test indicate that both children and adults who have well-developed fantasy lives are far less prone to assaultive behavior. Singer and Opler (1956), comparing Irish and Italian schizophrenic patients, found that the Irish showed greater imagination and were more cooperative and less assaultive in their ward behavior. Townsend (1968) found that Rorschach measures of imagination were significantly higher for boys who showed minimal direct aggression than for those who were observed to be regularly aggressive. Other studies with children bring clearly the important role of well-developed imagination in providing important controls for behavior (Pulaski, 1968; Gottlieb, 1968; Singer, 1961; Spivack & Levine, 1964; Biblow, 1970).

The implications of these studies for the effects of communication media would appear to be that very interesting fictional material, even if aggressive in content, will not necessarily impel the viewer to action but rather encourage further use of imagination. For the child or adult especially gifted in using imagination to distract himself or pass the time, the availability of interesting content from television will only abet further recourse to daydreaming and playful thought. It is possible that for those children or adults who do not have well-developed imaginations the "cathartic" or distraction effect of absorbing material, aggressive or nonaggressive, may not be evident. Indeed if modeling or incitement to direct action does occur from television, viewing it is likely to be chiefly for those children with little experience or opportunity for fantasy play. There seems little question that stories involving some degree of serious conflict, danger or suspense are generally most absorbing to boys or men (who make up the bulk of subjects in most experiments) The boxing film certainly seemed more interesting to most observers. It may be that this absorbing quality of aggressive movies alters an aggressive mood in many subjects or provides them with intriguing fantasies afterwards which because of their intrinsic interest distract the person from an aggressive intent or reduce a high level of psychological arousal (Tomkins, 1962).

Some recent findings point up the complexity of the problem of trying to generalize too readily about the effects of aggressive movie content on psychological states. In a study with adults Foulkes and Rechtshaffen (1964) showed films to Ss just before they went to sleep. Using EEG and rapid eye movement criteria of probable dreaming, they awakened their subjects to obtain dream reports during the night. These adult subjects seemed more disturbed and evidenced more aggression after seeing an aggressive rather than a neutral movie.

By contrast when the same study (Foulkes et al., 1967) was carried out with preadolescents very different results emerged. The children who saw a violent cowboy-Indian movie before sleep had fewer disturbing or aggressive dreams while those who saw a baseball movie showed greater hostility and distress in their dreams. In general the results suggested that an absorbing aggressive movie was less likely to lead to nightmares and aggressive-toned dreams than a neutral baseball film (admittedly somewhat less interesting to the children). Of course it would be hasty to move too quickly to generalize from the Foulkes et al. 1967 study to a proposal that aggressive movies make better bedtime watching than baseball. Nevertheless it seems clear that one cannot assume an automatically harmful effect of an absorbing adventure film. It is hard to believe, however, that a very mysterious film or one involving ghoulish practices or supernatural and sadistic events would, however absorbing, yield a night of pleasant dreams. Cowboys and Indians, with all the shooting and dying, have a faraway, clearly fantasy, stylized quality that seems different from a very realistic knife-fight or a convincingly portrayed horror film. The Foulkes studies do suggest an interesting methodological approach more like the true viewing situation, however, and worthy of further exploration.

Perhaps the study that comes closest to meeting reasonable criteria of comparability to a TV viewing situation is the recently completed but as yet unpublished study by Feshbach and Singer (1971). They studied young adolescent boys from middle and lower class backgrounds who were in private schools or residential treatment centers. They assigned half of each group regular "diets" of either aggressive (Western or detective-spy) or nonaggressive (comedy, family series, variety) TV shows to watch over a period of weeks. They obtained ratings *daily* of the actual aggressiveness, e.g., pushing, fighting of the boys before, during, and after their experimental diet. The results were especially striking for the lower-class boys. Those who watched aggressive films on TV were significantly lower in aggression than they had been initially while the nonaggressive film viewers increased, if anything, in their aggression. The greater the initial aggressive level of a boy, the more likely he was to reduce his aggressiveness if he had a steady diet of aggressive films! These boys reported that watching the more aggressive films increased their repulsion for aggression and so they apparently began suppressing their own somewhat. Of course it must be recalled that the boys who had the nonaggressive TV diet were habitual viewers with greater taste for aggressive films so that they were suffering some deprivation, which may account for their increased aggressiveness. Since no data are available on the imaginative predispositions of these children we cannot tell how many were stimulated to use more fantasy rather than to rely upon direct action.

This study is clearly the most intriguing yet to appear and generalizations must await full analysis of the data or formal publication. Nevertheless it provides at least two important methodological advances, *the use of directly observed aggression* (with physical and verbal aggression clearly separated) and *the use of regular TV watching continuing over a reasonable period of time.* If we are to really come to grips with the issue of the effects of TV violence on overt aggressive behavior, we will need several more studies of this type, controlling more effectively factors of interest, imagination, various inhibitory tendencies in the boys, and long-term viewing habits. By contrast the Bandura studies with the measure of aggression being the pummeling of an obvious toy seem artificial and less related to the urgent issues of overt violence.

An Evaluation of the Catharsis Theory

Viewed technically in the form in which it initially became popular, the catharsis theory essentially involves a hydraulic energy model or fits best in a drive-reduction model of learning. Within the past decade important advances in experimental studies of brain function and autonomic function as well as in studies of motivation have questioned the utility of simple drive-reduction models (Tomkins, 1962; White, 1959; Miller, 1963). The experimental literature reviewed above certainly does not provide any consistent evidence of an effect that fits the more traditional model. Indeed there is ample evidence that symbolic aggressive play in children may increase the likelihood that they will make aggressive responses. The research on humor appreciation (Levine, 1968) and related studies summarized above do call attention to the fact that modifications of aroused anger or aggressive impulsive reactions are possible. It seems more likely, however, that what happens is not a partial reduction of a certain quantum of an aggressive drive but rather a distracting effect, a change of moods or emotional arousal level, a shift of cognitive focus, which changes the initial situation. Indeed, as Meyerson (1967) has shown in a study with children, imitation of aggressive models by children requires a very specific marked similarity of the two situations to be effective. The effects of aggression on film may indeed yield some imitative effects *in play* but it may also be that the excitement and absorption of the content may well alter a depressed or angry mood and provide the observer with a somewhat different perspective on a situation. In this sense it is possible that cathartic effects occur through the enjoyment changes in mood and escape value of aggressive material.

A more profound question upon which the experimental literature is largely silent has to do with the reasons for the prevalence of violence in the communication media. This is of course partially cultural and it seems likely that part of the appeal of Western films in the U. S. (like Samurai films in Japan or Roman epics in Italy) grows from relations to the nation's historic past, to adventure more generally than to violence alone, and to opportunities, especially for males, to identify temporarily with demonstrations of physical prowess and daring which are absent from their own more workaday worlds. In this respect the relatively stylized quality of the most successful adventure films, mixed often enough with a certain degree of humor, makes it clear to the audience that they are absorbed temporarily in an unreal world. It seems unlikely that a comparable cathartic effect is obtained from witnessing true violence on news programs. The national revulsion experienced at specific scenes of violence, e.g., the shooting "in cold blood" of a Viet Cong guerilla by General Loan during the Tet offensive, the police dogs leaping at Birmingham demonstrators, etc. scarcely offer any cathartic relief.

Pending the needed research on the psychological effects of actual violence in news reports or documentaries, some implications may be drawn from the work on catharsis and modeling. It seems likely that violent material that is close to actual experience or that is in the realm of possibility for the viewer (e.g., a knife-fight between boys or a detailed fist-fight, a husband strangling a wife vividly depicted) would prove more disturbing and evoke less enjoyment and change of mood in an already upset or mildly angered person. Most of the evidence from surveys or experimental studies of modeling suggest that children are more upset by material close to their life situation, or will imitate models in situations almost identical with what they have viewed. The more remote the material in terms of historical past or costume (e.g., Westerns) or the more stylized and the more often some humor or period of exhilaration is associated with the material, the more likely a quasi-cathartic effect, a real change of mood. In a study like Foulkes *et al.* (1967) cited above, one characteristic of the Western film is its *closure* psychologically while this is less likely in the baseball film (which did not lead up to the victory of one team or another). To the extent that most TV adventure films end happily or with some clear resolution, the likelihood of a closing off of the situation is greater than where the material ends on a note of tension or failure of resolution (as is certainly the case for news reports of violence). As Breger (1967) has analyzed the nature of dream material and Singer (1968) the issue of daydream content, what gets into consciousness is the unfinished business of our lives. In this sense the specific effects of violence or non-violence of programming may be secondary to other factors such as *closure–non-closure, reality–unreality, justification–non-justification,* etc. Cathartic effects may therefore occur most often when material comes to a relatively acceptable conclusion.

CONCLUSIONS

1. A careful scrutiny of the formal scientific literature does not yield evidence that warrants a judgment linking the increased violence in the United States to the portrayal of violence in fiction or news reporting on TV or movie film. The occurrence of three major wars in a period of 25 years with the vast increase in military emphasis in the nation compared with the 1930's or 1920's, the far greater availability of weapons to the general public after World War II, and the frustration of the greatly increased hopes of the urban masses seem far more critical factors. Indeed if television has played a role, it may be as much by presenting the poor with daily images of the world outside the ghetto, of the affluence of the nation, and of the many desirable objects or commodities just out of reach of the poor. It also provides concrete examples of social or political action by poor persons all around the nation. The very heavy load of aggressive content in most popular media is certainly a fact but whether it has a direct impact on actual violent actions can simply not be known from our present evidence.

2. The experimental and survey research carried out does raise the possibility that specific children or adults strongly aroused by some external frustration immediately after viewing a television or movie depiction of violence could indeed imitate some of the aggression witnessed on the screen. Available evidence suggests that someone so influenced might most likely be a person who does not watch TV frequently or systematically, who lacks a well-developed imaginative life as a personality resource, and who has a pattern of impulsivity or hyperactivity.

What imitation does occur is only in situations bearing great similarity to what was actually depicted on the screen.

3. Experimental evidence suggests the possibility (which merits more extensive research) that the high content of *justified* aggression presented in films and television may systematically lower normal inhibitions and anxieties concerning the expression of aggression. There are some suggestions, however, that for boys already high in aggression, viewing aggressive material will not increase their aggressive response (Meyerson, 1967) and may even lead to a decrease in overt aggression (Feshbach & Singer, 1968).

4. Observation of aggressive behavior in fictional material may help reduce tensions under conditions where it is mixed with humor or cast in a clearly playful setting. Similarly, violence in stereotyped form (such as Westerns) or in situations far removed from the ordinary daily lives of viewers (historical or foreign settings, use of lances rather than switchblade knives) may be less distressing or provocative of imitation. This latter point merits significant research attention, for it implies new possibilities of programming if supported.

5. It is increasingly clear that the behavioral sciences have developed relatively sophisticated techniques for studying the problems of the impact of television or related media. Most of the research has been on an extremely small scale, however, has employed relatively unrepresentative samples of actual TV programming in the design, and has not yet satisfactorily duplicated the actual conditions of TV viewing in the home setting. Studies with lower middle or lower socioeconomic groups are sparse. Most research has used male adults or children and has only recently begun to examine actual aggressive behavior rather than aggressive *play* or simulated aggression. It seems important that formal research on the problem of violence in public media be carried out on the basis of serious research rather than the plethora of opinion or polemics in this area. The technology is available but there does not seem to be sufficient evidence for public or legal action at this time without jeopardizing other freedoms.

6. Pending more extensive experimental research, some self-scrutiny and perhaps internal restraint may be desirable in the popular media especially since the experimental research does open the possibility of some negative effects. The slow erosion of inhibitions agains violence, the excitement through observation of immediate events in the news broadcasts all seem to have cumulative effects which demand urgent study. Especially significant is the need for careful study of the impact of the increased vividness and pictorial effectiveness of documentary or ongoing films and radio reportage of incidents of violence or calls to action. Such

material has simply not been studied and its implications for influence on viewers seem currently more powerful than the content of clearly fictional programs.

REFERENCES

Albert, R. The role of mass media and the effect of aggressive film content upon children's aggressive response and identification choices. *Genetic Psychology Monographs,* 1957, **55,** 221–285.

Ancona, L. and Bertini, M. Effett di scarica dell' aggressivita per film a forte tensione emotiva. *Contributi dell'Instituto di Psichologia,* 1967, **28,** 1–18.

Bailyn, L. Mass media and children: A study of exposure habits and cognitive effects. *Psychological Monographs,* **73,** 1959, 1–48.

Baker, J. W. The effects of four types of vicarious aggression on physiological and psycological arousal. *Dissertation Abstracts,* 1967, **28**(5-B), 2132–2133.

Banay, R. S. Testimony before the subcommittee to investigate juvenile delinquency; Committee of the Judiciary, U. S. Senate, Eighty-fourth Congress, S. Res. 62, 1955, Washington, D. C., U. S. Government Printing Office.

Bandura, A. What TV violence can do to your child. *Look,* October 22, 1963, 46–52.

Bandura, A. & Houston, A. C. Identification as a process of incidental learning. *Journal of Abnormal and Social Psychology,* 1961, **63,** 311–318.

Bandura, A., Ross, D., & Ross, S. Transmission of aggression through imitation of aggressive models. *Journal of Abnormal and Social Psychology,* 1961, **63,** 575–582.

Bandura, A., Ross, D., & Ross, S. Imitation of film-mediated aggressive models. *Journal of Abnormal and Social Psychology,* 1963a, **66,** 3–11.

Bandura, A., Ross, D., & Ross, S. Vicarious reinforcement and imitative learning. *Journal of Abnormal and Social Psychology,* 1963b, **67,** 601–607.

Bandura, A. & Walters, R. H. *Social learning and personality development.* New York: Holt, Rinehart & Winston, 1963.

Berkowitz, L. Some aspects of observed aggression. *Journal of Personality and Social Psychology,* 1965, **2,** 359–369.

Berkowitz, L. Impulse, aggression and the gun. *Psychology Today,* 1968, **2,** 18–23.

Berkowitz, L., Corwin, R., & Heironimus, M. Film violence subsequent aggressive tendencies. *Public Opinion Quarterly,* 1962, **27,** 217–229.

Berkowitz, L. & Geen, R. Film violence and the cue properties of available targets. *Journal of Personality and Social Psychology,* 1966, **3,** 525–530.

Berkowitz, L. & Geen, R. Stimulus qualities of the target of aggression: A further study. *Journal of Personality and Social Psychology,* 1967, **5,** 364–368.

Berkowitz, L. & Rawlings, E. Effects of film violence on inhibitions against subsequent aggression. *Journal of Abnormal and Social Psychology,* 1963, **66,** 405–412.

Biblow, E. The role of fantasy in the reduction of aggression. Unpublished doctoral dissertation, City University of New York, 1970.

Blumer, H. & Hauser, P. *Movies, delinquency and crime.* New York: Macmillan, 1933.

Bokander, I. & Lindholm, K. The effects of aggressive films on minors. *Nordisk Psykologi,* 1967, **19,** (1).

Bramel, B., Taub, B., & Blum, B. An observer's reaction to the suffering of his enemy. *Journal of Personality and Social Psychology,* 1968, **8,** 384–392.

Breger, L. Function of dreams. *Journal of Abnormal and Social Psychology Monograph,* 1967, **72,** Whole No. 641.

Buss, A. *The Psychology of Aggression*. New York: Wiley, 1961.

Coffin, T. Television's impact on society. *American Psychologist*, 1955, **10**, 630–641.

Dworkin, E. & Efran, J. The angered: Their susceptibility to varieties of humor. *Journal of Personality and Social Psychology*, 1967, **6**, 233–236.

Emery, F. E. Psychological effects of the Western film: A study in television viewing: II. The experimental study. *Human Relations*, 1959, **12**, 215–232.

Eron, L. Relationships of TV viewing and aggressive behavior in children. *Journal of Abnormal and Social Psychology*, 1963, **34**, 849–867.

Feshbach, S. The drive-reducing function of fantasy behavior. *Journal of Abnormal and Social Psychology*, 1955, **50**, 3–11.

Feshbach, S. The catharsis hypothesis and some consequences of interaction with aggressive and neutral play objects. *Journal of Personality and Social Psychology*, 1956, **24**, 449–462.

Feshbach, S. The stimulating versus cathartic effects of a vicarious aggressive activity. *Journal of Abnormal and Social Psychology*, 1961, **63**, 381–385.

Feshbach, S. Effects of exposure to aggressive content in television upon aggression in boys. *Proceedings of the XVI International Congress of Applied Psychology, Copenhagen*, 1968, 669–672.

Feshbach, S. & Singer, R. D. *Television and aggression*. San Francisco: Josey-Bass, 1971.

Foulkes, D., Pivik, T., Steadman, H., Spear, P., & Symonds, J. Dreams of the male child: An EEG study. *Journal of Abnormal Psychology*, 1967, **72**, 457–467.

Foulkes, D. & Rechtshaffen, A. Presleep determinants of dream content: Effects of two films. *Perceptual and Motor Skills*, 1964, **19**, 983–1005.

Freud, S. *Civilization and its discontents*. In Strachey, J. (Ed.) *The complete psychological works of Sigmund Freud*. London: Hogarth, 1962.

Furu, T. *Television and children's life: A before-after study*. Tokyo, Japan: Radio and Television Culture Research Institute, 1962.

Geen, R. Effects of frustration, attack, and prior training in aggressiveness upon aggressive behavior. *Journal of Personality and Social Psychology*, 1968, **9**, 316–321.

Geen, R. & Berkowitz, L. Name-mediated aggressive cue properties. *Journal of Personality*, 1966, **34**, 456–465.

Geen, R. & Berkowitz, L. Some conditions facilitating the occurrence of aggression after the observation of violence. *Journal of Personality*, 1967, **35**, 666–676.

George, F. B. A study of the attitudes of selected officers of the California Congress of parents and teachers toward the relation of motion pictures and television to children. Unpublished doctoral dissertation, University of Southern California, 1965.

Gordon, J. E. & Cohen, F. Effect of fantasy arousal of affiliation drive on doll play aggression. *Journal of Abnormal and Social Psychology*, 1963, **66**, 301–307.

Gottlieb, S. Modeling effects on fantasy. Unpublished doctoral dissertation, City University of New York, 1968.

Hanratty, M., Liebert, R., Morris, L., & Fernandez, L. Imitation of film-mediated aggression against live and inanimate victims. *Proceedings, 77th Annual Convention, American Psychological Association*, 1969, 457–458.

Heinrich, K. Filmerleben, Filmwirkung, Filmerzeihung. *Der Einfluss des Films auf die Aggressivitat bei Jungendlichen, Experimentalle Untersuchungen und ihre lernpsychologischen Konsequenzen*. Berlin: Schroedel, 1961.

Hicks, D. Imitation and retention of film-mediated aggressive peer and adult models. *Journal of Personality and Social Psychology*, 1965, **2**, 97–100.

Himmelweit, H., Oppenheim, A. N., & Vance, P. *Television and the child: An empirical study of television viewing on the young*. New York: Oxford Univer. Press, 1958.

58

JEROME L. SINGER

Kaufmann, H. Definitions and methodology in the study of aggression. *Psychological Bulletin*, 1965, **64**, 351–364.
Kaufmann, H. & Feshbach, S. The influence of anti-aggressive communications upon response to provocation. *Journal of Personality*, 1963, **31**, 428–444.
Kenny, D. T. An experimental test of the catharsis theory of aggression. Unpublished doctoral dissertation, University of Michigan, 1953.
Klapper, J. (Ed.) *The effects of mass communication.* Glencoe, Ill.: The Free Press, 1960.
Larsen, O. N., Gray, L., & Fortis, J. Goals and goal achievement methods in television content: Models for anomie? *Sociological Inquiry*, 1963, 180–196.
Lazarus, S. & Opton, E. M. The study of psychological stress: A summary of theoretical formulations and experimental findings. In Spielberger, C. (Ed.) *Anxiety and Behavior.* New York: Academic Press, 1966.
Lefcourt, H., Barnes, K., Parke, R., & Schwartz, F. Anticipated social censure and aggression-conflict as mediators of response to aggression induction. *Journal of Social Psychology*, 1966, **70**, 251–263.
Lesser, L. N. An experimental investigation of children's behavior as a function of interpolated activities and individual differences in imaginative behavior. Unpublished doctoral dissertation, New York University, 1962. Also *Dissertation Abstracts*, 1963, **24**(2), 836–837.
Levine, S. *Motivation in humor.* New York: Atherton, 1968, in press.
Logan, C. S. What our children see. *Yearbook of the institute for education by radio*, 1950, 170–174.
Lorenz, K. *On aggression.* New York: Harcourt, Brace & World, 1966.
Lovaas, O. Effect of exposure to symbolic aggression on aggressive behavior, *Child Development*, 1961, **32**, 37–44.
Maccoby, E. Effects of the mass media. In Hoffman, M. & Hoffman, L. (Eds.) *Review of child development research.* New York: Russell Sage, 1964, Vol. I.
Maccoby, E. & Wilson, W. Identification and observational learning from films. *Journal of Abnormal and Social Psychology*, 1957, **55**, 76–87.
Masotti, L. H. (Ed.) Urban violence and disorder. *American Behavioral Scientists*, 1968, **2**(4).
McCasland, B. W. The relation of aggressive fantasy to aggressive behavior in children. Unpublished doctoral dissertation, Syracuse University, 1961.
McCord, J. & McCord, W. The effect of parental role models on criminality. *Journal of Social Issues*, 1958, **14**, 66–74.
Meyerson, L. J. The effects of filmed aggression on the aggressive responses of high and low aggressive subjects. *Dissertation Abstracts*, 1967, **27**(9-B), 3291. Unpublished doctoral dissertation, University of Iowa, 1966.
Miller, N. E. Some reflections on the law of effect produce a new alternative to drive reduction. In Mr. Jones, (Ed.) *Nebraska symposium on motivation.* Lincoln, Nebraska: Nebraska Univ. Press, 1963.
Mussen, P. & Rutherford, E. Effects of aggressive cartoons on children's aggressive play. *Journal of Abnormal and Social Psychology*, 1961, **62**, 461–464.
Pulaski, M. A. S. Play as a function of toy structure and fantasy predisposition. Doctoral dissertation, City University of New York, 1968. *Child Development*, 1970, **41**, 531–537.
Pytkowicz, A. R., Wagner, N., & Sarason, I. G. An experimental study of the reduction of hostility through fantasy. *Journal of Personality and Social Psychology*, 1967, **5**, 295–303.
Robins, L. *Deviant children grow up.* Baltimore, Md.: Williams & Wilkins, 1967.

Rosenbaum, M. E. & de Charms, R. Direct and vicarious reduction of hostility. *Journal of Abnormal and Social Psychology*, 1960, **60**, 105–111.

Rosenthal, R. *Experimenter effects in behavioral research*. New York: Appleton-Century-Crofts, 1966.

Schramm, W., Lyle, J., & Parker, R. *Television in the lives of our children*. Stanford, Calif.: Univer. of Stanford Press, 1961.

Scott, J. P. *Aggression*. Chicago, Ill.: Chicago Univer. Press, 1958.

Siegel, A. Film-mediated fantasy aggression and strength of aggressive drive. *Child Development*, 1956, **27**, 365–378.

Singer, J. L. Imagination and waiting ability in young children. *Journal of Personality*, 1961, **29**, 396–413.

Singer, J. L. *Daydreaming*. New York: Random House, 1966.

Singer, J. L. Research applications of the projective techniques. In A. I. Rabin (Ed.) *Projective techniques in personality assessment*. New York: Springer, 1968.

Singer, J. L. Drives, effects and daydreams: The adaptive role of spontaneous imagery and stimulus-independent mentation. Paper read at the Conference on Cognition, Center for Research in Cognition and Effect, City University of New York, June 1968.

Singer, J. L. & Opler, M. K. Contrasting patterns of fantasy and motility in Irish and Italian schizophrenics. *Journal of Abnormal and Social Psychology*, 1956, **53**, 42–47.

Singer, J. L. & Rowe, R. An experimental study of some relationships of daydreaming and anxiety. *Journal of Consulting Psychology*, 1962, **26**, 446–454.

Spivack, G. Some cognitive deficiencies in poorly self-controlled adolescents. Paper presented at the meeting of American Psychological Association, 1964.

Spivack, G. & Levine, M. Self-regulation and acting-out in normal adolescents. Progress Report for NIMH, Grant M-4531. Devon, Pennsylvania: Devereaux Foundation, 1964.

Thibaut, J. W. & Coules, J. The role of communication in the reduction of interpersonal hostility. *Journal of Abnormal and Social Psychology*, 1952, **47**, 770–777.

Tomkins, S. S. Affect, imagery consciousness. Vol. I. New York: Springer, 1962.

Townsend, J. K. The relation between Rorschach signs of aggression and behavioral aggression in emotionally-disturbed boys. *Journal of Projective Techniques and Personality Assessment*, 1968, **31**, 13–21.

Walters, R. H. Implications of laboratory studies of aggression for the control and regulation of violence. Annals of the American Academy of Science, 1965.

Walters, R. H., Leat, M., & Mezei, L. Inhibition and disinhibition of responses through empathetic learning. *Canadian Journal of Psychology*, 1963, **17**, 235–243.

Walters, R. H. & Parke, R. Influence of response consequences to a social model on resistance to deviation. *Journal of Experimental Child Psychology*, 1964, **1**, 269–280.

Walters, R. H., Parke, R., & Cane, V. Timing of punishment and the observation of consequences to others as determinants of response inhibition. *Journal of Experimental Child Psychology*, 1965, **2**, 10–30.

Walters, R. H. & Thomas, E. L. Enhancement of punitiveness by visual and audiovisual displays. *Canadian Journal of Psychology*, 1963, **16**, 244–255.

Walters, R. H., Thomas, E. L., & Acker, C. W. Enhancement of punitive behavior by audio-visual displays. *Science*, 1962, **136**, 872–873.

Wertham, F. *Seduction of the innocent*. New York: Rinehart, 1954.

Wertham, F. The scientific study of mass media effects. *American Journal of Psychiatry*, 1962, **119**, 306–311.

Wertham, F. Is TV hardening us to the war in Vietnam? *New York Times*, December 4, 1966, 50–54.

Whalen, R. *Crime and violence on television.* Ottawa, Canada: Canadian Broadcasting
    Corp., 1959.
White, R. W. Motivation reconsidered: The concept of competence. *Psychological Review,*
    1959, **66,** 297–333.
Wolfgang, M. & Ferracuti, F. *The subculture of violence.* London: Tavistock, 1967.

CHAPTER III

THE PHYSIOLOGY OF AGGRESSION AND THE IMPLICATIONS FOR AGGRESSION CONTROL

K. E. MOYER

CARNEGIE-MELLON UNIVERSITY

A MODEL FOR AGGRESSIVE BEHAVIOR

This paper will briefly outline a physiological model of aggressive behavior and the implication of the model for the physiological control of hostility and aggression. (See Moyer (1969) for a more complete statement of this model.)

It is important to recognize that aggression is not a unitary concept. There is considerable evidence that there are a number of different kinds of aggressive behavior and that each of them has a different physiological basis. Since this evidence has been discussed in detail elsewhere (Moyer, 1968), it will suffice to indicate here that each kind of aggression can be defined by the stimulus situation which elicits it and the particular topography of the response.

The following classification of aggressive behaviors may be useful: predatory, inter-male, fear-induced, irritable, territorial, maternal, sex related, and instrumental. Each of these, except instrumental, can be defined by the stimulus situation which elicits it. Instrumental aggression is a learned response which occurs in a given situation because it has, in the past, been reinforced. Thus, instrumental aggression does not have a specific physiological basis except in the sense that learning has a physiological basis.

The particular classification system suggested here may not be, and is probably not, the one which will ultimately be the most useful. However, although we may argue about the most efficacious classification system, the fact that there are different kinds of aggression now seems to be indisputable. Since a single model cannot fit all of the different kinds of aggression, an attempt will be made here to identify mechanisms or types of mechanisms which, although differing in detail, are similar for all or most aggression types.

The first premise of this model indicates that there are in the brains of animals and man, innately organized neural systems which, when active in the presence of particular stimuli, result in destructive behavior toward those stimuli. Thus, aggressive behavior is stimulus bound.

There is now a vast amount of data to support that basic premise. Flynn and his colleagues have accumulated a mass of evidence on the neural substrate for predatory and irritable aggression in the cat. It has been shown that if a friendly cat is stimulated in the lateral hypothalamus through an implanted electrode, it will ignore the experimenter and attack an available rat. However, if the cat is stimulated in the medial hypothalamus, it will ignore the rat and attack the experimenter (Egger & Flynn, 1963). Richard Bandler (1969), in my own laboratory, has provided strong evidence that the neural system for predatory aggression in the rat is cholinergic in nature.

Kaada (1967, pp. 195–234), in his extensive review of the literature on brain mechanisms related to aggression, cites numerous studies which differentiate between attack behavior (irritable aggression), defense behavior (fear-induced aggression) and flight. He concludes that "all three behavior patterns appear to have their separate although somewhat overlapping representations in the brain."

Although the evidence is limited, it appears clear that man for all of his encephalization, is not free of those neural aggression systems. King reports the case of a mild mannered female patient who became aggressive, verbally hostile, and threatened to strike the experimenter when she was electrically stimulated in the region of the amygdala. When the current was turned off, she again became mild mannered and apologetic for her behavior. Her hostile feelings and aggressive behavior could be turned on and off at the flick of a switch. She commented that she felt no pain, but that she did not like to feel so hostile (King, 1961, pp. 477–486). Other cases of brain stimulation in humans resulting in aggressive tendencies have been reported by Sem-Jacobsen (1966); Sem-Jacobsen and Torkildsen (1960, pp. 275–290); and by Ervin, Mark, and Sweet (1968).

There is also evidence from several sources that, like many other systems in the brain, there are suppressor systems which are antagonistic to the aggression systems. Karli has shown that lesions in the suppressor areas of the olfactory bulb will turn a peaceful rat into an irritable mouse killer (Karli *et al.,* 1969). Other authors also report great increases in irritability and aggressive behavior after lesions in the hypothalamus and amygdaloid region (Wheatly, 1944; Wood, 1958). Several studies show that the activation of suppressor systems in the brain will inhibit ongoing aggression.

Fortunately for man and animal alike, the aggression systems of the brain are not active most of the time. We must therefore consider how they become activated and deactivated. Briefly, there is good reason to believe that these different hostility systems are sensitized and desensitized by certain blood constituents. To give just one example, it has been known for centuries that the raging bull can be converted into the gentle steer by lowering its androgen level through castration. This finding has been verified experimentally in a wide variety of animals (Beeman, 1947; Collias, 1944). When a given hostility system is sensitized by a particular hormone balance, a variety of environmental conditions will evoke hostile feelings and hostile behavior. These environmental situations may involve frustration, stress in many forms, or if the neural systems are highly sensitized, simply the presence of an attackable entity. What types of entity will be attacked will depend in part on the reinforcement history of the organism and in part on the particular aggression system which is sensitized.

Aggressive behavior, like all other basic behaviors, is strongly influenced by experience. Just as an animal can be taught to overeat or to starve to death through the use of reinforcement, animals and man can be taught to exhibit or inhibit aggressive behavior by the same method. It is possible to increase the probability of occurrence of any aggressive or destructive response, no matter what its initial motivational source, if that response is followed by positive reinforcement. The law of effect operates just as effectively for responses which are labeled destructive as for those which are not.

Man, of course, learns better and faster than all other animals. It is therefore reasonable to expect that the internal impulses to aggressive behavior would be more subject to modification by experience in man than in any other animal. Also, because of man's additional ability to manipulate symbols and to substitute one symbol for another, one would expect to find a considerable diversity in the stimuli which will elicit or inhibit activity in the aggression systems. One would also expect that the modes of expression would be more varied, diverse, and less stereotyped in man than in other animals.

With the above brief model in mind, we can look at the kinds of aggression controls that are available now, and what the potential might be for further controls. Although the emphasis in this paper is on the physiological methods useful in the control of hostile behavior, this should not be construed to imply that other control methods are either ineffective or unimportant. There are, in fact, a number of nonphysiological methods which can be briefly mentioned.

Since the sensitized aggression system is activated by frustration, it should be possible, at least in part, to reduce aggressive behavior by changing the environment to reduce excessive frustration and deprivation. Just as it is possible for some obese persons to learn to eat less, some individuals can learn to inhibit aggressive tendencies. This can be accomplished by the positive reinforcement of nonaggressive responses in the presence of aggression eliciting stimuli or through the negative reinforcement of expressed aggression. Since negative reinforcement constitutes a stressor, the total effect of that approach must be carefully evaluated. It should also be possible to assist the individual to restructure his cognitive patterns as they relate to the objects of his hostility through the device of role playing (Toch, 1969). Finally, the expression of aggression can be reduced by removing some of the cues which instigate aggressive behaviors. Berkowitz (1967, pp. 243–266) summarizes an outstanding series of studies which demonstrate that individuals react with greater hostility in the presence of objects such as guns, which have been previously associated with aggressive incidents.

If the model outlined above has any validity, it should also be possible to control aggressive tendencies through the direct physiological manipulation of the internal environment.

INHIBITION OF AGGRESSION IN ANIMALS BY BRAIN LESIONS

If there are neural systems which are active during, and responsible for, aggressive behavior, it should be possible to reduce or eliminate aggressive tendencies by interrupting or interfering with these neural systems. There is now abundant evidence that such a procedure is possible. As might be suspected when dealing with neural systems rather than neural centers, there are a number of different brain areas which may be lesioned to delimit aggressive tendencies. Further, it should be emphasized that there are different kinds of aggressive behavior and although there must obviously be some overlap in the neurological substrates, particularly at the final common path, they are reasonably independent centrally and can be experimentally delineated (Moyer, 1968). This then is another reason to expect that lesions in a number of brain areas would produce a decrease in aggressive tendencies.

Because it has only recently been recognized that there are different kinds of aggressive behavior, it is frequently difficult to determine in any given experiment which type of aggression is being used as a dependent variable. However, it is not the purpose of this paper to deal with the physiology of the different kinds of aggression, but to emphasize those control measures which may be common to many types.

As early as 1937 it was shown that brain lesions could result in the physiological reduction of aggression. Using the very radical surgery of complete bilateral temporal lobe ablation, including the uncus and the greater part of the hippocampus, Kluver and Bucy (1937, 1938, 1939) produced tameness in vicious rhesus monkeys. They report that the loss of both fear and anger reactions were complete. It is important to note that the lesioned animals, although quite docile, were not in any sense sedated, but were in a generally more aroused state. The animals never resented any form of handling and were always eager to engage in playful activities with the experimenter. The normal, extreme hostility was replaced by a state of "hypomania." This change to extreme tameness was especially remarkable because these investigators took particular care to use only wild and aggressive monkeys.

Since 1937 many investigators have supported the work of Kluver and Bucy by showing that extensive damage to the temporal lobe results in an increase in docility in a variety of animals (Adey, Merrillees, & Sunderland, 1956; Thompson & Walker, 1950). The evidence seems to indicate that aggressive behaviors are not completely eliminated from the animals repertoire, but the threshold for such behavior is heightened. Monkeys and baboons with extensive lesions in the temporal region generally did not retaliate when attacked by other animals, but would sit and wince and grimace. However, if the lesioned animal was cornered, it would manifest enough aggression to extricate himself from that situation (Pribram & Bagshaw, 1953). Similar findings have been reported for the dog. The operated animals are less dominant, and more docile toward the handler, but were quite able to defend themselves when attacked (Fuller, Rosvold, & Pribram, 1957).

Social dominance, which involves aggressive components, can be directly manipulated by anterior temporal lobectomy. Plotnik (1968) assessed the dominance hierarchy in a group of squirrel monkeys in three different group competitive situations which involved both positive and negative reinforcement. He then operated on each dominant animal in succession, with testing between operations, and showed that the lesioned animal fell from the top of the hierarchy postoperatively. Behavior changes resulting from extensive temporal lesions (uncus and amygdala) are so deviate that the animal in the natural state is rejected by the social group and may eventually die. Free ranging rhesus monkeys, observed on Cayo Santiago Island, which were subjected to this operation, failed to show either appropriate aggressive or submissive gestures (Dicks, Myers, & Kling, 1969).

Much of the more recent work on the diminution of hostile reactions through the interruption of the neural systems which underlie those reactions has been concentrated on attempts to delineate more clearly the specific relevant brain areas. The temporal lobectomy studies did, in fact, demonstrate that brain lesions could reduce hostility. However, such massive damage produced many other changes as well including: hypersexuality, "psychic blindness," excessive orality, and a hyper-reactivity to all visual stimuli.

A number of contradictory studies clearly indicated that damage to the amygdala resulted in changes in the subject's aggressive potential. Although some investigators have found that bilateral amygdalectomy resulted in increases in irritability (Schreiner & Kling, 1953; Bard, 1950; Bard & Mountcastle, 1948), it has generally been found that aggressiveness is reduced by that operation. Bilateral amygdalectomy raises the threshold for at least three different kinds of aggressive behavior. Irritable aggression is dramatically reduced. Amygdalectomized cats do not aggress even when suspended by their tails or when they are generally roughed up (Schreiner & Kling, 1953). Amygdalectomy also eliminates predatory aggression in the cat (Summers & Kaelber, 1962) and in the rat (Woods, 1956). Fear reactions (escape tendencies) are also reduced by amygdalectomy in a variety of animals with consequent reduction in fear-induced aggressive behavior. This is true of the monkey (Rosvold, Mirsky, & Pribram, 1954; Schreiner & Kling, 1953, 1956; Shealy & Peele, 1957) the cat (Ursin, 1965) the wild Norway rat (Woods, 1956; Galef, 1970; Karli, 1956) as well as the lynx and agouti (Schreiner & Kling, 1956).

Even amygdalectomy, which involves a relatively small, histologically separable structure, turns out to be a rather gross operation as far as aggressive behavior is concerned. The amygdala includes at least eight identifiable nuclei (Gloor, 1960, pp. 1395–1416). Some of these nuclei function to facilitate certain kinds of aggressive behavior, while others are inhibitory. Recent research indicates that some of the contradictory results in the studies involving total amygdalectomy were probably due to subtotal ablation. Thus, it seems likely that in those studies where increased aggressiveness occurred, one of the aggression facilitating nuclei was missed (Siegel & Flynn, 1968).

While the exact relationships between the various nuclei in the amygdala and aggressive behavior remain to be worked out in detail [see Moyer (1968) for a recent attempt], it is clear from the results of a number of studies (Siegel & Flynn, 1968; Fonberg, 1965; Ursin, 1965; Karli & Vergnes, 1965) that aggressive behaviors of different kinds, in a variety of species can be blocked by the removal of very tiny amounts of precisely the right brain tissue. In the cat, for example, this may involve as little as 1/2 cu cm.

Lesions in a number of brain structures other than the amygdala also result in a reduction of hostile behavior. Bilateral removal of 50% to 90% of the hippocampus in the monkey, baboon, or cat without damage to the overlying cortex or adjacent structures results in an increase in docility (Gol, Kellaway, Shapiro, & Hurst, 1963). Delgado and Kitahata (1967) offer support for the role of the hippocampus in aggressive tendencies. They were able to produce functional reversible lesions in the hippocampus of monkeys by injecting anesthetics through permanently implanted cannulae. The injection of dibucaine, phenobarbital, and xylocaine all produced a decrease in aggressiveness. The monkeys did not show their teeth or attempt to bite a glove even when struck lightly in the face with it. The above findings are contrary to a study by Green, Clemente, and de Groot (1957) which showed an increase in aggression after hippocampectomy, but it seems likely, as they suggest, that the aggression increase resulted from "tissue irritation."

Studies on the effects of lesions of the cingulum emphasize the need for caution in generalizing results of studies on one species of animal to another. Anand and Dua (1956) and Kennard (1955a, 1955b) have reported an increase in irritability in cats after cingulectomy, although a recent study by Ursin (1969) found no effect of that operation on cats. Brutkowski, Fonberg, and Mempel (1961) also found hyperirritability in dogs after lesions in the cingulum. However, cingulectomy in monkeys reduces fear and makes them more docile (Kennard, 1955a; Glees, Cole, Whitty, & Cairns, 1950; Ward, 1948).

Lesions in the posteromedial hypothalamus (Sano, 1966), anterior thalamic nuclei (Schreiner & Kling, 1953), dorsomedial thalamus (Spiegel & Wycis, 1949), midbrain (Brown & Hunsperger, 1963), and lateral hypothalamus (Karli & Vergnes, 1965) have all been shown to result in a reduction of one or another kind of aggressive behavior.

INHIBITION OF AGGRESSION IN HUMANS BY BRAIN LESIONS

Just as there are wild cats and wild monkeys, there are wild men, men who have so much spontaneous activity in the neural systems which underlie aggressive behavior that they are a constant threat to themselves and to those around them. These are individuals who are confined to the back wards of mental hospitals under either constant sedation or constant restraint. The homicidal hostility of these persons can also be reduced if appropriate brain lesions are made to interrupt the functioning of these systems for irascibility. In some cases they have gone from the back wards out into society to lead useful lives.

There is now abundant evidence that pathological hyperirritability and aggressive behavior in humans is associated with several types of brain dysfunction. Tumors with an irritative focus frequently result in increased irritability and rage attacks. Cases manifesting this syndrome have been described with tumors in the temporal lobe (Kreshner, Bender, & Strauss, 1936; Vonderahe, 1944; Mulder & Daly, 1952), the frontal lobe (Strauss & Keschner, 1935), the hypothalamus (Alpers, 1940), and the septal region (Zeman & King, 1958). More recently, Sano (1962) has reported on 1800 cases of brain tumor and found the irritability syndrome in those involving the temporal lobe and the anterior hypothalamus.

Gibbs (1951) has estimated that approximately half of the patients with epilepsy who have an anterior temporal lobe focus have some psychiatric disorder, those non-ictal psychiatric symptoms are not directly related to electroencephalographic abnormalities (also see Gibbs, 1956). Gloor (1960, pp. 1395–1416) has suggested that there is a "propensity for these patients to be provoked into explosive and violent anger, often for causes of the most trifling nature."

EEG abnormalities in the temporal lobe have been correlated with behavioral aberrations in individuals diagnosed as having episodic behavior disorders (Robinson & Guerrero-Figueroa, 1967). In 36 out of 100 consecutive temporal lobe epileptic patients selected for temporal lobectomy, Serafetinides (1965) found overt physical aggressiveness as a part of the behavior pattern. (See Wilder (1968) for a further discussion of epilepsy and aggressive behavior.)

In some individuals manifesting the dyscontrol syndrome, the EEG appears to be normal. However, there is evidence that the patient's disturbed behavior is accompanied by hypersynchronous activity recorded from depth electrodes placed in rhinencephalic structures (Monroe, 1959; Ervin, Mark, & Stevens, 1969, pp. 54–65; Heath, 1962). It has been repeatedly shown that the surgical excision of the epileptogenic focus may result in an alleviation of the pathology. This indicates that the cause was due to abnormal discharges and not to lesions in the brain (Gloor, 1960, pp. 1395–1416). It is important to note that many of these inter-ictal, aggressive, dyscontrol symptoms are episodic just as epilepsy is episodic. Between episodes, the individual may behave in a completely normal manner. It should also be recognized that individuals manifesting inter-ictal or sub-ictal dyscontrol syndromes are on a continuum which varies from homicidal behavior to occasional "normal" irritability. As Jonas (1965) points out so succinctly,

Biological laws would demand the existence of a continuum extending from the intense focal and generalized electrical discharges in grand mal down to the normally firing brain. It is also probable that the brain, in its complexity, could not function unceasingly without the occurrence of abnormal discharges resulting from occasionally overburdened circuits. Such manifestations, however, may escape detection because of the innocuous and inconsequential aspects of the symptoms (p. 15).

Jonas goes on to make the important point that spontaneous firing in the motor system may result in the twitching eyelid or the activation of whole muscle groups such as in nocturnal jactations during light sleep. Thus, it is most reasonable to expect that spontaneous firing in the temporal lobe might result in feelings of irritation, anger, or rage. If this activity is sufficiently intense, the hostile impulses may be acted out. When J. P. Scott (1965) says, "There is no known physiological mechanism by which spontaneous internal stimulation for fighting arises," he chooses to ignore all of the data presented here.

The experimental work of Kluver and Bucy, which involved bilateral temporal lobe ablation and resulted in surgically induced docility, inspired some surgeons to attempt the same operation on man in an attempt to modify aggressive behavior and agitation in schizophrenic patients (Terzian & Ore, 1955). As might be suspected from the results of Kluver and Bucy, this radical operation resulted in a variety of dysfunctions. In one case report presented in detail by Terzian & Ore (1955), bilateral removal of the temporal lobes including most of the uncus and hippocampus, exactly reproduced the Kluver and Bucy syndrome, including rage and fear reduction, loss of recognition of people, increased sex activity, bulimia, and serious memory deficiencies. Prior to the operation the patient had frequent attacks of aggressive and violent behavior during which he had attempted to strangle his mother and to crush his younger brother under his feet. After unilateral temporal lobectomy, he attacked the nurses and doctors and threatened some with death. After the second temporal lobe was removed, he became extremely meek with everyone and was "absolutely resistant to any attempt to arouse aggressiveness and violent reactions in him."

Temporal lobe lesions, both unilateral and bilateral have been extensively used in man to control epilepsy which is not susceptible to drug therapy. A frequent side effect of the operation, in addition to seizure control, has been a general reduction in hostility compared to the individuals reactions prior to the operation (Green, Duisberg, & McGrath, 1951; Terzian, 1958; Scoville & Milner, 1957; Pool, 1954). Although cases have been reported in which aggressive behavior has been increased by the operation, (Sawa, Ueki, Arita, & Harada, 1954; Woringer, Thomalske, & Klinger, 1953) the increase is generally temporary. Some authors report no change in psychiatric symptoms (Gibbs, Amador, & Rich, 1958, pp. 358–367). Bailey (1958, p. 551) indicates that temporal lesions do not generally reduce the psychiatric problems of the patient except that in certain subjects, the attacks of aggressive behavior were reduced or completely eliminated. He believes that the aggressive attacks were in fact psychomotor seizures. Falconer, Hill, Meyer, and Wilson, (1958, pp. 396–410) report definite personality changes for the better after temporal lobe lesions and conclude that the most striking way in which they improved was in the reduction of aggressiveness. "Whereas, previously, the relatives of the patient might be very careful as to what they said to the patient for fear of provoking an aggressive outbreak, they can now talk freely and joke with him (Falconer, 1958, p. 486)."

It is clear that radical ablation of the temporal lobes can reduce pathological hostility in man. However, as with animals, the production of surgical docility in man is not limited to temporal lobe lesions. Following Ward's demonstration of the calming effects of cingulectomy on monkeys, Le Beau (1952) did cingulum ablations on humans in an attempt to control agitated behavior, obsessive compulsive states, and epilepsy. He concluded that "Cingulectomy is specially indicated in intractable cases of anger, violence, aggressiveness, and permanent agitation." Other investigators have found that lesions in the anterior cingular gyrus while not eliminating outbursts of anger, have reduced the intensity and duration of such outbursts (Tow & Whitty, 1953; Whitty, Duffield, Tow & Cairns, 1952; Sano, 1962).

Operating on the theory that pathological aggression is due to an imbalance in the ergotropic circuits and the tropotropic circuits with a dominance of ergotropic (Sano, 1962; Sano, Yoshioko, Ogashiwa, Ishijima, & Ohye, 1966), Sano has performed what he calls "sedative surgery." This involves lesioning the ergotropic zone (posterior hypothalamus) in order to normalize the balance. He reports remarkable success with patients showing intractable violent behavior. They became markedly calm, passive, and tractable showing decreased spontaneity. Although they showed a recovery of the spontaneity within a month, the other changes persisted for up to three years and seven months, as long as the patients were followed up. Of course, one need not accept Sano's theory in order to accept his results. He may very well be getting the right results for the wrong reasons. Sano's theory implies that aggressive behavior is the result of excessive arousal and can thus be eliminated by sedation. Sedation can, of course, reduce hostile behavior as it does all other behavior. Sedation, however, is not essential to the limiting of aggression. It is quite possible to be hyperactive without being aggressive. For example, the Kluver-Bucy monkeys were extremely friendly but at the same time, they were hypomanic and always ready to engage in play.

Lesions in a number of other brain areas have resulted in reductions in aggressive behavior in humans. Bilateral lesions of the dorsomedial nuclei of the thalamus result in a reduction in tension, anxiety states, agitation, and aggressiveness (Spiegel, Wycis, Freed, & Orchinik, 1951). Other areas resulting in calming effects after lesioning are the fornix, the upper mesencephalon (Sano, 1966) and the frontal lobes (Liddell, 1953).

The most precise control of aggressive behavior through brain lesions, and the one which involves the greatest promise, has been more recently developed and involves stereotaxic lesions in the amygdala. Lesions 8 to 10 mm in diameter have been produced by an injection of 0.6 to 0.8 ml of oil to which lipiodol had been added (Narabayashi, Nagao, Saito, Yoshida & Nagahata, 1963; Narabayashi & Uno, 1966). These authors report that 85% of 51 patients showed a marked reduction in emotional excitability and a normalization of their social behavior. It should be emphasized that except for the reduction in hostility, none of the signs of the Kluver-Bucy syndrome resulted from the bilateral destruction of the amygdaloid nuclei.

Similar results have been reported by Heimburger, Whitlock, and Kalsbeck (1966). They have lesioned approximately half of the maygdala using cryosurgery. The lesions were 8 to 10 mm in diameter. This operation has resulted in dramatic improvement in some patients and an overall improvement in 23 of 25 patients. Destructiveness, hostility, and aggression toward others were the behavior symptoms most frequently improved by the operation. The improvement in two of the patients was so great that they were released from mental institutions. Others were moved from solitary confinement to open wards. Some of them were observed to smile and laugh for the first time in their lives after the operation. Heimburger, et al. (1966) conclude "Stereotaxic amygdalotomy is a safe and relatively easy procedure for treatment of a select group of patients who have previously been considered untreatable."

Similar results have been reported by Schwab, Sweet, Mark, Kjellberg, and Ervin (1965). They use a very promising technique of implanting 48 pairs of recording electrodes bilaterally through the limbic system. Then they carry out a program of recording and stimulation over a period of several weeks in order to localize and limit as much as possible the precise area which, when destroyed, will relieve the symptoms. A radio-frequency lesion is then made through the indwelling electrodes. Ervin indicates that there is good reason to believe from their observations that the neural and neurochemical substrate for the motor seizure and for the interseizure assaultive and aggressive behavior are different. It is possible to eliminate the one without affecting the other (Ervin, personal communication).

AGGRESSION CONTROL BY BRAIN STIMULATION

The control of aggressive behavior can also be achieved by the activation of those neural systems which send inhibitory fibers to the aggression systems. Delgado has repeatedly shown that vicious rhesus monkeys can be tamed by the stimulation of aggression suppressor areas. A normally aggressive female monkey which had to be handled with gloves and would bite anything that came within range was implanted with an electrode in the caudate nucleus. As soon as the electrode was activated, the animal became docile. She closed her normally open and threatening mouth and if objects or the experimenters hands were placed near her mouth, she either pushed them away or turned her head. Delgado emphasizes that this reaction was not one of "general arrest" in which the animal was immobilized by a generalized motor inhibition. She showed good coordination and no loss of mobility. She responded well to sensory stimulation and gave the impression that she was well "aware of her surroundings" (Delgado, 1960). In another case, it was possible for the experimenter to put his finger in the monkey's mouth during the period when its aggressive behavior was blocked by caudate stimulation (Delgado, 1967). As soon as the current was turned off, the animal was as dangerous as ever.

In order to eliminate the need for restraint and the necessity for connecting wires to the head, a technique was developed by which the brain of the subject could be stimulated by remote, radio control. The monkey wore a small stimulating device on its back which was connected by subcutaneous leads to the electrodes which were implanted in various locations in the brain. The leads were connected through a very small switching relay which could be closed by an impulse from a miniature radio receiver which was bolted to the animal's skull. The radio receiver could then be activated by a transmitter which was effective up to several hundred feet away. With this system it was possible to study the monkeys while permitting them free range in the colony. The experimenter could control the brain stimulation by activating the radio transmitter from outside the cage. With this experimental set up it was possible to change the normal social hierarchy in the colony. Stimulation of the caudate

nucleus of the boss monkey blocked his spontaneous aggressive tendencies. His territoriality diminished and the other monkeys in the colony
reacted to him differently. They made fewer submissive gestures and
showed less fear of the boss. When the caudate nucleus was being stimulated, it was possible for the experimenter to enter the cage and catch
the monkey with bare hands (Delgado, 1963, 1965). Reduction in aggressive behavior by caudate stimulation has also been demonstrated
in the chimpanzee (Delgado, Bradley, Johnston, Weiss, & Wallace, 1969).

During one phase of the experiment described above, the button for
the transmitter was placed inside the cage near the feeding tray and thus
made available to all of the monkeys in the colony. One of the submissive
monkeys learned to press the button during periods when the boss monkey
showed aggressive tendencies. When the boss would make threatening
gestures, the smaller monkey would frequently look him straight in the
eye and press the button thus directly calming him down and reducing his
hostile tendencies (Delgado, 1963, 1965). (Whether or not any political
implications can be drawn from this series of experiments, I shall leave
to the reader to decide.)

Man also has neural systems in the brain which, when activated, function to block ongoing aggressive behavior. Sem-Jacobsen and Torkildsen
(1960, pp. 275–290) report that stimulation in the ventromedial frontal
lobes had a calming effect on a violent manic patient. A similar effect
resulted from stimulating the central area of the temporal lobe. When
both points were stimulated in rapid succession the calming antihostility
effect was greater and of some duration. Peterson in a discussion of the
above paper, also reports that actively disturbed and antagonistic patients
become quite placid and talk well after about 15 minutes of stimulation
in the frontal medial area of the brain. This period of calmness might last
for a day or even longer.

Stimulation in the septal region of animals can function as a reinforcer.
In man, septal stimulation results in a variety of subjective positive feelings, not infrequently linked with sexual ideation (Heath, 1964). Septal
stimulation can also block intractable pain. One 15 minute session may
control the pain for several days (Heath & Mickle, 1960, pp. 214–247).
Stimulation in the same general brain area can also dramatically inhibit
the rage response.

. . . Patient No. B-10, the psychomotor epileptic was stimulated in the septal region during
a period when he was exhibiting agitated violent psychotic behavior. The stimulus was
introduced without his knowledge. Almost instantly his behavioral state changed from one
of disorganization, rage, and persecution to one of happiness and mild euphoria. He described the beginning of a sexual motive state. He was unable, when questioned directly,
to explain the sudden shift in his feelings and thoughts (Heath, 1963, p. 575).

Heath goes on to point out that the case described above is not unique, but has been repeated in a large number of patients in his laboratory. The same kind of dramatic change can also be produced by direct application of acetylcholine to the septal area through permanently implanted cannulae. In one patient described by Heath, the electrical recording characterized by spike and slow wave activity in the septal area was normalized by the application of acetylcholine at the same time that the rage responses associated with it were reduced (Heath, 1964).

Direct brain stimulation as a means of aggression control has some obvious problems connected with it, but a number of developments may resolve these difficulties and make this technique practicable in certain cases. It is already technically feasible to avoid the necessity of bringing the patient into the laboratory, plugging him in and stimulating at periodic intervals. Heath (1954) has developed a transisterized self-contained unit which the patient can wear on his belt. The unit generates a preset train of stimulus pulses each time it is activated. This stimulator could be connected to an electrode implanted in an area of the brain which reduces aggressive tendencies. The patient would then have his own "antihostility button" which he could press to calm himself down whenever his irrational feelings of hostility occurred. The fact that septal stimulation also produces pleasurable sensations would be a bonus. This device has already been used with a narcoleptic patient who, whenever he felt himself drifting off to sleep, could reach down and press his "on button" and once again become alert. His friends soon learned that they could press the button to get him back into the conversation if he fell asleep too rapidly to press it himself (Heath, 1963).

Remote radio control of intracerebral stimulation is also possible in the completely free patient just as it is in the free ranging monkey. Delgado, Mark, Sweet, Ervin, Weiss, Bach-Y-Rita, and Hagiwara (1968) have already implanted electrodes in the brains of four patients and brought the leads out to a radio receiver which was attached to the patient's head and covered by the head bandages. It is thus possible to stimulate these patients from a considerable distance by activating the radio transmitter. Various effects have been reported to result from radio stimulation with this device including, "pleasant sensations, elation, deep thoughtful concentration, odd feelings, super relaxation, and colored vision." In one patient outbursts of rage and assaultive behavior, similar to her spontaneous episodic anger responses, resulted from stimulation in the right amygdala. It is also possible to record from the electrodes because the unit on the head includes a very small RF transmitter. If the electrodes were implanted in an aggression inhibitory area, it would be quite possible to permit the patient to engage in his normal activities as long as he was within the range of the transmitter. Periodically then, the stimulator could be activated thus keeping the patient in a nonaggressive state of mind.

Even though the unit described above weighs only about 70 grams, there are still some obvious difficulties with it. It must be worn under bandages on the head (although one patient was able to hide the device completely with a wig), and it is necessary for the leads to the electrodes to penetrate the skin thus producing a constant source of irritation as well as the ever present possibility of infection. However, even these difficulties have been resolved by the recent developments in microminiaturization. At a recent symposium, Delgado (1969) reported that an entire stimulation unit had been reduced in size and shaped so that it could be implanted under the skin. It is therefore possible for an individual to have an electrode implant in an aggression inhibiting area attached to one of these devices. As soon as his hair grows back, he will look no different than any other individual. He could then return to all normal activities as long as he stayed within the range of the transmitter. Obviously, what that range would be, would depend on the transmitter's power.

One further development would also contribute to the use of brain stimulation as a means of aggression control. Devices are now in the process of development which will, in time, permit the stimulation of precise brain locations without the necessity of opening the skull. One of these devices involves the use of two parabolic reflectors to focus sound energy in such a way that only at the point of intersection of the two sources will there be an effect. This device is currently successfully used as a stereotaxic lesioning instrument (Baltimore Instrument Co., Baltimore, Md.). However, according to one of the developers, there is the distinct possibility that it could be modified to use as a stimulator (C. Dickey, personal communication). If the effects of brain stimulation in reducing aggressive potential are reasonably long lasting as they are for the inhibition of pain, (Heath & Mickle, 1960, pp. 214–247), it would be possible for the patient with intractable hostility to stop in for brain stimulation every several days and have his intractable hostility controlled without the necessity of surgery. It should be emphasized that this device and technique have not yet been developed. However, they are clearly within the range of possibility.

AGGRESSION CONTROL BY HORMONE THERAPY

Our physiological model of aggressive behavior indicates that the neurological systems for aggressive behavior are sensitized by chemical factors in the blood stream, these are primarily but not exclusively hormones. An understanding of the endocrinology and blood chemistry in-

fluences on aggression should ultimately lead to a rational therapy for
certain kinds of hostility in man.

The importance of androgens in the blood stream for intermale and
irritable aggression has already been mentioned and is well documented.
Thus, any manipulation of the blood chemistry which results in a reduction in the androgen level should raise the threshold for those aggressive tendencies. Castration as a means of accomplishing androgen reduction has been repeatedly reported to reduce fighting in animals (Beeman, 1947; Seward, 1945; Sigg, 1969; Urich, 1938). The same procedure,
although certainly a drastic one, has been found useful in the control of
certain violent sex crimes in man (LeMaire, 1956; Hawke, 1950).

There are now several substances available which have demonstrated
antiandrogenic activity (Lerner, 1964). A-Norprogesterone (Lerner,
Bianchi, & Borman, 1960) chlormadinone acetate (Rocky & Neri, 1968)
and cyproterone acetate (Neumann, Von Berswordt-Wallrabe, Elger,
& Steinbeck, 1968) have all been shown to be potent antagonists of androgens. In intact animals, the administration of these substances works
similarly to castration (Neumann et al., 1968). Although there have not
yet been extensive clinical trials, it certainly seems reasonable to suggest
as Neumann, Elger, and Von Berswordt-Wallrabe (1967) do, that these
substances may be of particular value for the control of males with disturbed sex drive, particularly those who are unable to discontinue com-
mitting violent sexual offenses.

There is some evidence from animals that estrogenic substances may
function to inhibit aggressive behavior. Clark and Birch (1945), working
with castrated chimpanzees, found that aggressiveness was reduced by
estrogen. The animal given the estrogen became subordinate to its cage
mate. Suchowski (1969) has recently reported that the fighting behavior
usually found in isolated mice was completely inhibited by injections of
estradiol. He concluded "that an androgenic effect may be masked or
inhibited by an impeded estrogenic side-effect or by estrogens themselves
. . . The strongest inhibitors of aggressiveness are represented by
estrogens and followed by pregnane derivatives which seem to be longer
lasting." The aggressive behavior of the female, golden hamster toward
the male can be drastically reduced by the administration of six daily
injections of estrogen followed by a single injection of progesterone (Kislak & Beach, 1955).

So far, there are a limited number of studies which indicate that female
hormones may be used in the control of aggressive tendencies in man.
Golla (quoted in Sands, 1954), suggested that estrogenic substances
could be used as a form of chemical castration in man. This approach, he
suggested, would be more efficient than an actual castration because the

estrogens would block the effects of the adrenal androgens which would not be affected by the operation. Sands (1954) reports a series of cases in which the aggressive tendencies of adolescents and young adults were controlled by the use of stilbestrol. Another case in which irritable aggression and excessive libido were controlled by the administration of stilbestrol is described in some detail by Dunn (1941). This patient was a 27 year old male under maximum sentence for sexual offenses against female minors. He was a persistent trouble maker in prison and was frequently placed in solitary confinement for insubordination. The prisoner had abnormal amounts of male hormone and gonadatropic hormone in the urine before therapy and was preoccupied with his sex life. After four weeks of daily treatment with stilbestrol he reported that his sexual responses both physical and mental were reduced. He had also adapted much better to prison discipline and was no longer considered a trouble maker. He continued relatively symptom free for more than three months after discontinuance of therapy. Subsequently, however, he had a return of his symptoms and requested a resumption of therapy.

Although the above case reports can hardly be considered as definitive, they certainly indicate that further work should be done in this area and they present another possibility for the direct physiological manipulation of hostile behavior.

A significant number of women show a premenstrual syndrome which includes an increase in irritability and feelings of hostility (Dalton, 1964; Greene & Dalton, 1953; Hamburg, 1966). In individuals with inadequate controls, these feelings are acted upon with resulting aggressive behavior. In a study of female prison inmates, it was shown that 51% of the adult population, mean age of 32.4 years, showed premenstrual tension. Thirty three percent of the reformatory population, mean age 21.4 years, manifested premenstrual tension. A study of the prison records revealed that 62% of the crimes of violence were committed during the premenstrual week and only 2% at the end of the period (Morton, Additon, Addison, Hunt, & Sullivan, 1953). A similar finding is reported by Dalton (1961). He found that 49% of all crimes were committed by women during menstruation or in the premenstrum. Thus, the association between menstruation and crime is highly significant. One would expect only 29% of all crimes to be committed during the eight day period if they were normally distributed. The probability of the obtained distribution occurring by chance is less than one in a thousand. Dalton (1961) reports further that women prisoners were more frequently reported for "bad behavior" during the menstrual or premenstrual period.

Feelings of irritability and hostility during the premenstrum are not confined to a few asocial individuals who get into difficulties with the law.

Moderate or severe degrees of the premenstrual syndrome occur in about a quarter of all women (Coppen & Kessel, 1963; Hamburg, Moos & Yalom, 1968). Janowsky, Gorney, & Mandell (1967) estimate that up to 90% of women claim to undergo some irritability, hopelessness, or depression prior to or during menstration.

The underlying physiology of the irritability associated with premenstrual tension is obscure. It seems clear that the syndrome is associated with a fall in the progesterone level in the blood (Hamburg *et al.*, 1968). Several studies have also shown that the symptoms can be alleviated by the administration of this hormone (Dalton, 1964; Greene & Dalton, 1953). It has also been shown that women who take oral contraceptives which contain progestagenic agents show significantly less irritability than do women who are not taking the pill (Hamburg *et al.*, 1968). It may be that the irritability reducing effects of the progestogens are a function of their direct effect on the neural systems in the brain which relate to hostility. However, the explanation may be much less direct. Janowsky *et al.* (1967) hypothesize that the irritability results from the cyclic increase in the aldosterone inasmuch as weight changes, behavioral changes, and aldosterone changes seem to parallel each other. The resulting increase in sodium and water retention caused by the aldosterone results in a secondary neuronal irritability and consequent psychic symptoms. The therapeutic effects of lithium and diuretics in treating premenstrual tension may then be due to their tendency to reverse the aldosterone effect on sodium metabolism.

Another possible explanation relates to the tendency for a cyclic hypoglycemic reaction. Morton *et al.* (1953) reported that a sugar tolerance test during the premenstrual period resulted in a typical hypoglycemic type curve in the female prisoners they studied. A reduction in premenstrual symptoms occurred under treatment, including improvement in behavior and attitude and less punishment for infraction of rules. Their therapeutic regimen consisted of placebo, high protein diet alone and with ammonium chloride. Although the greatest improvement occurred with the combined therapy, 39% improved with the high protein diet which is a recommended therapy for hypoglycemia (Lyght, 1966).

Hypoglycemia, from whatever cause, is, in many cases, associated with tendencies to hostility, and is another dysfunction in the blood chemistry which evidently sensitizes the neural substrates for aggression. There has, unfortunately been relatively little systematic study of this relationship. However, Gyland (quoted in Frederichs & Goodman, 1969) studied six hundred patients with hypoglycemia and indicates that 89% of them showed hyperirritability and 45% manifested "unsocial, asocial, or anti-social behavior." A study of Salzer (quoted in Frederichs & Goodman, 1969), indicated that irritability was found in 45% and unsocial or anti-social behavior in 22% of patients with low blood sugar. Gloor (1967, p. 86) suggests that some of the most aggressive patients are those with Islet cell tumors during the periods when they are hypoglycemic. When their blood sugar is raised, they again become "quite civilized."

A much neglected paper by Wilder (1947) compiles a remarkable amount of evidence which implicates low blood sugar as a causal factor in hostility and crime. He indicates that the aggressive tendency associated with hypoglycemic states is manifest in matrimonial relationships, homicidal threats and acts, destructiveness, and cruelty towards children. Wilder suggests that the hypoglycemic state may represent a temporary state of "moral insanity." Although there is a clear cut need for further work on this problem, particularly experimental studies with control groups, there appears to be a reasonable evidence of this relationship.

Hypoglycemia and the psychological effects related to it are readily treated by altering the blood chemistry through diet or through the use of adrenocortical steroids (Lyght, 1966).

Low blood sugar tends to intensify allergic reactions and although the physiological mechanism has not yet been found, a frequent component of allergic reactions is an increase in aggressive tendencies. These reactions may vary from slight irritability through argumentativeness to obviously abnormal aggressive behavior (Randolph, 1962). Some highly allergic individuals respond to specific foods with a full blown rage reaction within half an hour after ingestion. Observations by the mother of a child so affected rather dramatically illustrate this point.

You wouldn't believe bananas. Within twenty minutes of eating a banana this child would be in the worst temper tantrum – no seizures – you have ever seen. I tried this five times because I couldn't believe my own eyes. He reacted with behavior to all sugars except maple sugar. We went to California the Christmas of 1962 to be with my parents. Robbie's Christmas treats were all made from maple sugar. He was asking for some other candy. My mother wanted him to have it and I told her alright if she wanted to take care of the tantrum. Of course she didn't believe me – but predictably within thirty minutes she had her hands full with Robbie in a tantrum. It made a believer of her. These discussions did not take place in front of the child if you're wondering about the power of suggestion.

If you go into this food reaction thing it will make you feel so sorry for people you can't stand it. After bad behavior from food Robbie would cry and say he couldn't help it and feel so badly about it. You won't be able to read of a Crime of Violence without wondering if a chemical reaction controlled the aggressor – in fact you'll be unable to condemn anyone for anything – or maybe you're less impressionable.[1]

[1]Quoted from a letter to the author.

Allergies can, of course, be treated by the direct or indirect manipulation of the blood chemistry.

Aggression Control by Drugs

The activity of the neural systems responsible for aggressive behavior and feelings of hostility can also be reduced by the use of drugs. Although there is currently no drug which is a completely specific antihostility agent, there are available a significant number of preparations which do reduce aggressive tendencies as one component of their action. The current state of the art is summarized nicely by Resnick (1969) when he says the following.

There is ample evidence to indicate that psychotropic drugs now available may help individuals who are aggressive, irritable, unstable, egocentric, easily offended, obsessive compulsive and dependent, who demonstrate such symptoms as anxiety, depression, hysteria, agony, unexplainable and motiveless behavior, recurrent violent emotional upsets including temper tantrums and violent rages.

Some kind of a measure for aggressiveness is a part of the battery of screening tests used in the initial evaluation of psychotropic drugs on animals and many standard drugs are being evaluated for antiaggression effects. A review article by Valzelli (1967) provides some notion of the extent of these investigations. He reported two hundred and four animal studies which dealt with the drug-aggression interaction. Eight of these studies reported drugs which produced an increase in aggressiveness; twenty-four reported no effect on the particular behavior studied. Of the eighty drugs covered in the studies reported by Valzelli, seventy-four of them inhibited some form of aggression in some animal studied. Thus, the potential for the development of aggression inhibiting drugs for humans is very great. It is important, however, to recognize that drug effects may be both species specific and situation specific. Valzelli is one of the few authors who makes an attempt to discriminate among the different kinds of aggressive behavior. His table of drug effects shows that some drugs tend to block one kind of aggression and facilitate another within the same species and that a given drug may block aggression in one species but facilitate it in another. In addition, there are wide individual differences in the susceptibility to the taming effects of various drugs.

All of the above factors are significant in the treatment of hostile tendencies in humans. Aggressive behavior has many causes, and can result from an overactivity, or dysfunction in a number of different neural systems. It is therefore not surprising that a specific drug may be effective in reducing the hostility of some individuals and have no effect on others with similar symptoms. Nevertheless, a large number of cases, in which hostility is a major disturbing factor, can be successfully treated with pharmacotherapy.

The advent of the widespread use of phenothiazines less than 15 years ago led to a significant reduction in psychotic hostility. Kline (1962) suggests that "wards formerly filled with screaming denudative, assultive patients now have window curtains and flowers on the table." Quantitative estimates of the reduction of destructive, assaultive behavior are difficult to find, but Kline (1962) offers one which is dramatic in its simplicity. In 1955 prior to the use of the major tranquilizers in the Rockland State Hospital, there were 8,000 window panes broken and three full time glaziers were needed to keep the windows in repair. By 1960 when full use was being made of the psychotropic drugs, the window pane breakage was down to 1900 panes a year. It has been suggested that the sedative action of the phenothiazines alone could account for the improved picture in the mental hospitals. However, it must be recognized that potent sedative hypnotics such as chloral hydrate and paraldehyde have been known and used for three quarters of a century.

The phenothiazines, or major tranquilizers, all appear to have a taming effect over and above their sedative action (Goodman & Gilman, 1965; Ban, 1969). However, some tend to exacerbate hostility symptoms in some patients, others appear to be particularly effective in the reduction of those symptoms. Perphenazine alone or in combination with the antidepressant amitriptyline has been useful in reducing the aggressive tendencies of depressed patients (Pennington, 1964), aggressive mental defectives (Mises & Beauchesne, 1963), sex deviated criminals (Buki, 1964), and aggressive alcoholics (Bartholomew, 1963). The hostile tendencies of a wide variety of patients from epileptic psychotics (Wolpowitz, 1966) to disturbed adolescents (Rosenberg, 1966) and hyperactive children (Alderton & Hoddinott, 1964) have been successfully controlled with thioridazine. A survey of the studies on thioridazine is given by Cohen (1966).

Dilantin (sodium diphenylhydantoin) is a drug which has been used with considerable success in the control of seizures. It has recently come into popular prominence because of its apparent tendency to control hyperexcitability and hostility in nonepileptic patients (Rosenfeld, 1967). Zimmerman (1956) as early as 1956 studied 200 children with severe behavior disorders and reported that 70% of them improved under sodium diphenylhydantoin therapy showing less excitability, as well as less frequent and less severe temper tantrums.

Turner (1967) in a study of 72 subjects seen in psychiatric practice found that 86% showed drug related improvement particularly in relation to anger, irritability, and tension. The drug is effective with individuals having both abnormal and normal EEG records (Glueck & Boelhouwer, 1967; Ross & Jackson, 1940). There seems to be little question that dilantin is useful in a wide variety of disorders including neurotics, psychotics, psychopaths, and emotionally disturbed children. The behavioral syndrome which seems to be common in such a diverse group of patients includes explosiveness, low frustration tolerance, irritability, impulsive behavior, compulsive behavior, aggressive behavior, erratic behavior, inability to delay gratification, mood swings, short attention span, undirected activity, and similar symptoms (Resnick, 1967). The general findings above were supported in an excellent double blind study of behavior modification in selected prisoners and juvenile delinquents (Resnick, 1967). Resnick (1967) gives excerpts from tape recordings of interviews with the prisoners during the study which reveal the potency of the drug in manipulating negative affect. Certainly, a great many more studies must be done, but there is every reason to believe that drug administration to selected prisoners would not only make them feel better, but would also facilitate prison management.

Hyperkinetic children present a behavior disorder syndrome which includes overactivity, restlessness, aggressiveness, temper tantrums, disobedience, impulsivity, and poor concentration. There are now a variety of drugs which dramatically reduce these symptoms without appreciable sedation. One of the earliest and most effective drugs which is still being used is the stimulant amphetamine (Bradley, 1937). Although there is no adequate explanation for the effect, it is clear that aggressively noisy children and those inclined toward antisocial acting out behavior are "normalized" by amphetamines (Heath & Buddlington, 1967). The same class of drugs also seems to be useful with adult patients who have immature personalities with outbursts of spontaneous aggression (Ban, 1969). A variety of other drugs quell the outbursts of hostility in children with behavior disorders. Benadryl is useful in children below the age of ten years but is considerably less effective in older children (Fish, 1960). Several studies have shown that haloperidol is particularly effective in the treatment of children with severe behavior disorders. Barker and Fraser (1968) in a double blind crossover study showed that children with the hyperactive aggressive syndrome were significantly improved on haloperidol. Similar findings have been reported by Cunningham, Pillai and Rogers (1968). They suggest that the reduction in overactivity, destructiveness, teasing, and bullying should provide greater opportunity to positively reinforce more desirable forms of behavior.

Two more classes of drugs which effectively reduce irritability should be mentioned because of their extensive use and their potential for even greater use. These are the so-called minor tranquilizers which include the propanediols (meprobamate and tybamate) and the benzodiazepines (including chlordiazepoxide, diazepam, and oxazepam). Although the propanediols have a taming effect on vicious monkeys and aggressive cats (Berger, 1954; Hendley, 1954), the benzodiazepines seem to be effective at a dose level which produces neither sedation nor ataxia (Scheckel & Boff, 1966). (See Cook and Kelleher (1963) for an extensive review of these findings). Meprobamate effectively controls tension and anxiety symptoms which are associated with irritability in humans (Ban, 1969) and is effective in the reduction of premenstrual tension. A large number of studies have shown that the benzodiazepines can effectively reduce aggressive excitability, hostility, and irritability. (Denham, 1963; De-Craene, 1964; Barsa & Saunder, 1964 are a few.) Diazepam has been used with "remarkable success" in eliminating the destructive rampages of psychotic criminals (Kalina, 1962). Kalina indicates that schizophrenia is unaffected by the drug, but the aggressive and destructive elements which make the patient difficult and dangerous to manage are eliminated.

FURTHER IMPLICATIONS

There can be little doubt that when certain physiological conditions occur, both men and animals will react with hostility toward any appropriate stimulus object. If the organism is manipulated physiologically so as to alter or prevent those internal conditions, aggressive behavior will not occur. In the light of the studies presented above it is naive to suggest as does Montagu (1966) that, "all of man's natural inclinations are toward the development of goodness." Or, that, "there is not a shred of evidence that man is born with 'hostile' or 'evil' impulses which must be watched and disciplined (Montagu, 1966, p. 44)." Whether man is born good or evil is a value judgment and depends on the frame of reference of the evaluator. However, there is abundant evidence that man has innate, neural and endocrine organizations which when activated result in hostile thoughts and behaviors. To ignore these data is to forfeit means of control which are valuable to both the victims and the aggressors.

Although there is still much to learn about the physiological control of aggression, there can be little doubt that such control is now possible through brain lesions, brain stimulation, or manipulation of the internal environment with hormones or drugs. The emphasis so far in the paper has been on pathological hostility where the need is the greatest and where the results are the most obvious. However, further implications must be considered. It seems clear as in many of the cases described above, that the man who is ill with pathological aggressive tendencies should have available to him the cures developed by research. But, what of the "normal" person? What is the potential effect on the reader of this book and the author of this chapter?

I once had a neighbor who met all of the accepted criteria of freedom from pathology. She certainly should not and could not have been committed. However, her aggression circuits were easily fired. She felt hostile much of the time. She was irascible and uncomfortable. Though she reported that she tried very hard to inhibit her hostile behavior, she found herself frequently shouting at her children and her husband. Certainly, most men would agree that she should be free of this unreasonable hostility if she could find a drug which would help her control it. There may very well be drugs available now (diphenylhydantoin, meprobamate, or diazepam, for example) which would help her handle her hostile moods, and if there are not, there will be within a few years. These are the clear and unmixed blessings of research. Certainly the world will be a more peaceful place for all when each of us has the opportunity, if we choose, to reduce our irrational irritability by physiological means.

That, however, is not the end of the story. We must also examine the other edge of the two-edged sword of progress. Knowledge is accumulating at an ever increasing rate and that accumulation cannot be terminated; we can only hope to consider wisely the manner in which that knowledge is used. Airplanes are now being built which are longer than the initial flight of the Wright Brothers. If there is a comparable advance in our understanding of the chemistry and the physiology of aggression (and there is every reason to believe that there will be), what physiological means of aggression control will be available 65 years from now?

In my laboratory at Carnegie-Mellon we have squirrel monkeys which are vicious and untameable. A hand put in the cage to touch or pet them will be savagely and repeatedly bitten. They can only be handled with heavy gauntlet gloves. Judy Gibbons Parkman and I have recently shown that it is possible to put a few thousands of a gram of diazepam in the milk that we give them. They evidently cannot taste it, or could I. When the drug begins to take effect, they lose their hostility and can be handled with bare hands. As others have reported, the drug does not sedate them, it simply makes them more friendly. Most of the milk available today is pasteurized and homogenized and has Vitamin D added. Will the milk available tomorrow have an antihostility drug added or will such a drug be added to the water supply? Will this make for a peaceful population, and if so, will it be worth it? Resnick (1969) has suggested that by the year 2000 we will have a drug-controlled society or a society that will self-destruct. But, who will make the controlling decisions? The absolute physiological control of some kinds of aggression in individuals is here now. The control of hostility in masses of people is close enough that we should be concerned about it. We should begin to seriously ask the question, "Who will control the controllers of the mind?"

REFERENCES

Adey, W. R., Merrillees, N. C. R., & Sunderland, S. The entorhinal area; behavioral, evoked potential, and histological studies of its inter-relationships with brain stem regions. *Brain,* 1956, **79,** 414–438.

Alderton, H., & Hoddinott, B. A. A controlled study of the use of thioridazine in the treatment of hyperactive and aggressive children in a children's psychiatric hospital. *Canadian Psychiatric Association Journal,* 1964, **9,** 239–247.

Alpers, B. J. Personality and emotional disorders associated with hypothalamic lesions. *Association for Research in Nervous and Mental Disease,* 1940, **20,** 725–748. Baltimore: Williams & Wilkins Co.

Anand, B. K. & Dua, S. Electrical stimulation of the limbic system of the brain ('visceral brain') in the waking animals. *Indiana Journal of Medical Research,* 1956, **44,** 107–119.

Bailey, P. Discussion. In M. Baldwin & P. Bailey (Eds.), *Temporal lobe epilepsy.* Springfield, Ill.: Charles C. Thomas, 1958.

Ban, T. A. *Psychopharmacology.* Baltimore: Williams & Wilkins, 1969.

Bandler, R. Neurochemical basis of predatory aggression in the rat. Doctoral dissertation, Carnegie-Mellon University, Pittsburgh, Pa., 1969.

Bard, P. Central nervous mechanisms for the expression of anger in animals. In M. L. Reymert (Ed.), *Feelings and emotions.* The Mooseheart Symposium. New York: McGraw-Hill, 1950.

Bard, P. & Mountcastle, V. B. Some forebrain mechanisms involved in expression of rage with special reference to suppression of angry behavior. *Research Publications, Association for Research in Nervous and Mental Disease,* 1948, **27,** 362–404.

Barker, P., & Fraser, I. A. A controlled trial of haloperidol in children. *British Journal of Psychiatry,* 1968, **114,** 855–857.

Barsa, J., & Saunder, J. C. Comparative study of chlordiazepoxide and diazepam. *Diseases of the Nervous System,* 1964, **25,** 244–246.

Bartholomew, A. A. Perphenazine (Trilafon) in the immediate management of acutely disturbed chronic alocholics. *Medical Journal of Australia,* 1963, **1,** 812–14.

Beeman, E. A. The effect of male hormone on aggressive behavior in mice. *Physiological Zoology,* 1947, **20,** 373–405.

Berger, F. M. The pharmacological properties of 2-methyl-2-N-propyl-1,3-propanediol dicarbamate (Miltown) and a new interneuronal blocking agent. *Journal of Pharmacology and Experimental Therapeutics,* 1954, **112,** 412.

Berkowitz, L. Experiments on automatism and intent in human aggression. In C. D. Clemente & D. B. Lindsley (Eds.), *Aggression and Defense.* Berkeley, Calif.: Univ. of California Press, 1967.

Bradley, C. The behavior of children receiving benzedrine. *American Journal of Psychiatry,* 1937, **94,** 577.

Brown, J. L., & Hunsperger, R. W. Neuroethology and the motivation of agonistic behavior. *Animal Behaviour*, 1963, **11**, 439–448.

Brutkowski, S., Fonberg, E., & Mempel, E. Angry behavior in dogs following bilateral lesions in the genual portion of the rostral cingulate gyrus. *Acta Biologiae Experimentalis, Polish Academy of Sciences*, 1961, **21**, 199–205.

Buki, R. A. The use of psychotropic drugs in the rehabilitation of sex-deviated criminals. *American Journal of Psychiatry*, 1964, **120**, 1170–1175.

Clark, G., & Birch, H. G. Hormonal modifications of social behavior. The effect of sex-hormone administration on the social status of a male-castrate chimpanzee. *Psychosomatic Medicine*, 1945, **7**, 321–329.

Cohen, S. Thioridazine (Mellaril): Recent developments. *Journal of Psychopharmacology*, 1966, **1**, 1–15.

Collias, N. E. Aggressive behavior among vertebrate animals. *Physiological Zoology*, 1944, **17**, 83–123.

Cook, L., & Kelleher, R. T. Effects of drugs on behavior. *Annual Review of Pharmacology*, 1963, **3**, 205–222.

Coppen, A., & Kessel, N. Menstruation and personality. *British Journal of Psychiatry*, 1963, **109**, 711–721.

Cunningham, M. A., Pillai, V., & Rogers, W. J. B. Haloperidol in the treatment of children with severe behavior disorders. *British Journal of Psychiatry*, 1968, **114**, 512.

Dalton, K. Menstruation and crime. *British Medical Journal*, 1961, **3**, 1752–1753.

Dalton, K. *The premenstrual syndrome*. Springfield, Ill.: Charles C. Thomas, 1964.

DeCraene, O. Nervoses et therapeutique tranquillisante. *Scalpel*, 1964, **117**, 1044–1050.

Delgado, J. M. R. Emotional behavior in animals and humans. *Psychiatric Research Reports*, 1960, **12**, 259–271.

Delgado, J. M. R. Cerebral heterostimulation in a monkey colony. *Science*, 1963, **141**, 161–163.

Delgado, J. M. R. Pharmacology of spontaneous and conditioned behavior in the monkey. Pharmacology of conditioning, learning and retention. Proceedings of the Second International Pharmacological Meeting, Prague, August 20–23, 1965, 133–156.

Delgado, J. M. R. Brain research and behavioral activity. *Endeavour*, 1967, **26**, 149–154.

Delgado, J. M. R. Aggression in free monkeys modified by electrical and chemical stimulation of the brain. Paper presented at the Symposium on Aggression, Interdepartmental Institute for Training in Research in the Behavioral and Neurologic Sciences, Albert Einstein College of Medicine, New York, June 5, 1969.

Delgado, J. M. R., Bradley, R. J., Johnston, V. S., Weiss, G., & Wallace, J. D. Implantation of multi-lead electrode assemblies and radio stimulation of the brain in chimpanzees. Technical Report, ARL-TR-69-2, 6571st Aeromedical Research Laboratory. Aerospace Medical Division, Air Force Systems Command, Holloman Air Force Base, New Mexico, 1969.

Delgado, J. M. R., & Kitahata, L. M. Reversible depression of hippocampus by local injections of anesthetics in monkeys. *Electroencephalogy and Clinical Neurophysiology*, 1967, **22**, 453–464.

Delgado, J. M. R., Mark, V., Sweet, W., Ervin, F., Weiss, G. Bach-Y-Rita, & Hagiwara, R. Intracerebral radio stimulation and recording in completely free patients. *Journal of Nervous & Mental Disease*, 1968, **147**, 329–340.

Denham, J. Psychotherapy of obsessional neurosis assisted by Librium. Topical problems of psychotherapy. *Supplementum ad acta psychotherapeutica et psychosomatica*, 1963, **4**, 195–198.

Dicks, D., Myers, R. D., & Kling, A. Uncus and amygdala lesions: Effects on social behavior in the free-ranging rhesus monkey. *Science*, 1969, **165**, 69–71.

Dunn, G. W. Stilbestrol induced testicular degeneration in hypersexual males. *Journal of Clinical Endocrinology*, 1941, **1**, 643–648.

Egger, M. D., & Flynn, J. P. Effect of electrical stimulation of the amygdala on hypothalamically elicited attack behavior in cats. *Journal of Neurophysiology*, 1963, **26**, 705–720.

Ervin, F., Mark, V., & Sweet, W. Focal brain disease and assaultive behavior. Proceedings of the Symposium on the Biology of Aggressive Behaviour, Milan, May, 1968. Excerpta Medica, Amsterdam, 1969.

Ervin, F. R., Mark, V. H. & Stevens, J. Behavioral and affective responses to brain stimulation in man. In J. Zubin & Shagass (Eds.), *Neurobiological aspects of psychopathology*. New York: Grune & Stratton, 1969.

Falconer, M. A. Discussion. In M. Baldwin & P. Bailey (Eds.), *Temporal lobe epilepsy*. Springfield, Ill.: Charles C. Thomas, 1958.

Falconer, M. A., Hill, D., Meyer, A., & Wilson, J. L. Clinical, radiological and EEG correlations with pathological changes in temporal lobe epilepsy and their significance in surgical treatment. In Baldwin, M., & Bailey, P. (Eds.), *Temporal lobe epilepsy*. Springfield, Ill.: Charles C. Thomas, 1958.

Fish, B. Drug therapy in child psychiatry: Pharmacological aspects. *Comparative Psychiatry*, 1960, **1**, 212–227.

Fonberg, E. Effect of partial destruction of the amygdaloid complex on the emotional-defensive behavior of dogs. *Bulletin de l'Academic Polonaise des Sciences*, 1965, **13**, 429–431.

Frederichs, C., & Goodman, H. *Low blood sugar and you*. New York: Constellation International, 1969.

Fuller, J. L., Rosvold, H. E., & Pribram, K. H. The effect on affective and cognitive behavior in the dog of lesions of the pyriform-amygdala-hippocampal complex. *Journal of Comparative & Physiological Psychology*, 1957, **50**, 89–96.

Galef, B. G. Aggression and timidity: Response to novelty in feral Norway rats. *Journal of Comparative & Physiological Psychology*, 1970, **70**, 370–375.

Gibbs, F. A. Ictal and non-ictal psychiatric disorders in temporal lobe epilepsy. *Journal of Nervous Mental Disease*, 1951, **113**, 522–528.

Gibbs, F. A. Abnormal electrical activity in the temporal regions and its relationship to abnormalities of behavior. *Research Publications Association for Research in Nervous and Mental Disease*, 1956, **36**, 278–294.

Gibbs, F. A., Amador, L., & Rich, C. Electroencephalographic findings and therapeutic results in surgical treatment of psychomotor epilepsy. In M. Baldwin & P. Bailey (Eds.), *Temporal lobe epilepsy*. Springfield, Ill.: Charles C. Thomas, 1958.

Glees, P., Cole, J., Whitty, C., & Cairns, H. The effects of lesions in the cingular gyrus and adjacent areas in monkeys. *Journal of Neurology Neurosurgery and Psychiatry*, 1950, **13**, 178–190.

Gloor, P. Amygdala. In J. Field, H. W. Magoun, & V. E. Hall (Eds.), *American physiological society handbook of physiology*, Section I: Neurophysiology, Vol. II. Baltimore, Md.: Williams & Wilkins, 1960.

Gloor, P. In discussion of a paper by Eibl-Eibesfeldt, I., Ontogenetic and maturational studies on aggressive behavior. In C. D. Clemente & D. B. Lindsley (Eds.), *Aggression and defense: Neural mechanisms and social patterns* (Brain function, Vol. V UCLA Forum Med. Sci. No.) Los Angeles: Univ. of California Press, 1967.

Glueck & Boelhouwer. Paper presented at the American Psychiatric Association, May, 1967.

Gol, A., Kellaway, P., Shapiro, M., & Hurst, C. M. Studies of hippocampectomy in the monkey, baboon and cat. *Neurology*, 1963, **13**, 1031.

Goodman, L. S., & Gilman, A. *The pharmacological basis of therapeutics.* New York: Macmillan Co., 1965.

Green, J. D., Clemente, C. D., & de Groot, J. Rhinencephalic lesions and behavior in cats. *Journal of Comparative Neurology,* 1957, **108,** 505–536.

Green, J. R., Duisberg, R. E. H., & McGrath, W. B. Focal epilepsy of psychomotor type, a preliminary report of observations on effects of surgical therapy. *Journal of Neurosurgery,* 1951, **8,** 157–172.

Greene, R., & Dalton, K. The premenstrual syndrom. *British Medical Journal,* 1953, **1,** 1007–1014.

Hamburg, D. A. Effects of progesterone on behavior. In R. Levine (Ed.), *Endocrines and the central nervous system.* Baltimore: Williams & Wilkins, 1966.

Hamburg, D. A., Moos, R. H., & Yalom, I. D. Studies of distress in the menstrual cycle and the postpartum period. In R. P. Michael (Ed.), *Endocrinology and human behaviour.* London: Oxford Univ. Press, 1968.

Hawke, C. C. Castration and sex crimes. *American Journal of Mental Deficiency,* 1950, **55,** 220–226.

Heath, R. G. Common characteristics of epilepsy and schizophrenia – clinical observation and depth electrode studies. *American Journal of Psychiatry,* 1962, **118,** 1013–1026.

Heath, R. G. Electrical self stimulation of the brain in man. *American Journal of Psychiatry,* 1963, **120,** 571–577.

Heath, R. G. Developments toward new physiologic treatments in psychiatry. *Journal of Neuropsychiatry,* 1964, **5,** 318–331.

Heath, R. G. Pleasure response of human subjects to direct stimulation of the brain: Physiologic and psychodynamic considerations. In R. G. Heath (Ed.), *The role of pleasure in behavior.* New York: Hoeber Inc., 1964.

Heath, R. G., & Buddington, W. Drugs for stimulation of mental and physical activity. In W. Modell (Ed.), *Drugs of choice 1968–1969.* St. Louis: Mosby, 1967.

Heath, R. G. *et al. Studies in schizophrenia.* Cambridge: Harvard Univ. Press, 1954.

Heath, R. G., & Mickle, W. A. Evaluation of seven years experience with depth electrode studies in human patients. In E. R. Ramey & D. S. O'Doherty (Eds.), *Electrical studies on the unanesthetized brain.* New York: Hoeber Inc., 1960.

Heimburger, R. F., Whitlock, C. C., & Kalsbeck, J. E. Stereotaxic amygdalotomy for epilepsy with aggressive behavior. *Journal of the American Medical Association,* 1966, **198,** 165–169.

Hendley, C. D., *et al.* Effect of 2-methyl-2-N-propyl-1,3-propanediol dicarbamate (Miltown) on central nervous system. *Proceedings of the Society for Experimental Biology and Medicine,* 1954, **87,** 608.

Janowsky, E. S., Gorney, R., & Mandell, A. J. The menstrual cycle: Psychiatric and ovarian-adrenocortical hormone correlates; Case study and literature review. *Archives of General Psychiatry,* 1967, **17,** 459–469.

Jonas, A. D. *Ictal and subictal neurosis: Diagnosis and treatment.* Springfield, Ill.: Charles C. Thomas, 1965.

Kaada, B. Brain mechanisms related to aggressive behavior. In C. D. Clemente & D. B. Lindsley (Eds.), *Aggression and defense.* Berkeley, Calif.: Univ. of California Press, 1967.

Kalina, R. K. Use of diazepam in the violent psychotic patient: A preliminary report. *Colorado GP,* 1962, **4,** 11–14.

Karli, P. The Norway rat's killing response to the white mouse. *Behavior,* 1956, **10,** 81–103.

Karli, P., & Vergnes, M. Role des differentes composantes du complexe nucleaire amygadalien dans la facilitation de l'agressivite interspecifique du rat. *Comptes Rendus de la Societe de Biologie,* 1965, **159,** 754.

Karli, P., Vergnes, M., & Didiergeorges, F. Rat-mouse interspecific aggressive behaviour and its manipulation by brain ablation and by brain stimulation. Proceedings of the Symposium on the Biology of Aggressive Behaviour, Milan, May, 1968, Excerpta Medica, Amsterdam, 1969.

Kennard, M. A. The cingulate gyrus in relation to consciousness. *Journal of Nervous Mental Disease*, 1955a, **121**, 34–39.

Kennard, M. A. Effect of bilateral ablation of cingulate area on behaviour of cats. *Journal of Neurophysiology*, 1955b, **18**, 159–169.

King, H. E. Psychological effects of excitation in the limbic system. In D. E. Sheer (Ed.), *Electrical stimulation of the brain*. Austin: Univ. of Texas Press, 1961.

Kislak, J. W., & Beach, F. A. Inhibition of aggressiveness by ovarian hormones. *Endocrinology*, 1955, **56**, 684–692.

Kline, N. Drugs are the greatest practical advance in the history of psychiatry. *New Medical Material*, 1962, 49.

Kluver, H., & Bucy, P. C. "Psychic blindness" and other symptoms following bilateral temporal lobectomy in Rhesus monkeys. *American Journal of Physiology*, 1937, **119**, 352–353.

Kluver, H., & Bucy, P. C. An analysis of certain effects of bilteral temporal lobectomy in the rhesus monkey, with special reference to "psychic blindness." *Journal of Psychology*, 1938, **5**, 33–54.

Kluver, H., & Bucy, P. C. Preliminary analysis of functions of the temporal lobes in monkeys. *Archives of Neurology & Psychiatry*, 1939, **42**, 979–1000.

Kreschner, M., Bender, M., & Strauss, I. Mental symptoms in cases of tumor of the temporal lobe. *Archives of Neurology and Psychiatry*, 1936, **35**, 572–596.

LeBeau, J. The cingular and precingular areas in psychosurgery (agitated behaviour, obsessive compulsive states, epilepsy), *Acta Psychiatrica et Neurologica*, 1952, **27**, 305–316.

LeMaire, L. Danish experiences regarding the castration of sexual offenders. *Journal of Criminal Law and Criminology*, 1956, **47**, 294–310.

Lerner, L. J. Hormone antagonists: Inhibitors of specific activities of estrogen and androgen. *Recent Progress in Hormone Research*, 1964, **20**, 435–490.

Lerner, L. J., Bianchi, A., & Borman, A. A-Norprogesterone an Androgen antagonist. *Proceedings of the Society for Experimental Biology and Medicine*, 1960, **103**, 172–175.

Liddell, D. W. Observation on epileptic automatism in a mental hospital population. *Journal of Mental Science*, 1953, **99**, 731–748.

Lyght, C. E. (Ed.). *The merck manual of diagnosis and therapy*. West Point, Pa.: Merck & Co., 1966.

Mises, R., & Beauchesne, H. Essai de la perphenazine chez l'enfant, et l'adolescent. *Annales Medico Psychologiques*, 1963, **2**, 89–92.

Monroe, R. R. Episodic behavioral disorders — Schizophrenia or epilespy. *AMA Archives of General Psychiatry*, 1959, **1**, 205–214.

Montagu, A. *On being human*. New York: Hawthorn Books, 1966.

Morton, J. H., Additon, H., Addison, R. G., Hunt, L., & Sullivan. A Clinical study of premenstrual tension. *American Journal of Obstetrics & Gynecology*, 1953, **65**, 1182–1191.

Moyer, K. E. Kinds of aggression and their physiological basis. *Communications in Behavioral Biology*, 1968, **2**, 65–87.

Moyer, K. E. A preliminary physiological model of aggressive behavior. In J. P. Scott & B. E. Eleftheriou (Eds.), *The physiology of fighting and defeat*. Chicago, Ill.: Univ. of Chicago Press, 1969, (In press).

Mulder, D., & Daly, D. Psychiatric symptoms associated with lesions of temporal lobe. *Journal American Medical Association*, 1952, **150**, 173–176.

Narabayashi, H., Nagao, T., Saito, Y., Yoshida, M. & Nagahata, M. Stereotaxic amygdalotomy for behavioral disorder. *Archives of Neurology (Chicago)*, 1963, **9**, 1–16.

Narabayashi, H., Uno, M. Long range results of stereotaxic amygdalotomy for behavior disorders. Second International Symposium Stereoencephalotomy, *Confinia Neurolologica*, 1966, **27**, 168–171.

Neumann, F., Elger, W., & Von Berswordt-Wallrabe, R. Inter-sexuality of male foetuses and inhibition of androgenic functions in adult animals with a testosterone blocker. *German Medical Monthly*, 1967, **12**, 1–17.

Neumann, F., Von Berswordt-Wallrabe, R., Elger, W., & Steinbeck, H. Activities of anti-androgens. Experiments in prepuberal and puberal animals and in foetuses. In J. Tamm (Ed.) *Testosterone*. Proceedings of the work shop conference, April 20–22, 1967, Tremsbuettel, Georg Thieme Verlag, Stuttgart, 1968, 134–143.

Pennington, V. M. The phrenotropic action of perphenazine amytriptyline. *American Journal of Psychiatry*, 1964, **120**, 1115–1116.

Plotnik, R. Changes in social behavior of squirrel monkeys after anterior temporal lobectomy. *Journal of Comparative and Physiological Psychology*, 1968, **66**, 369–377.

Pool, J. L. The visceral brain of man. *Journal of Neurosurgery*, 1954, **11**, 45–63.

Pribram, K. H., & Bagshaw, M. Further analysis of the temporal lobe syndrome utilizing fronto temporal ablations. *Journal of Comparative Neurology*, 1953, **99**, 347–375.

Randolph, T. G. *Human ecology and susceptibility to the chemical environment*. Springfield, Ill.: Charles C. Thomas, 1962.

Resnick, O. The psychoactive properties of diphenlylhydantoin: Experiences with prisoners and juvenile delinquents. *International Journal of Neuropsychiatry*, 1967, **3**, Suppl. 2, S20–S47.

Resnick, O. Use of psychotropic drugs with criminals. *Psychopharmacology Bulletin*, 1969, **5**, 17.

Robinson, W. G., & Guerrero-Figueroa, R. Electrophysiological studies during wakefulness and natural sleep in patients with episodic behavioral disorders. In. R. Guerrero-Figueroa (Ed.), *Clinical and experimental research approaches to problems in mental illness*. Louisiana State Univ. Press, 1967 (In press).

Rocky, S., & Neri, R. O. Comparative biological properties of SCH 12600 (6-chloro 4, 6 pregnadien 16-methylene 17- ol-3, 20-dione-17-acetate) and chlormadinone acetate. *Federation Proceedings*, 1968, **27**.

Rosenberg, P. H. Management of disturbed adolescents. *Diseases of the Nervous System*, 1966, **27**, 60–61.

Rosenfeld, A. 10,000-to-1 payoff. *Life Magazine*, 1967, **63**, 121–128.

Ross, A. T., & Jackson, V. A. B. Dilantin sodium: Its influence on conduct and on psychometric ratings of institutionalized epileptics. *Annals of Internal Medicine*, 1940, **14**, 770–773.

Rosvold, H. E., Mirsky, A. F., & Pribram, K. H. Influences of amygdalectomy on social behavior in monkeys. *Journal of Comparative and Physiological Psychology*, 1954, **47**, 173–178.

Sands, D. E. Further studies on endocrine treatment in adolescence and early adult life. *Journal of Mental Science*, 1954, **100**, 211–219.

Sano, K. Sedative neurosurgery: With special reference to postero-medial hypothalamotomy. *Neurologia medico chirrurgica*, 1962, **4**, 112–142.

Sano, K. Sedative stereoencephalotomy: Fornicotomy, upper mesencephalic reticulotomy and posteromedial hypothalamotomy. *Progress in Brain Research,* Vol. 21B, 350–372. Correlative neuroscience Part B: *Clinical Studies.* Elseiver, Amsterdam, 1966.

Sano, K., Yoshioka, M., Ogashiwa, M., Ishijima, B., & Ohye, C. Postero-medial hypothalamotomy in the treatment of aggressive behaviors. *Confinia Neurologica,* 1966, 27, 164–167.

Sawa, M., Ueki, Y., Arita, M., & Harada, T. Preliminary report on the amygdaloidectomy on the psychotic patients, with interpretation of oral-emotional manifestation in schizophrenics. *Folio Psychiatrican et Neurologica Japonica,* 1954, 7, 309–329.

Scheckel, C. L., & Boff, E. Effects of drugs on aggressive behavior in monkeys, Excerpta Medica International Congress Series No. 129, Proceedings of the Fifth International Congress of the Collegium Internationale Neuropsychopharmacologicum, 1966, 789–795.

Schreiner, L., & Kling, A. Behavioral changes following rhinencephalic injury in cat. *Journal of Neurophysiology,* 1953, 16, 643–658.

Schreiner, L. & Kling, A. Rhinencephalon and behavior. *American Journal of Physiology,* 1956, 184, 486–490.

Schwab, R. S., Sweet, W. H , Mark, V. H., Kjellberg, R. N., Ervin, F. R. Treatment of intractable temporal lobe epilepsy by stereotactic amygdala lesions. *Transactions of the American Neurological Association,* 1965, 12–19.

Scott, J. P. Review of J. D. Carthy & F. J. Ebling, The natural history of aggression. *Science,* 1965, 148, 820–821.

Scoville, W. B., & Milner, B. Loss of recent memory after bilateral hippocampal lesions. *Journal of Neurological & Neurosurgical Psychiatry,* 1957, 20, 11–21.

Sem-Jacobsen, C. W. Depth-electrographic observations related to Parkinson's disease. *Journal of Neurosurgery,* 1966, 24, 388–402.

Sem-Jacobsen, C. W., & Torkildsen, A. Depth recording and electrical stimulation in the human brain. In E. R. Ramey & O'Doherty, D. S. (Eds.), *Electrical studies on the unanesthetized brain.* New York: Hoeber, Inc., 1960.

Serafetinides, E. A. Aggressiveness in temporal lobe epileptics and its relation to cerebral dysfunction and environmental factors. *Epilepsia,* 1965, 6, 33–42.

Seward, J. P. Aggressive behavior in the rat: I. General characteristics; age and sex differences. *Journal of Comparative Psychology,* 1945, 38, 175–197.

Shealy, C., & Peele, J. Studies on amygdaloid nucleus of cat. *Journal of Neurophysiology,* 1957, 20, 125–139.

Siegel, A., & Flynn, J. P. Differential effects of electrical stimulation and lesions of the hippocampus and adjacent regions upon attack behavior in cats. *Brain Research,* 1968, 7, 252–267.

Sigg, E. B. Relationship of aggressive behavior to adrenal and gonadal function in male mice. Proceedings of the Symposium on the Biology of Aggressive Behaviour, Milan, May, 1968, Excerpta Medica, Amsterdam, 1969.

Spiegel, E. A., & Wycis, H. T. Physiological and psychological results of thalamotomy. *Proceedings of the Royal Society of Medicine Supplement,* 1949, 42, 84–93.

Spiegel, E. A., Wycis, H. T., Freed, H., & Orchinik, C. The central mechanism of the emotions. *American Journal of Psychiatry,* 1951, 108, 426–432.

Strauss, I., & Keschner, M. Mental symptoms in cases of tumor of the frontal lobe. *Archives of Neurological Psychiatry,* 1935, 33, 986–1005.

Suchowski, G. K. Sexual hormones and aggressive behavior. Proceedings of the Sumposium on the Biology of Aggressive Behaviour, Milan, May, 1968, Excerpta Medica, Amsterdam, 1969.

Summers, T. B., & Kaelber, W. W. Amygdalectomy: Effects in cats and a survey of its present status. *American Journal of Physiology*, 1962, **203**, 1117–1119.

Terzian, H. Observations on the clinical symptomatology of bilateral partial or total removal of the temporal lobes in man. In M. Baldwin & P. Bailey (Eds.), *Temporal Lobe epilepsy*. Springfield, Ill.: Charles C. Thomas, 1958, 510–529.

Terzian, H., & Ore, G. D. Syndrome of Kluver and Bucy. Reproduced in man by bilateral removal of the temporal lobes. *Neurology*, 1955, **5**, 378–380.

Thompson, A., & Walker, E. A. Behavioral alterations following lesions of the medial surface of the temporal lobe. *Folia Psychiatrica Neurologica et Neurochirurgicao Neerlandica*, 1950, **53**, 444–452.

Toch, H. *Violent men*. Chicago, Ill.: Aldine, 1969.

Tow, P. M., & Whitty, C. W. Personality changes after operations on the cingulate gyrus in man. *Journal of Neurological and Neurosurgical Psychiatry*, 1953, **16**, 186–193.

Turner, W. J. Therapeutic use of diphenylhydantoin in neuroses. *International Journal of Neuropsychiatry*, 1967, **3**, 94–105.

Urich, J. The social hierarchy in albino mice. *Journal of Comparative Physiology*, 1938, **25**, 373–413.

Ursin, H. The effect of amygdaloid lesions on flight and defense behavior in cats. *Experimental Neurology*, 1965, **11**, 61–79.

Ursin, H. The cingulate gyrus – A fear zone. *Journal of Comparative and Physiological Psychology*, 1969, **68**, 235–238.

Valzelli, L. Drugs and aggressiveness. *Advances in Pharmacology*, 1967, **5**, 79–108.

Vonderahe, A. R. The anatomic substratum of emotion. *The New Scholasticism*, 1944, **18**, 76–95.

Ward, A. A. The cingular gyrus: Area 24. *Journal of Neurophysiology*, 1948, **11**, 13–23.

Wheatly, M. D. The hypothalamus and affective behavior in cats. *Archives of Neurological Psychiatry*, 1944, **52**, 296–316.

Whitty, C. W., Duffield, J. E., Tow, P. M., & Cairns, H. Anterior cingulectomy in the treatment of mental disease. *Lancet*, 1952, **1**, 475–481.

Wilder, J. Sugar metabolism in its relation to criminology. In Linduer & Seliger, *Handbook of correctional psychology*. New York: Philosoph. Library, 1947.

Wilder, B. J. The clinical neurophysiology of epilepsy, a survey of current research. Public Health Service, NINDB Monograph #8, 1968.

Wolpowitz, E. The use of thioridazine (Melleril) in cases of epileptic psychosis. *South African Medical Journal*, 1966, **40**, 143–144.

Wood, C. D. Behavioral changes following discrete lesions of temporal lobe structures. *Neurology*, 1958, **8**(Suppl. 1), 215–220.

Woods, J. W. "Taming" of the wild Norway rat by rhinencephalic lesions. *Nature*, 1956, **178**, 869.

Woringer, E., Thomalske, G., & Klinger, J. Less rapports anatomiques du noyau amygdalien et la technique de son extirpation neurochirurgicale. *Revue Neurologique*, 1953, **89**, 553–560.

Zeman, W., & King, F. A. Tumors of the septum pellucidum and adjacent structures with abnormal effective behavior: An anterior midline structure syndrome. *Journal of Nervous Mental Disease*, 1958, **127**, 490–502.

Zimmerman, F. T. Explosive behavior anomalies in children of an epileptic basis. *New York State Journal of Medicine*, 1956, **56**, 2537–2543.

THE LEARNING AND UNLEARNING OF AGGRESSION

The Role of Anxiety, Empathy, Efficacy, and Prosocial Values

ERVIN STAUB

HARVARD UNIVERSITY

Aggression is older than man. It is discouraging that despite its age, aggression shows no sign of weakening. It does not seem that there has been much decline in the course of history in violence, in the tendency of man to hurt other men. This is in contrast to recurrent hopes of the perfectibility of man. Aggression today seems to dominate our problems in the world: the war in Vietnam, the high crime rate, and the violence in the cities and on the campuses are some of the more predominant examples. Less attention-getting but also relevant is the fact that most psychotherapists find a majority of their patients, I believe, to have great difficulties with the expression of appropriate forms of self-assertion, that is, with the management of aggression.

In this paper the development of aggressive antisocial tendencies and strategies for their decrease or elimination will be considered. In a less detailed manner, overly strong inhibition of self-assertive behavior, together with strategies for the decrease of inhibitions, will also be considered. In preparation for this, determinants of aggression will be discussed. It is the differential effect on people of potential instigators or differences in the inhibition of aggression, or differences in the knowledge of ways to deal with aggression from others, that will determine individual differences in aggression. Moreover, in order to change aggressive tend-

93

encies it is necessary to understand the influences that lead to aggression. Although attention will be focused on aggression, to some degree aggression will be considered within the general framework of moral development and moral behavior. The limitation and management of aggression is an important part of our moral concerns, and therefore the understanding of the internalization of moral values and norms and the learning of moral conduct may help us to understand and to deal with problems related to aggression.

INSTIGATION FOR AGGRESSION

Research findings indicate that *frustration,* interference with reaching a goal, may, but does not necessarily, lead to aggression. There are individual differences in the extent to which people respond to frustration at all, that is, in frustration tolerance. Moreover, animal research shows that frustration may lead to enhanced goal seeking, more energetic attempts to reach the goal. The well-known study by Davitz (1952) showed that children reacted to frustration with aggression or with constructive activity depending on the type of training they had received beforehand.

Another generally agreed upon antecedent of aggression is *threat* to the satisfaction of basic needs, or threat of attack. The importance of these factors was originally suggested by Maslow (1941) and Rosenzweig (1944). Since then, the effects on aggression of insult and verbal or physical attacks of various forms have been extensively investigated in laboratory experiments. The attacks usually take the form of a confederate or the Experimenter insulting Subjects, telling them or implying that they are stupid or incompetent, making unreasonable demands on them, and generally behaving in a rude, unpleasant, insulting, and belittling manner. The effects of such treatment on various forms of aggression by the Subjects, ranging from responses to TAT stories to evaluation of the instigator or to the administration of shocks to the instigator, have been examined. In a few experiments, S's aggressive responses to physical attacks, that is, to receiving painful electric shocks, have been investigated (Taylor, 1967; Berkowitz, Green, & Macauley, 1962). Generally people respond to such treatment with one or all of the available forms of aggression that were mentioned. Geen (1968) found that the aggressive response to insult was greater than to frustration, particularly when Ss were reinforced for aggression by the E observing and approving S's activities in the course of S's administering electric shocks to the presumed instigator.

Recent research findings have begun to show that subjecting people to instigation, particularly to insult or attack, tends to make subsequent suffering by the instigator reinforcing for them. That this should be the case is implied in the usual definition of aggression, as behavior that aims at inflicting injury or pain on others, but has only recently been actually demonstrated. In one experiment (Hartman, 1969), Subjects who were either insulted by a presumed partner in the experiment, or were not insulted, viewed either a neutral movie, or a movie that concentrated on the instrumental aspects of physical aggression, that is, on the behavior of the aggressor, or a movie that concentrated on the pain cues of a victim of physical aggression. Insulted Subjects who viewed others' pain subsequently aggressed against the person who had insulted them to a significantly greater degree than Subjects who viewed either of the other two movies, while Subjects who were not insulted aggressed significantly less if they saw pain cues of a victim than if they observed the instrumental aspects of aggression. Subjects' aggression took the form of administering electric shocks. The findings suggest that observation of others' pain following insult, which possibly produced anger, may have been a reinforcing event, while it seems to have been negatively reinforcing without the prior experience of insult. For Subjects who were not previously insulted the pain cues may have activated empathy, the vicarious experience of others' suffering. The Subjects in this experiment were male adolescents under court commitment who were detained at least six weeks in an institution. Another finding of significance was that those Ss who had a history of more offenses tended to administer more shocks than those who had a history of fewer or less severe offenses, with the difference greatest in the group of Ss who were insulted and viewed a movie showing the pain responses of the victim of aggression. For more antisocial individuals, the observation of pain cues following insult may have been more reinforcing than for less antisocial individuals.

In another experiment, Feshbach, Stiles, and Bitter (1967) found that administration of shocks to a person who behaved in an insulting and unpleasant manner toward the female Subjects served as positive reinforcement in a verbal conditioning type situation, while it seemed to serve as a negative reinforcement for noninsulted Ss, with a significant difference in the learning rate between the two groups. Berkowitz, Green, and Macauley (1962) found that "angered" Subjects, those who received a large number of electric shocks, reported feeling better after hearing that their tormentor performed poorly than after hearing that he had performed well on an assigned task. These individuals were also more aggressive toward the instigator than others. In a study less directly relevant but suggesting a similar phenomenon Aronson and Cope (1968) found that Ss were more willing to do a favor both for a person who behaved pleasantly toward someone who behaved pleasantly toward them and a person who behaved unpleasantly toward someone who behaved unpleasantly toward them, than in the case of the two reverse variations. These findings suggest, in a direct or indirect manner, that people gain satisfaction out of the suffering of their "enemy." Some of the findings show individual differences in this tendency. An important question for the control of aggression is: What are the limits of this tendency? Do people gain satisfaction out of observing the agony and death of someone who was mildly insulting to them, or is there an equitable relationship between the suffering one has experienced and the amount of suffering of the person who caused this suffering, that one enjoys? How individual differences in getting satisfaction out of one's "enemy's" suffering develop is a further important question.

Various interpretations have been offered for the mediation that takes place between frustration, threat, or attack, on the one hand, and aggression on the other. According to Berkowitz, instigation enhances physiological arousal, and the presence or absence of aggressive cues will determine whether this enhanced arousal will lead to aggression or not. The importance of the presence of prior exposure to aggressive cues, such as movies or a gun, on the amount of subsequent aggression, especially by "angered," that is, previously insulted or "instigated" Subjects, has been demonstrated by Berkowitz and his associated (Berkowitz, 1964; Geen & Berkowitz, 1967; Berkowitz & LePage, 1967). In a recent formulation, Berkowitz et al. (1969) suggested that response to instigation will depend on the interpretation of a combination of internal and external cues. That is, external cues will influence the interpretation of internal reactions to the instigating stimuli. Berkowitz et al. (1969) have shown that information provided to Ss by an "anger meter" that they had experienced different degrees of anger affected the magnitude of aggression following instigation. In another study, Geen and O'Neal (1969) found that following exposure to an aggressive film, Ss who were exposed to noise, which presumably enhanced arousal, administered more shocks to another person than Ss who did not hear the noise.

Presumably, the same stimuli usually lead to internal reactions and provide a source of interpretation of these reactions. To view it another way, the interpretation of external stimuli would often determine whether there will be any reaction to them at all, and if so, what kind. Interpretative tendencies that are the result of past experiences may, therefore, be important determinants of reactions to instigating stimuli. External stimuli may, however, also lead to aggression through relatively automatic habitual responses (Miller et al., 1961) or may activate fantasy aggression that, in turn, activates aggressive response sequences.

Reciprocation—The Need for Balance

In addition to the desire to harm others, produced by frustration and threats or attack, aggression may be motivated by a need to reciprocate (retaliate) or to balance the physical or psychological harm that one has suffered through others' actions and the perceived injustice or unfairness against one's self or others. The concept of a norm of reciprocity has been proposed to explain prosocial behavior, the willingness of people to make sacrifices for the sake of others. Gouldner (1960), for example, suggested that it is a widely recognized norm that people should help those who helped them and that they should not harm those who helped them. Investigations related to this norm are relatively few, but they tend to support its influence in the realm of prosocial behavior (Goranson & Berkowitz, 1966; Staub & Sherk, 1970). Reciprocity may, however, also be considered a principle of retaliation. People try to even out, or balance the harm or injustice or unfair treatment they have experienced. For example, in a study we did (Staub & Sherk, 1970), we found that children who had been selfish in sharing candy with their partner subsequently were allowed, by the same partner, to use a crayon that was needed for drawing a picture for a shorter time than children who were generous. A few children, who were obviously and particularly selfish, in that they ate candy in the presence of the other child but shared none with him, received the crayon from the other child only for extremely brief periods of time, if at all. It seems that negative reciprocity, or retaliation, took place.

Retaliation or balancing may take a variety of different forms, and it may be accomplished through means other than aggression. But what is the source of a balancing or retaliating tendency, and what are its goals? Two sources may be suggested. One is direct tuition; children are taught values and ideas such as justice, equality, reciprocity, or equality of opportunity. Deviation from these ideals or internalized values may motivate action to eliminate the deviation. Secondly, as Piaget (1932) and Kohlberg (1964) have suggested, the development of concepts of justice, fairness, equality, and reciprocity may be a function of social experience, may naturally grow out of experiences in interaction with others, and come to be perceived as the "logic" of interpersonal relations. Probably it is a combination of experience and direct tuition that lead to the development of these concepts and ideals.

One goal of reciprocity, or balancing, may be to achieve justice. Another goal may be to maintain or restore status in the eyes of others and to maintain self-respect. A number of recent experiments suggest that when a harm-doer does not compensate his victim he tends to derogate him and justify the victim's suffering, which may increase the probability that the harm-doer will hurt the victim again (Berscheid, Boye, & Darley, 1968; Berscheid, Boye, & Walster, 1968). Retaliation may, on the other hand, restore to equity an inequitable relationship. A recent study has shown (Berscheid, Boye, & Walster, 1968) that a harm-doer will derogate his victim less if he anticipates retaliation from the victim, that is, if he expects that he will receive electric shocks from the victim after he has administered electric shocks to him, than if he does not expect retaliation. Retaliation or balancing may re-establish an equitable relationship, maintain one's status, and help to regain or retain self respect which may depend on these.

Another aspect of a balancing tendency may be that harm suffered by others may lead to self-sacrificial behavior that benefits others and balances the harm. Rawlings (1968) found, for example, that female Ss whose partners received electric shocks, whether due to Ss' fault or not, subsequently delivered electric shocks of less duration to a third girl, and therefore of greater duration to themselves, than girls whose partners did not receive electric shocks. Other research showed that having caused harm to someone increases willingness to perform self-sacrificial acts that benefit others (Darlington & Macker, 1966; Freedman *et al.*, 1967). In these experiments the harm that was caused was unintended by the actor. Although the concept of guilt has been used to explain the latter findings, a balancing tendency motivated by the desire to adhere to principles of fairness, justice and equity, and to the self image of a just person may be a reasonable alternative explanation.

Not only others' behavior, and the harm or suffering it has caused, but the motives attributed to the actor may determine the victim's reaction. The degree of arbitrariness of a frustrator's behavior has been found, for example, to affect subsequent aggression toward him with greater arbitrariness leading to greater aggression (Pastore, 1952; Fishman, 1965). The same may be found with regard to threat or attack, if its arbitrariness was varied. In a number of other experiments, most of them not in the area of aggression, attribution of intent has affected reactions to others' behavior. Shopler and Thompson (1968) found that a favor was reciprocated only if circumstances made the behavior appear as unselfish or not manipulative in intent. Mallick and McCandless (1966) had third grade children frustrated by older children who interfered with the completion of work on several tasks and deprived Ss of winning money. Subsequent aggression, that is, attempts to hinder their frustrator from working on tasks (really a straightforward retaliation) was reduced greatly when the frustrator's behavior was explained to Ss as not malicious in intent but probably mainly the result of tiredness and clumsiness.

Hostile attitudes toward others, the tendency to negatively evaluate, mistrust, and suspect others, may increase the probability of aggression toward others (Buss, 1961; Lovaas, 1961; Loew, 1967), because they enhance the perception of malicious intent and the desire to retaliate. (Hostility may also enhance the perceived need for defense against aggression; see the next section.) That hostility influences people's judgment or evaluation of others has been found in two experiments by Murstein (1961; 1966). Individuals who were judged as hostile by others, for example, their fraternity brothers (Murstein, 1961), tended to deviate in their judgment of others' hostility from the rest of the group. The nature of this deviation was not indicated; it seems more likely that they would judge others more, rather than less, hostile, but there is no data on this point. Murstein (1961) also found that less "insightful" individuals also deviated in their judgment of others' hostility from the rest of the group. Aggressive antisocial individuals, juvenile delinquents, for example, tend to be hostile and show little insight about reasons for their own or others' behavior (Staub & Conn, 1970; Slavson, 1965). This may make it more likely that they would respond to others' behavior with aggression.

Perceived injustice, unfairness, or physical or psychological harm that was suffered may lead to anger; when it is felt that balance has been achieved, anger may subside. The inability to retaliate or to establish a balance may itself enhance anger and hostility. Thibault and Coules (1952) had individuals exchange written communications with a presumed partner. When Ss were insulted in one communication and their chance to respond with a communication of their own was temporarily eliminated, they subsequently showed a significantly greater level of hostility toward this person than Ss who had the opportunity to communicate following the insult.

The notion of establishing a balance may also apply to violent social conflicts, including revolution. Relative deprivation, a concept of recent prominence (Pettigrew, 1967) suggests that the knowledge that one is deprived of what others have leads to frustration. However, this knowledge may also lead to anger on account of injustice or unfairness toward one's self or others. The fact that many of the people who participate in social movements, violent or otherwise, do not themselves experience the relative deprivation that they try to eliminate may suggest that it is the perception of injustice and the desire to create balance that is involved (Rosenhan, 1970).

Reciprocation, balancing, or justice may be brought about through aggression, but also through nonaggressive means. Rothaus and Worchel (1964) found, for example, that of several treatment groups, Subjects were least aggressive toward the Experimenter who insulted them when, in response to verbal comments or complaints by a subject-confederate, the Experimenter stopped insulting them. The effectiveness of the communication in eliminating further insults may have implied that Ss were previously wronged, and may have provided "satisfaction" or served to balance the previous injury.

Decreasing Instigation — The Value of Efficacy

In addition to producing a desire to hurt another person or to balance or retaliate, frustration, threat, or attack may be responded to with aggression in order to reduce subsequent and possibly more intense frustration, threat, or attack. Aggression may be a defensive measure. However, defensive action need not be aggressive, if acts other than aggressive ones can successfully eliminate the probability of being victimized again. Moreover, confidence in one's ability to respond effectively to frustration, threat, or attack or to unfair treatment by others may decrease the arousal or anger-producing potential of instigation.

With regard to the latter point, a variety of experiments have shown with both animals and man that the ability to control or predict aversive experiences decreases both tension and disruption of ongoing behavior. Individuals were less tense when they could determine the sequence in which subtests of an intelligence test would be taken, even though this had no functional value, than others who could not do so (Stotland & Blumenthal, 1964). Fearful individuals were willing to approach a feared stimulus when they could control their own approach (Staub, 1968). Male Subjects who could control the administration of shocks to themselves and could, consequently, predict the timing and exact size of the shocks both tolerated stronger shocks, perceived lower levels of shocks as less uncomfortable and showed less tension at lower levels of shocks than Subjects who had the shocks administered by someone else (Staub, Tursky, & Schwartz, in press). Confidence in one's ability to respond appropriately to instigating stimuli and to deal successfully with them (i.e., control them) may decrease tension, anger, or the need to attempt to control them by aggressive means. This hypothesis needs to be investigated directly; all the evidence for it is indirect.

In addition to decreasing instigation, the ability to respond successfully to, or to defend against, further instigation with nonaggressive or moderately aggressive means may also decrease aggressive behavior. Stone and Hokanson (1969) reviewed several experiments in which friendly or passive responses following instigation, usually insult or aggression by others who administered electric shocks to the Subjects, were associated with reduction in autonomic indices of arousal. This suggests that cathartic-like reactions can result from other than aggressive behavior. Although lack of physiological tension is no guarantee of lack of violence, this evidence is suggestive. In their experiment Stone and Hokanson (1969) have shown that when Ss could avoid stronger shocks from another person by administering shocks to themselves, they tended to respond to others' aggression by self-administration of shocks instead of administering shocks to the aggressor. Those self-punitive responses came to be followed by vascular arousal-reduction, similar to those that were previously found to follow aggressive responses to instigation (Hokanson et al., 1963). Finally, the experiment by Rothaus and Worchel (1964) that was previously interpreted to show that injustice may be balanced without aggression, may be interpreted to show that aggression will be minimal when nonaggressive defenses against instigation by others are successful. In this study an instrumental communication by a subject-confederate was successful in eliminating further insults by the Experimenter; it also reduced subsequent hostility toward the Experimenter.

Reinforcement for Aggression

Perhaps the most general and most important influence on aggression is the probability of reward or punishment for aggressive behavior. A number of writers have differentiated between anger aggression, which aims to inflict pain or injury, and behavior that aims to accomplish other goals, any kind of goal, but inflicts injury and pain in the process (Bandura & Walters, 1963a, 1963b; Feshbach, 1964; Berkowitz, 1962; Buss, 1961). This latter type of aggression, instrumental aggression, may have an unlimited variety of reinforcers. The probability of performing aggressive acts in response to instigation may also be greatly influenced by an individual's history of rewards and punishment for aggression. Patterson, Littman, and Bricker (1967) have shown through extensive observation of children in nursery schools that aggressive behavior is very strongly influenced by reinforcement by other children in the form of withdrawal, letting go of a toy, crying, or other rewards. Although an aggressive disposition tended to be persistent, with the children who started out as most aggressive also ending up as most aggressive, many children became more aggressive as a result of their successful counteraggression or other reinforcement for aggression. Patterson et al. suggest that aggressive habits result from reinforcement for aggression, and only subsequently will emotional states become elicitors of the previously acquired instrumental responses.

Many other studies show that both direct and vicarious reinforcement for aggression, or even the observation of aggressive models who are not punished, enhance subsequent aggression (Bandura, Ross, & Ross, 1963; Bandura & Walters, 1963a, 1963b). Observing violence that was described to *S*s as justified, was also found to enhance subsequent aggression (Berkowitz & Rawlings, 1963). Most of this research did not examine the long range effects of reinforcement or modeling; the study by Patterson *et al.* (1967) was an exception. In a naturalistic study of a street corner gang, Miller *et al.* (1961) noted that most of the aggression in the group seemed to be governed by norms that prescribed appropriate forms of aggression for various occasions. Members of the group seldom showed anger in the course of aggressive behavior. Under the influence of norms that condone or encourage aggression, aggression may become a socially desirable behavior that is rewarded in various ways, including prestige for the successful aggressor.

INHIBITION OF AGGRESSION

I would like to consider next influences that may inhibit aggression. One class of these is fear of punishment, anxiety about aggression, and guilt; while the first of these is likely to be situation-specific, the other two are considered internalized inhibitors of aggression. People vary greatly in the extent that they are afraid to aggress against others or feel guilty about hurting others. It is generally agreed that aggressive antisocial individuals have little anxiety or guilt about aggression. This conclusion comes, in large part, from research with projective and other assessment measures, which shows that stories or responses of aggressive antisocial individuals contain little indication of aggression anxiety. In general, research in this area (Staub & Conn, 1970) shows that the ability to predict overt aggression from Thematic Apperception Test responses improves a great deal if, instead of considering only the amount of aggression expressed in stories, the amount of anxiety and guilt, that is, internal or self-punishment, is also taken into consideration.

Anxiety or guilt are accepted and known inhibitors of aggression. Another neglected but probably important inhibitor of aggression is *empathy,* the capacity to view events from the standpoint of others and to experience vicariously others' emotions. The cognitive component of empathy, the capacity to view events from another's point of view and to recognize the nature of the emotional experience of another, is probably a precondition for the emotional component, the vicarious experience of another's emotion. The motives or intentions perceived as guiding others' actions was proposed as an important influence on the amount and kind of reciprocation or balancing that would take place following instigation. The ability to view events from another's point of view is likely to determine whether and to what extent others' intentions, or their reasons for their actions, are considered at all.

Viewing or perceiving events from another's point of view may lead to the vicarious experience of another's emotion. Vicarious experience of others' pain and suffering may decrease the willingness to inflict pain or suffering on others. In a recent experiment, Feshbach and Feshbach (1969) demonstrated an association between empathy and aggression for boys at two age levels, although not for girls. Among younger boys (4–5 years old) they found a positive association between aggression, as measured by teachers' ratings of children's behavior in class, and empathy, as measured by the degree of correspondence between children's description of how characters in pictures felt and their own reported feelings. Among younger children, activity level, social maturity, and greater social participation may lead to both greater empathy and more aggressive behavior. A similar finding of Murphy (1937) showed a positive relationship between sympathetic behavior and aggression among nursery school children, the two presumably linked by Ss activity level. Among boys six to seven years old, however, the relationship was negative. Children who showed greater empathy or similarity of emotion to those of characters in pictures behaved less aggressively in class.

Previously reviewed research findings, which showed that exposure to others' suffering may be negatively reinforcing for subjects who did not experience prior instigation (Feshbach et al., 1967) and may reduce subsequent aggression (Hartman, 1969), may also be an indication of empathic reactions. So may be findings reported by Buss (1966). Subjects in this study found out before administering shocks to a second victim, that they had harmed the first person to whom they presumably administered shocks, specifically, that this person now cannot move the finger to which shocks were administered. When the victims were females, this resulted in a reduction of the amount of shock administered to the second victim; the same held, to a smaller degree, for female Subjects. The effect was greatest when both the victim and the Subject were females. Information about the harmful consequences of the shocks for the first victim may have activated empathy. An alternative explanation is also just as reasonable, however; aggression anxiety, guilt, and fear of consequences may have been enhanced by the knowledge of the harm suffered by the victim.

Empathy may limit both instrumental aggression and aggression following instigation, since presumably, even when angry, the more a person vicariously experiences others' emotion, the less reinforcing or satisfying will others' suffering be for him. Consequently, individual differences in empathy may be important determinants of aggressive behavior. However, although direct experimental evidence is not available, it is likely that following instigation—threat, attack, or frustrating behavior—by another person, empathy would be less aroused by this person's or perhaps anyone's suffering than under other conditions.

In sum, a variety of influences on aggression were proposed. Frustration, threat, insult, or attack may all instigate aggression. Reinforcement for aggression and subcultural norms that tolerate or encourage aggression are likely to lead to habitually aggressive responses. A reciprocating and balancing tendency will influence reactions to others' behavior that causes physical or psychological damage or perpetrates injustice; however, others' intentions or motives are also considered, and evaluative tendencies, such as hostility, may affect retaliative action. In addition to aiming to hurt others or to establishing a balance, aggression following instigation may also serve as a defense against further aggression. Both defense and retaliation may, however, take nonaggressive forms; finally, anxiety or guilt, and empathy were suggested as internalized inhibitors of aggression.

THE ACQUISITION OF AGGRESSIVE ANTISOCIAL TENDENCIES

In the next section, aggressive antisocial tendencies and overly strong inhibition of assertive behavior will be discussed, with emphasis on the former. The manifestation of these problems, their development, and strategies for change will be of concern.

Aggressive-antisocial tendencies are exemplified by overt aggressiveness and destructiveness, often accompanied by or manifested through delinquency or criminality. Violent physical acts against individuals and property for verbal aggression may be characteristic of individuals even if their difficulties with society result from theft or burglary. How do these tendencies develop and what are the characteristics of aggressive antisocial individuals?

Child Rearing

Lack of cohesiveness and inconsistency of discipline were found to characterize the families of delinquent and aggressive children (McCord et al., 1959; Elder, 1968). The usual technique of disciplining children in these families, sometimes referred to as power assertion (Hoffman, 1970), is characterized by physical punishment, threats, and verbal attacks. Love oriented techniques are rarely employed (Sears et al., 1957; Aronfreed, 1968; Elder, 1968). Aronfreed calls these techniques sensitization techniques; the child learns that transgression will be punished but does not acquire internal standards that would guide his behavior. Specifically, aggression toward the parents is severely punished. In contrast aggression toward peers may even be encouraged as a masculine-type behavior. "Induction" techniques of discipline (Aronfreed, 1968), which are thought to lead to the internalization of norms, including prohibitions against aggression, are usually not practiced. These techniques emphasize the communication of reasons for the undesirability of certain behaviors, including pointing out to children the consequences of their behavior for others (Aronfreed, 1968; Hoffman, 1970). The use of verbal reasoning, or a verbal medium of discipline, close control over children's behavior, the use of withdrawal of affection to motivate the child to adhere to the verbalized standards or values, and concern about intentions behind the behavior are likely to produce internal governors of behavior (Aronfreed, 1968). These practices are usually absent in lower class families and particularly in families of aggressive antisocial individuals. The result, as the evidence suggests, is a lack of anxiety or guilt about aggression, that is, a lack of internal inhibition of aggression. McCord and McCord (1956) found, for example, that children diagnosed as behavior disorders or psychopaths gave fewer guilt responses on a test with incomplete stories describing situations in which the central character has violated some standard of behavior than children diagnosed in various other ways. Bandura and Walters (1959) found that aggressive boys were deterred from antisocial acts primarily by fear of external punishment instead of guilt or other forms of internal control. Additional evidence that aggressive children lack internal controls was reviewed elsewhere (Staub & Conn, 1970). Although empathy was not evaluated in these studies, the child rearing experiences of these children do not seem conducive to the development of the capacity for empathy. Pointing out to children the consequences of their behavior for others and alerting them to others' internal states seem, for example, important for the development of empathy (Hoffman, 1970).

The literature suggests that parental warmth is not characteristic of the background of aggressive-antisocial individuals. Lack of affection by parents for children was reported, for example, as characterisitic of families with delinquent children (Glueck, 1966). However, the atmosphere of warmth seems important as a background for learning and internalizing parental standards (Maccoby, 1968). Moreover, in a study by Bossard and Boll (1957) adult Ss reported, in autobiographical material and questionnaire responses, that a few persons, often parents but sometimes others, influenced them greatly. Toward these persons strong emotional attitudes developed in the early years of these adults' life. When there were positive emotional attitudes toward these persons, they tried to emulate them more or less consciously in their traits, values, habits, and even occupations. When there was a feeling of aversion, or negative emotional attitudes, they tried to develop opposing traits. These emotional attitudes, Ss reported, influenced their reactions toward the methods of child rearing or other conditions that constituted their experience. These findings may suggest one reason why, through positive emotional attitudes toward individuals outside the home, an environment that may be expected to lead to aggressive-antisocial tendencies will not always do so. The influence of identification with parents on moral development has been supported by recent findings of Hoffman (1970) and Rutherford and Mussen (1968). Bandura and Walters (1959) reported that aggressive adolescent boys in their study experienced conditions that were highly unfavorable for identification with parents. Relationships between fathers and sons were especially poor, with either a severe break in the relationship, or a generally poor relationship in which fathers were typically hostile and rejecting. Bandura and Walters (1959) suggest that serious delinquency may be related not only to a lack of internalization of parental standards, but also to the development of hate and hostility toward the parents and the learning of active opposition to parents and parental norms. In addition to the generally poor relationship, the use of physical punishment, threat, and verbal attack may further engender hostility. The result seems to be a pattern of aggression with insistence on self-reliance and rejection of interference; such boys fear, avoid, and repel close involvements except perhaps with members of their own group. A pattern of active rebellion and rejection of approach by others has also been reported by other writers (Redl & Wineman, 1951; McCord & McCord, 1964; Slavson, 1965). Others' behavior is easily interpreted as a threat, insult, or challenge. It is interesting in this regard, that in a recent study (Kinzel, 1969) it was shown that prisoners who committed violent crimes perceived an Experimenter who was approaching them, while they were sitting in the middle of a room, as threatening, looming over them, or rushing at them, more than prisoners who were committed for nonviolent crimes. Certain individuals may perceive physical approach toward them, or simply the presence of others at close quarters, as an attack.

The availability of aggressive models and *subcultural norms* that permit or even encourage aggression is also likely to contribute to the development of aggressive tendencies. Children may learn aggression through observation of their parents' aggression directed toward themselves or their siblings. Moreover, parental values may support rather than inhibit aggression. Often fathers of aggressive antisocial children present a model for the children through their antisocial behavior outside the home. Identification with aggressive prototypes outside the home may also be important. Finally, a subculture in which toughness, aggressiveness, and criminality is encouraged or rewarded both by prestige and security also contributes to the development of aggressive antisocial tendencies (Bandura & Walters, 1959, 1963a, 1963b). With regard to security, even in institutions for the detention of juvenile delinquents, adolescent boys who are less aggressive than others often fare badly; they are victimized, attacked, used as scapegoats by others. An important question, although beyond the scope of this paper, is: What are the conditions that lead to the development and maintenance of such subcultural norms, and how could they be changed?

Another factor that probably importantly contributes to aggressive tendencies may be called insufficient ego development. Aggressive anti-social individuals tend to be implusive, poor in the ability to delay grati-fication, and distractible (Slavson, 1965; Elder, 1968). Not surprisingly, they are relatively easily frustrated. Their skill or competence in dealing with their environment seems to be poor and attempts to do so by ag-gressive means may predominate for this reason. It may be noted with regard to this, that Kohlberg (1964) has suggested on the basis of avail-able evidence, that "ego strength," particularly competence or mastery, may be important determinants of moral behavior. Aggressive antisocial individuals often lack socially acceptable goals; they probably also lack, however, availability of opportunities for achieving economic rewards (Cloward & Ohlin, 1960). Seeking alternative sources of reinforcement may lead to the development of subcultures that reward aggression, such as gangs, as recent sociological theories emphasize (Elder, 1968).

To sum up, aggressive antisocial adolescents, and the somewhat sparser research indicates adults too (McCord & McCord, 1964), have strong aggressive habits, lack internal controls, are implusive and are easily frustrated, lack skills, competence, and the opportunity to achieve socially acceptable goals and often lack such goals. They are hostile and suspicious of others, and easily react to others' behavior as an instigation for aggression.

TREATMENT: UNLEARNING AGGRESSIVE ANTISOCIAL TENDENCIES

In attempting to treat aggressive antisocial individuals, there are several difficulties to overcome. One is their hostility and negativism and rejection of approach toward them. They do not normally see any mean-ing or value in, or necessity for, treatment, and to be in treatment is socially undesirable in their subculture (Slack, 1960; Schwitzgebel, 1965). Poor verbal ability and lack of introspective inclination present problems for verbal-interpretative therapy. Finally, lack of interest in socially acceptable goals may make therapy particularly difficult, since unless such interest develops therapy is not likely to have lasting effect. McCord and McCord (1964) began their chapter on the treatment of psychopathy with a quotation from the Doctor in Macbeth: "This disease is beyond my practice," appropriately signifying the difficulty of treatment.

In the following, a set of hypotheses will be offered in the form of recommendations for treatment. These recommendations are guided by the notion that learning may take place at the behavioral, cognitive, and affective level, and that experimental findings and clinical experience may both be used to derive principles and techniques for learning. In specific instances, specific goals for therapy should be defined as clearly as possible, and treatment techniques applied that are appropriate for the specific case.

In the clinical literature on the treatment of aggressive antisocial children, adolescents, or adults, reported success can be found in a few instances when some form of milieu or group therapy has been employed (Redl & Wineman, 1952; Slavson, 1943, 1965; Maxwell Jones, 1953). Once the crucial formative years of the child's socialization have passed, and hostile and aggressive tendencies have developed, the best method of socialization or resocialization may be *within a peer group*. In a group, aggressive habits may be eliminated through changed reinforcement contingencies; hostile feelings and active dislike for others may be diminished; and through cohesion within the group and the development of group norms, individuals may learn to internalize standards that will inhibit or modify aggressive behavior. With children and adolescents the presence of adults who may be the source of new values, who show positive affect combined with a certain degree of firmness, and who come to be, in consequence, liked and respected by the children may be important. I wonder whether entirely new policies should not be introduced in the selection of adults to lead such groups; for example, bright, trained, rehabilitated criminals may serve very well in this capacity. Such individuals may command the respect of those whom they treat and provide a bridge between their values and the values that are to be acquired.

In the following, principles and specific techniques of treatment will be discussed. Most, but not all, of the suggested treatment approaches may be applicable to both group and individual therapy.

The Use of Reinforcement Strategies

Direct reinforcement techniques may be used to get aggressive antisocial individuals into treatment, and also as part of therapy.

With adolescent delinquents, experimenter-subject psychotherapy has been reported as a successful strategy to get these individuals into treatment (Slack, 1960; Schwitzgebel, 1965). The "subjects" were recruited at the usual hangout of delinquents, the street-corner, the pool hall; they were offered a part-time job of talking into a tape recorder. By the use of various reinforcers in addition to salary, like bonus money for specific actions, the availability of food at the laboratory, etc., regular attendance was usually achieved. In one study (Schwitzgebel & Kolb, 1964) a "three-year follow-up showed a significant reduction in the frequency and severity of crime when compared to a matched-pair control group." Members of the control group were never contacted but matched and followed up on the basis of correctional institutes' records.

This procedure is enlightening as a method of getting delinquents into treatment; the therapy itself was varied, since the inverviewer-counselors were volunteers who varied in background from social worker to priest. The comments and behavior of the boys indicated that they got involved with their jobs, and later the experience itself became more important than the money.

In contrast to the patient-subjects just described, usually antisocial aggressive individuals are in treatment because they are captive in an institution and they have little choice. Money incentives may be employed in this setting also. For example, in treating 14- to 16-year-old insti-tutionalized delinquent boys, in group therapy, the present author em-ployed a reinforcement procedure that seemed successful in getting the patients involved in therapy. These boys frequently displayed aggressive behavior and showed a tendency for explosions of anger. Activities re-lated to the task of the group — the modification of behavior, feelings, and attitudes — was difficult to maintain. Behavior was often disorderly. To change these conditions a system of reinforcement was introduced. Participants were told that they could "win" up to 75 cents in each session. Two preconditions for winning the money were stated: orderly behavior and talking; without these the third requirement for winning money could not be fulfilled. This third requirement, the content of the talk that would be reinforced, the group members had to figure out them-selves. This arrangement made the differential reinforcement and shap-ing of the content of discussion possible and the "task" more interesting. The group leader had a pile of dimes in front of him, and rewarded task-related contributions to the discussion such as participants' description of their own behavior and feelings, suggestions for change, comments about family, parents, conditions of life at home and in the children's center. Interaction between members of the group that was judged appro-priate was also rewarded. Orderly participation was sometimes specifically rewarded by money bonuses at the end of the session. The most obvious change was increased orderliness, and continuous, intensive, task-related participation in the discussion.

These two examples suggest that direct rewards may be used to get aggressive and antisocial adolescents involved with treatment. In addition to its reward value, money may provide such individuals with an excuse to do something they would have liked to do anyway, like talking about things that concern them, but were inhibited from doing by the norms of their subculture. Talking about problems with an adult may mean you are a sissy. Getting money for talking means that you are getting the better of a situation.

In addition to its initial use, direct reinforcement may be an important part of treatment. As mentioned before, aggressive antisocial subcultures provide reinforcement for aggression in terms of prestige, security, or in other ways. Rewards, particularly money, may be given to individuals, and also to the group as a whole, on condition of not engaging in aggressive acts. By making rewards for the group contingent on the behavior of individual members, pressure may arise within the group to reduce aggression, which may lead to changed reinforcement patterns within the group. These recommendations are supported by findings of Piliavin, Hardyck, and Vadum (1968), that perceived cost greatly effects transgression; they suggested that the cost of transgression may be increased through money wages given on condition that the recipient will stay out of trouble. While reducing aggressive behavior, other procedures, some described below, should aim at the development of prosocial behavior incompatible with aggressive acts. In addition to money, a system of increasing privileges may be used in an institution to reward appropriate behavior. The effectiveness of rewards cannot be taken for granted, and their value for the patients needs to be evaluated. The judicious use of rewards is crucial, so that they will not be pitted against important motives, such as group solidarity and the need for acceptance.

To facilitate cohesion and the development of new group norms and to affect the relationship of group members toward each other, group tasks may be employed. These may include sports, and within- and between-group competition. They may also involve occupational activities and contribute to the development of interest in socially acceptable goals. Slavson's (1943) so-called activity groups, although they included children who were probably only moderately aggressive, used activities as seemingly effective means of treatment. Permissiveness and praise and recognition for constructive behavior in the course of activities, like handicrafts, plays, and trips, seemed to lead to the development of group organization and orderly activities by 8–13-year-old children.

The selection of tasks appropriate for the group is crucial; one reason for the ineffectiveness of occupational therapy in hospitals and juvenile treatment centers is that most of the available activities insult the intelligence and lead to no practical skills.

Increasing Inhibitions

Increase in anxiety and empathy are likely to decrease aggression. Specific techniques may be employed to condition anxiety to aggressive behavior. One technique, aversive conditioning, employs the pairing of electric shocks or other unpleasant physical stimuli with the undesirable responses which may be performed or simply imagined (Wolpe & Lazarus, 1966). A variant of this procedure employs images as aversive stimuli (Cautela, 1966). Through association with images that produce discomfort, the imagined or performed undesirable behavior comes to evoke discomfort also. With problems of obesity and alcoholism Cautela used images that produced nausea. This writer used an extension of this procedure with a 14-year-old boy to decrease his inclination for stealing cars. He was to imagine himself stealing a car; the circumstances were realistically described. As he got into the car and was about to start it, the owner ran to the car, pulled him out and beat him up, or a policeman grabbed him and he was taken to the station; or the car blew up and injured him, and as he got out of the car bleeding, the police got him for trying to steal the car. The realistic description of these events seemed to result in the experience of strong discomfort by the patient. The procedure was repeated with different makes of cars to ensure maximum generalization. In five months following the application of this procedure, the patient was not caught stealing a car, nor did he report the stealing of a car to the therapist, although he did report other illegal acts. While clinical experience suggests the usefulness of aversive imagery in aversive conditioning (Cautela, 1966; Kolvin, 1967), no experimental demonstration of its efficacy is yet available.

Aversive conditioning and covert sensitization (Cautela, 1966), the procedure that uses images to create discomfort, may both be ineffective in increasing anxiety of patients who have an extremely diminished capacity for anxiety. Psychopaths, for example, have been reported generally poor in affective capacity (Cleckley, 1950), even to the extent that they have difficulties in learning to avoid a painful stimulus (Lykken, 1957).

Schachter and Latane (1964) found, nevertheless, that even chronically unemotional criminals showed signs of sympathetic hyperactivity. The two-factor theory of Schachter and Singer (1962) states that emotion is a function of both physiological arousal and interpretation of arousal. Using this theory as a starting point, Valins (1967) suggests that "sociopaths may be unemotional because they ignore or do not utilize as cues whatever internal reactions they do experience," i.e., because they do not interpret their arousal.

The research by Schachter and Latane (1964) and their review of earlier studies suggest that sociopaths overreact to a variety of stimulation, so that their autonomic reactivity is great in response to both frightening and relatively trivial and unimportant events. If such individuals do not interpret their arousal this may be so because they cannot discriminate on the basis of internal cues between important and unimportant events. If this is the case, if there is too much internal confusion, then the attempted treatment may demand two steps: that of enhancing variation in internal reactions so that unimportant events will produce less arousal than important ones, and that of teaching sociopaths to attend to and to interpret their internal arousal.

Variation in physiological reactivity may be produced by relaxation training. Behavior therapists have used relaxation training as part of desensitization, a procedure to eliminate anxiety. The purpose of relaxation training is to help patients reduce tension. Patients are taught to relax their muscles, and over time many of them learn to relax themselves in a very short period of time, without going through the laborious procedure that they initially use. One reason for this is that they learn the internal cues that are involved in relaxation, and ways to bring them about directly. In the case of aggressive-antisocial individuals, who have problems with their autonomic reactivity, pairing of stimuli with relaxation may diminish responsiveness to relatively trivial stimuli, and thereby increase the variability and discriminability of internal reactions. My experience suggests, unfortunately, that it may be difficult to train this type of individual in relaxation. For one thing, many of these people are restless and have difficulty in concentrating; for another thing many of them are unwilling to relinquish a sense of control, and relaxation has that implication for them. If the use of tried procedures turns out to be difficult, combining the use of relaxing drugs and the relaxation exercises so that resistance to the latter decreases may achieve the desired effect.

Another part of the task may be that of teaching the patient to attend to and interpret his internal arousal. Theoretically this may be done by pointing out connections between external cues and the appropriate emotional reactions to those cues, and attempting to link the external cues, and the description of relevant emotional reactions, to internal physiological states. The external cues, as well as internal reactions, may be created through role playing of specific events or scenes. Fights or quarrels that the patient has taken part in, so that aggressive situations will be involved, as well as pleasant events so that emotional reactivity may be enhanced to a variety of types of stimuli may be employed. In addition, less structured role playing or psychodrama may be used, so that spontaneously enacted important experiences of the patients will be included. The use of psychodrama may help patients to understand better not only their own, but also others' emotional reactions, and to view events from the standpoint of others. The capacity for empathy may be enhanced by the changes in perspective and by experiencing affect together with others.

There is evidence that emotional role playing may effect subsequent behavior, for example, smoking (Janis & Mann, 1965). Other evidence that role playing may lead to behavior or attitude change is also available (Goldstein, Heller, & Sechrest, 1966). However, changing emotional capacity and empathy through role playing has not been investigated. In a study we just completed (Staub, in press a), tangentially relevant data was provided. The study investigated two procedures in increasing prosocial behavior—role playing and "induction," or pointing out to children the positive consequences of helping others for the recipient of help. In role playing, children enacted situations in which one person needed help and another one provided help; then they exchanged roles. Kindergarten children were the Subjects in this study. Role playing increased subsequent attempts by girls, but not by boys, to help a distressed girl. Role playing also increased the subsequent sharing of candy by boys with a boy who was described as unhappy because he would not receive any presents for his birthday. Since nothing remotely similar to this was role played, and since this effect was found to be even stronger 4 to 7 days after the treatment than immediately afterwards, it may be concluded that role playing had a general effect of some kind, possibly increasing the capacity to share the feelings of the needy child. These findings are encouraging in that they suggest that perhaps a proclivity toward prosocial behavior, maybe through increased empathy, can be acquired by means of specific training.

Decreasing Instigation—Learning "Appropriate" Aggression

In a previous section it was suggested that aggression in response to frustration, threats or attacks, and perceived injustices may be decreased by increasing skill or mastery in dealing with instigations in a nonaggressive manner. Depending on the area where control or mastery is lacking, training would take different forms. Frustration about one's inability to deal with occupational goals needs to take the form of training in occupational skills. It is my impression that in the few cases of success of individual psychotherapy with psychopaths, reported by McCord and McCord (1964) the patients developed interest in a socially acceptable occupational activity. This may have been crucial for success. It is unfortunate that few opportunities are open for aggressive antisocial individuals, adolescents or adults, for occupational training. How this could be changed is an important social issue.

Another important type of training may aim at teaching aggressive antisocial individuals to deal with threat, attack, or hostility directed at them with moderate forms of self assertive, angry, or aggressive acts. *Assertive training* (Wolpe & Lazarus, 1966; Wolpe, 1958) has been employed by behavior therapists to decrease the inhibitions of overly inhibited patients, but may be highly effective in accomplishing the opposite effect also (Staub 1970b). The training usually includes role playing or behavior rehearsal of specific interactions that are likely to present the patient with problems. The patient may show how he usually behaves in the course of such interactions; then the therapist may show the patient how he acted and enact alternative types of responses. The appropriate behavior may be decided upon through discussion, and may be learned by the patient through rehearsal, reinforcement, and modeling by the therapist. Hostile-aggressive individuals often perceive others' behavior as a challenge, threat, or attack, but they seldom realize that their own behavior may serve as an instigator of others' aggressive acts. In the course of role playing, behaviors that may serve as an instigation to others' aggression may be pointed out, and alternative forms of behavior may be developed. Since nonaggressive defenses against others' aggression are important, assertive training should include the rehearsal of acts that may forestall and inhibit others' aggression and lead to reinforcement from the environment, including prosocial acts. Assertive training overlaps with psychodrama and role playing as discussed before, but it emphasizes training in specific types of behavior.

Assertive techniques seemed effective, in my experience, in decreasing the tendency for angry outbursts and verbal and physical aggressiveness by delinquent and neglected adolescents. The techniques of role playing and behavior rehearsal seemed suitable for use with individuals who enjoy motoric action and can deal with external events verbally, but have difficulties with introspection. Values that prescribe avoiding aggressive behavior may also be communicated during assertive training. Kaufmann and Feshbach (1963) found that a communication that suggested constructive, rational approaches for dealing with instigation of aggression resulted in less aggression of Subjects during a discussion following instigation of aggression by the Experimenter than any one of several other experimental treatments. Over a longer period of time a similar effect may be accomplished with aggressive individuals also.

Verbal Modes of Treatment

Cognitive clarification. Aggressive antisocial individuals show little understanding of the influence of their own and others' motives on behavior. The therapist may point out consistencies in an individual's behavior, or between antecedent events and behavior. The patient's norms, values, beliefs, that determine where, how, and when the expression of hostility is appropriate may be clarified. Evaluation of the appropriateness of these beliefs, information about societal norms, and clarification of positive and negative consequences of various courses of action may all be included in the discussion. The rationale and strategies of cognitive clarification in behavior therapy (Wolpe & Lazarus, 1966), of rational therapy (Ellis, 1962) and of alternative constructs (Kelley, 1955) may all be combined in cognitive clarification. Slavson (1965) suggests that antisocial adolescents do not accept responsibility for their actions, but blame others instead. He suggests, moreover, that the assumption or realization of their responsibility is a crucial component of therapy. Cognitive clarification may contribute to this.

An aspect of cognitive clarification may be to teach, through a verbal medium of exchange, values, standards, and norms that were not learned in the course of socialization. In order for such values to be internalized, there should be close affective ties between therapist and patient which provide the motive, like the affection between parent and child, for the acceptance and internalization of these values. Verbal discussion in a group may decrease resistance to new values, and increase the probability that they will be incorporated into the functioning of the group.

A form of verbal therapy may aim at decreasing aggressive fantasy. Fantasy aggression may increase the likelihood of aggressive behavior. Megargee (1966) writes, for example, that case reports indicate that in a number of instances violent fantasy behavior may have been used to predict a violent act. Holmes (1966) found that the elimination of aggressive cues from the environment resulted in a decrease of physiological arousal of insulted subjects to the level of non-insulted ones, even though the former had no opportunity to express hostility. Reduction of aggressive fantasy may have a similar effect. Patients may describe their fantasies or they may be asked to make up stories in response to TAT and other stimulus materials with content relevant to the patient's life. Then specific images and behavioral sequences that are neutral or incompatible with aggression may be introduced into the flow of images, or patients may be asked to develop themes incompatible with aggression and be rewarded for doing so. Procedures used in the development of achievement imagery may be employed (McClelland, 1965).

OVERLY STRONG INHIBITION OF AGGRESSION

Reactions to instigation vary widely. Some individuals may react with anger. Others, fearing harm to themselves, may react with anxiety (Funkenstein, 1955), particularly in the case of threat or attack. Still others may either escape or attack with seemingly little intervening emotional reactions.

Even when people react to instigating stimuli with anger, resentment, or hostility, strong internalized norms may prohibit any form of expression of anger or resentment, and result in a feeling of anxiety or guilt when aggressive acts are performed or even contemplated. In addition to these internal inhibitors, the fear of retaliation for aggression, fear of loss of love or of censure, may effectively inhibit aggressive, angry, or self-assertive behavior. While the source and nature of development of such inhibitions is viewed differently in different theoretical frameworks, there is agreement that in neurosis, problems with inhibited anger, aggression, and hostility are present. In the psychoanalytic view, for example, repressed hostility is a central element of the neurosis (White, 1964). Behavior therapists consider insufficient assertiveness, when strong anxiety prohibits even appropriate expression of self-assertion and justified resentment and anger, a frequent problem (Salter, 1965; Wolpe, 1958). Previous discussion of the antecedents of internalized morality suggests that overly strong inhibitions may result from child rearing techniques that lead to the development of internalized norms, but include generalized prohibition of angry, self-assertive behavior on the part of the child, or of expressions of independence. However, research is scant in this area.

Recent research findings suggest that overly strong inhibition or overcontrol may be associated with violent crime (Megargee, 1966; Megargee, Cook & Mendelsohn, 1967). Megargee suggested that many individuals who commit extremely aggressive crimes, violent or assaultive behavior with sometimes relatively little apparent justification, are characterized by overcontrol, or strong inhibition of impulses, particularly aggressive ones. The findings are suggestive of hostile tendencies on the part of these individuals, which are apparently kept in check until, for reasons that are not entirely clear because the immediate provocation is often minimal (Megargee, 1966), they result in a violent crime. This research has, so far, aimed primarily at showing that people who commit extremely aggressive acts are not necessarily undercontrolled individuals. In contrast to aggressive-antisocial individuals, overcontrolled violent adolescents seem to have been relatively well adjusted until they commit a violent act (Megargee, 1966). However, other characteristics of these individuals have not been thoroughly investigated yet and therefore it is not yet established whether they are like the overly inhibited neurotic individuals that were previously referred to, or not.

The goal of treatment in the case of overly strong inhibitions would be to decrease anxiety associated with aggression, to change values that prohibit any form of expression of anger or self-assertion, and to teach moderate, appropriate forms of assertive behavior.

Desensitization procedures may be employed to decrease anxiety about aggression (Wolpe, 1958; Wolpe & Lazarus, 1966). In this procedure, stimuli that evoke anxiety for the patient are determined and then arranged in a hierarchy from least to most anxiety provoking. Patients are trained in relaxation and, while relaxed, scenes or images representing the anxiety-producing stimuli are presented to them verbally by the therapist. Relaxation and anxiety are viewed as incompatible responses, and relaxation is thus expected to inhibit anxiety evoked by stimuli presented to the patient.

In addition to desensitization, assertive training would be used, as described above, but with the goal of teaching patients expressions of moderate forms of self-assertion. According to Wolpe (1958) assertive training is important because assertive responses reciprocally inhibit anxiety. However, the primary importance of assertive training probably lies in teaching people forms of behavior that express their anger and balance the injustice they may feel they have suffered, but in a manner that is socially acceptable and leads to reinforcement instead of punishment from the environment.

In assertive training it is important to encourage patients to apply their new skill in asserting themselves in graduated steps so that they will avoid strong negative reinforcement from the environment in the initial part of the training which would again enhance anxiety about self-assertion. The therapist may accompany the patient into real life settings to provide security, and if necessary to take over and protect the patient from negative consequences of self-assertive action (Wolpe & Lazarus, 1966; Wolpe, 1958; Salter, 1965).

Sometimes anxiety may be so strong that desensitization has to precede role playing, because the patient is inhibited by anxiety from even play-acting assertive responses. An adult male patient, for example, seemed incapable of attempting to rehearse a request to ask his sister, who used to type in a room beside his bedroom after he went to bed in the evening, to type in another room. This patient was afraid that if he started to assert himself he would lose control. There was justification for his fear; once he got furious and attacked and knocked down a fellow waiter in a restaurant, a form of behavior that one would expect from the over-controlled individuals Megargee (1966) investigated.

Cognitive clarification would also be used in treatment. By clarifying assumptions of patients about aggressive behavior, values may be influenced so that appropriately assertive responses will be viewed as justified and permissible. The use of desensitization, assertive training, and cognitive clarification together may lead to change that is consistent and accompanied by relatively little conflict.

Most of the discussion so far has dealt with adolescents and adults, and only some of it is applicable to children. In the case of very young children, no clear-cut pattern of behavior can be found such as the one described for aggressive-antisocial individuals; neither is their inhibition of aggression usually as strong as in the case of adults. A number of reports show that negative reinforcement for aggressive behavior and positive reinforcement for incompatible prosocial behavior results in decreased aggression (Brown & Elliott, 1965; O'Leary et al., 1967). With inhibited children, in traditional therapy, opportunities are provided for the expression of aggression in play, by observing aggressive puppets, or in other ways (White, 1964; Staub & Conn, 1970). The opportunity to express aggression without punishment is helpful, of course, because it decreases inhibition. In addition, through verbal therapy, children's values and feelings may be modified. However, a guiding principle of this form of therapy is that catharsis, the expression or observation of aggression, reduces subsequent aggression. Research findings suggest that aggression has cathartic effects only under specific conditions, when directed at certain types of targets. Moreover, the reduction in arousal associated with the expression of anger may be reinforcing, increasing future probability of aggression. Consequently, cathartic type treatment should be employed judiciously.

LIMITING INDIVIDUAL VIOLENCE

Much of the foregoing may be summarized in response to the question: How might individual violence be minimized? The acquisition of competence and a related sense of personal efficacy in achieving important occupational and interpersonal goals and in dealing with instigation in a nonaggressive or moderately aggressive manner may decrease felt or perceived instigation, and may enable people to respond to frustration in a constructive manner and to defend against or retailiate threat or attack with relatively little aggression. Childhood experience, including childrearing practices and moral education in schools, may contribute to these goals.

Learning strong internalized norms which prohibit aggression may also reduce aggression. However, good discrimination learning is necessary, so that appropriate self-assertion and expression of anger or resentment remains possible. In order to effectively inhibit aggression it is desirable, I think, that children be not only taught norms that prohibit aggression, but also prosocial values, norms and behavior. Learning to esteem others' well-being may be an extremely important principle in inhibiting aggression, because it leads to behavior antithetical to aggression – prosocial behavior. It is more likely that aggression will be minimal when not only prohibitions are learned but also values and behavior that are incompatible with inflicting suffering on others.

Unfortunately, I do not think that teaching children to esteem other people's well-being is widely practiced. Some of our research findings suggest this (Staub, 1970a; Staub, in press b). In investigating developmental changes in children helping another child in distress, we found that helping increases with age until second grade, but then it decreases from second to sixth grade (Staub, 1970a). On the basis of the responses of Ss to questions by the Experimenter we hypothesized that older children, who have learned to behave according to rules and regulations, were afraid of disapproval for possibly inappropriate behavior in a situation where norms of appropriate behavior were unknown.

To investigate this hypothesis, another study was conducted (Staub, in press b) in which a group of children received indirect permission to go into an adjoining room (permission to get drawing pencils from that room, if needed). Subsequently these children helped a child in distress who was in that room significantly more than children who did not receive such permission. This finding was replicated in a second study (Staub, in press b) with girls alone. A prohibition group was added to the permission and no information (i.e., no permission) groups; children in the prohibition group were prohibited for an irrelevant reason from going into the adjoining room. The findings of the first study were replicated; children in the permission group helped significantly more than children in either of the other two groups, while no information and prohibition did not have differential effects.

Those findings suggest to me that children – our subjects were 7th graders – learn to fear disapproval for possibly inappropriate behavior more than they learn responsibility for helping others in distress. It seems that the Subjects were more concerned about doing the wrong thing than they were about not helping someone, a child of their own age, who sounded as if she were in serious distress. Their moral education seems to have overemphasized prohibitions and underemphasized prosocial values.

Considering that difficulty with the management of hostility and anger are widespread, and that most children have probably very poor training in empathy or instruction in values that emphasize the importance of others' welfare and well being, a question that arises is whether our educational system should not include instruction that aims at accomplishing these goals? We may be too bashful about bringing moral education into a public sphere, leaving it to parents whether and how effectively they will teach their children that they should not hurt others.

A final but important point in considering how aggression may be limited is whether cultural and particularly subcultural conditions may be changed to decrease aggression. First, conditions need to be changed to enhance the stability of relationships and affectional ties within the family so that the family climate and child rearing practices will contribute to the internalization of socially desirable ways of managing aggression. Secondly, frustration may be reduced by providing opportunities and teaching skills to achieve socially acceptable goals in a socially acceptable manner, so that alternative, aggressive ways of seeking rewards and accomplishing goals will be minimized. Would decrease in poverty, better jobs, and general improvement in living conditions contribute to this? How this may be accomplished will be an important concern in our society probably for a long time.

REFERENCES

Aronfreed, J. *Conduct and conscience,* New York: Academic Press, 1968.

Aronson, E. and Cope, V. My enemy's enemy is my friend. *Journal of Personality and Social Psychology,* 1968, **8,** 13–19.

Bandura, A., Ross, D., & Ross, S. A. Imitation of film-mediated aggressive models. *Journal of Abnormal and Social Psychology,* 1963, **66,** 3–11.

Bandura, A. & Walters, R. H. *Adolescent aggression: A study of the influence of child training practices and family interrelationship.* New York: Ronald Press, 1959.

Bandura, A. & Walters, R. H. *Social learning and personality development.* New York: Holt, Rinehart, and Winston, 1963a.

Bandura, A. & Walters, R. H. Aggression. In H. W. Stevenson (Ed.), *Child psychology: The sixty-second yearbook of the National Society for the Study of Education,* Part I. Chicago: N.S.S.E., 1963b.

Berscheid, E., Boye, D., & Darley, J. M. Effects of forced association on voluntary choice to associate. *Journal of Personality and Social Psychology,* 1968, **7,** 13–19.

Berscheid, E., Boye, D., & Walster, E. Retaliation as a means of restoring equity. *Journal of Personality and Social Psychology,* 1968, **10,** 370–376.

Berkowitz, L. *Aggression: A social psychological analysis.* New York: McGraw-Hill, 1962.

Berkowitz, L. Aggressive cues in aggressive behavior and hostility catharsis. *Psychological Review,* 1964, **71,** 104–122.

Berkowitz, L. & LePage, A. Weapons as aggression-eliciting stimuli. *Journal of Personality and Social Psychology,* 1967, **7,** 202–207.

Berkowitz, L. & Rawlings, E. Effects of film violence on inhibitions against subsequent aggression. *Journal of Abnormal and Social Psychology*, 1963, **66**, 405–412.

Berkowitz, L., Green, J. A., & Macauley, J. F. Hostility catharsis as the reduction of emotional tension. *Psychiatry*, 1962, **25**, 23–31.

Berkowitz, L., Lipinski, J. P., & Angulo, E.·J. Awareness of own anger level and subsequent aggression. *Journal of Personality and Social Psychology*, 1969, **11**, 293–300.

Bossard, J. H. S. & Boll, Eleanor Stoker. Child behavior and the empathic complex. *Child Development*, 1957, **28**, 37–43.

Brown, P. & Elliott, R. Control of aggression in a nursery school class. *Journal of Experimental Child Psychology*, 1965, **2**, 103–107.

Buss, A. H. *The psychology of aggression*. New York: Wiley, 1961.

Buss, A. H. The effect of harm on subsequent aggression. *Journal of Experimental Research in Personality*, 1966, **1**, 249–255.

Cautela, J. R. Treatment of compulsive behavior by covert sensitization. *Psychological Record*, 1966, **16**, 33–42.

Cleckley, H. *The mask of sanity*. (2nd ed.) St. Louis: C. V. Mosby, 1950.

Cloward, R. A. & Ohlen, L. E. *Delinquency and opportunity*. Glencoe, Ill.: Free Press, 1960.

Darlington, R. B. & Macker, C. E. Displacement of guilt-produced altruistic behavior. *Journal of Personality and Social Psychology*, 1966, **4**, 442–443.

Davitz, J. R. The effects of previous training on post-frustration behavior. *Journal of Abnormal and Social Psychology*, 1952, **47**, 309–315.

Elder Jr., G. H. Adolescent Socialization and Development in Borgotta, E. R. and Lambert, W. W. *Handbook of personality theory and research*. Chicago: Rand McNally, 1968.

Ellis, A. *Reason and emotion in psychotherapy*. New York: Lyle Stuart, 1962.

Feshbach, S. The function of aggression and the regulation of aggressive drive. *Psychological Review*, 1964, **71**, 257–272.

Feshbach, N. D. & Feshbach, S. The relationship between empathy and aggression in two age groups. *Developmental Psychology*, 1969, **1**, 102–107.

Feshbach, S., Stiles, W. B., & Bitter, E. The reinforcing effect of witnessing aggression. *Journal of Experimental Research in Personality*, 1967, **2**, 133–139.

Fishman, C. Need for approval and the expression of aggression under varying conditions of frustration. *Journal of Personality and Social Psychology*, 1965, **2**, 809–815.

Freedman, J. L., Wallington, S. A., & Bless, E. Compliance and pressure: The effect of guilt. *Journal of Personality and Social Psychology*, 1967, **7**, 117–124.

Funkenstein, D. H. The physiology of fear and anger. *Scientific American*, 1955, **192**, 74–80.

Geen, R. G. Effects of frustration, attack, and prior training in aggressiveness upon aggressive behavior. *Journal of Personality and Social Psychology*, 1968, **9**, 316–321.

Geen, R. G. & Berkowitz, L. Some conditions facilitating the occurrence of aggression after the observance of violence. *Journal of Personality*, 1967, **35**, 666–676.

Green, R. G. & O'Neal, E. C. Activation of cue-elicited aggression by general arousal. *Journal of Personality and Social Psychology*, 1969, **11**, 289–292.

Glueck, G. Identification of potential delinquents at 2–3 years of age. *International Journal of Psychiatry*, **12**, 1966, 5–17.

Goldstein, A. P., Heller, K., & Sechrest, L. B. *Psychotherapy and the psychology of behavior change*. New York: Wiley, 1966.

Goranson, R. E. & Berkowitz, L. Reciprocity and responsibility reactions to prior help. *Journal of Personality and Social Psychology*, 1966, **3**, 227–232.

Gouldner, A. W. The norm of reciprocity. *American Sociological Review*, 1960, **25**, 161–178.

Hartman, D. Influence of symbolically modeled instrumental aggression and pain cues on aggressive behavior. *Journal of Personality and Social Psychology,* 1969, **11**, 280–288.

Hoffman, M. L. Moral development. In Mussen, P. H. (Ed.), *Carmichael's Manual of Child Psychology.* New York: John Wiley and Sons, 1970.

Hokanson, J. E., Burgess, M., & Cohen, M. F. Effect of displaced aggression on systolic blood pressure. *Journal of Abnormal and Social Psychology,* 1963, **67**, 214–218.

Holmes, D. C. Effects of overt aggression on level of physiological arousal. *Journal of Personality and Social Psychology,* 1966, **4**, 189–194.

Janis, I. L. & Mann, L. Effectiveness of emotional role playing in modifying smoking habits and attitudes. *Journal of Experiment Research in Personality,* 1965, **1**, 84–90.

Jones, M. *The therapeutic community: A new treatment method in psychiatry.* New York: Basic Books, 1953.

Kaufman, H. & Feshbach, S. Displaced aggression and its modification through exposure to antiaggressive communications. *Journal of Abnormal and Social Psychology,* 1963, **67**, 79–83.

Kelley, G. A. *The psychology of personal constructs.* New York: Norton, 1955.

Kinzel. Paper presented at the Americal Psychiatric Association Meetings, Miami, Florida, May 1969.

Kohlberg, L. Development of moral character and ideology. In M. L. Hoffman (Ed.). *Review of child development research.* Vol. I, New York: Russel Sage Foundation, 1964.

Kolvin, I. "Aversive imagery" treatment in adolescents. *Behavior Therapy and Research,* 1967, **5**, 245, 249.

Loew, C. A. Acquisition of a hostile attitude and its relationship to aggressive behavior. *Journal of Personality and Social Psychology,* 1967, **5**, 335–341.

Lovaas, O. I. Effect of exposure to symbolic aggression on aggressive behavior. *Child Development,* 1961, **32**, 37–44.

Lykken, D. T. A study of anxiety in the sociopathic personality. *Journal of Abnormal and Social Psychology,* 1957, **55**, 6–10.

Maccoby, E. E. The development of moral values and behavior in childhood. In J. A. Clausen (Ed.), *Socialization and society.* Boston: Little, Brown and Co., 1968.

Mallick, S. & McCandless, B. A study of catharsis of aggression. *Journal of Personality and Social Psychology,* 1966, **4**, 591–596.

Maslow, A. H. Deprivation, threat, and frustration. *Psychological Review,* 1941, **48**, 364–366.

McClelland, D. C. Towards a theory of motive acquisition. *American Psychologist,* 1965, **20**, 321–333.

McCord, W. & McCord, J. *Psychotherapy and delinquency.* New York: Grune & Stratton, 1956.

McCord, W. & McCord, J. *The psychopath: An essay on the criminal mind.* Princeton: Van Nostrand, 1964.

McCord, W., McCord, J., & Zola, I. *Origins of crime.* New York: Columbia Univer. Press, 1959.

Megargee, E. I. Undercontrolled and overcontrolled personality types in extreme antisocial aggression. *Psychological Monographs,* 1966, **80** (3, Whole No. 611).

Megargee, E. I., Cook, P. E., & Mendelsohn, G. A. Development and validation of an MMPI scale of assaultiveness in overcontrolled individuals. *Journal of Abnormal Psychology,* 1967, **72**, 519–528.

Miller, W. B., Geretz, H., & Culter, H. S. Aggression in a boys' street corner group. *Psychiatry,* 1961, **24**, 283–298.

Murphy, Lois B. *Social behavior and child personality: An exploratory study of some roots of sympathy.* New York: Columbia Univer. Press, 1937.

Murstein, B. I. The effect of amount of possessions of the trait of hostility on accuracy of perception of hostility in others. *Journal of Abnormal and Social Psychology,* 1961, **62,** 216–220.

Murstein, B. I. Possession of hostility and accuracy of perception of it in others; A cross-sex replication. *Journal of Projective Techniques,* 1966, **30,** 46–50.

O'Leary, D. K., O'Leary, S., & Becker, W. L. Modification of deviant sibling interactions patterns in the home. *Behavior Research and Therapy,* 1967, **5,** 113–121.

Pastore, N. The role of arbitrariness in the frustration-aggression hypothesis. *Journal of Abnormal and Social Psychology,* 1952, **47,** 728–731.

Patterson, G. R., Littman, R. A., and Bricker, W. Assertive behavior in children. *Monographs of the Society for Research in Child Development,* 1967, **32,** (4, Whole No. 113).

Pettigrew, Th. F. *Social Evaluation Theory: Convergences and Applications.* In Levine, D. (Ed.) Nebraska Symposium on Motivation, Univer. of Nebraska Press, 1967.

Piaget, J. *The moral judgment of the child.* London: Hegan, Paul, Trench, Trubner, 1932.

Piliavin, I. M., Hardyck, J. A., & Vadum, A. C. Constraining effects of personal costs on the transgressions of juveniles. *Journal of Personality and Social Psychology,* 1968, **10,** 227–231.

Rawlings, Edna I. Witnessing harm to others: A reassessment of the role of guilt in altruistic behavior. *Journal of Personality and Social Psychology,* 1968, **10,** 337–380.

Redl, F. & Wineman, D. *Children who hate.* Glencoe, Ill.: Free Press, 1951.

Redl, F. & Wineman, D. *Controls from within: Techniques for the treatment of the aggressive child.* Glencoe, Ill.: Free Press, 1952.

Rosenhan, D. The natural socialization of altruistic autonomy. In J. Macauley and L. Berkowitz (Eds.). *Altruism and Helping.* New York: Academic Press, 1970.

Rosenzweig, S. An outline of frustration theory. In J. McV. Hunt (Ed.), *Personality and the behavior disorders.* New York: Ronald, 1944.

Rothaus, P. & Worchel, P. Ego-support, communication, catharsis, and hostility. *Journal of Personality,* 1964, **32,** 296–312.

Rutherford, E. & Mussen, P. Generosity in nursery school boys. *Child Development,* 1968, **39,** 755–765.

Salter, A. The theory and practice of conditioned reflex therapy. In J. Wolpe, A. Salter, and L. J. Reyna (Eds.). *The conditioning therapies: The challenge in psychotherapies.* New York: Holt, Rinehart, and Winston, 1965.

Schachter, S. & Latane, B. Crime, cognition, and the nervous system. In D. Levine (Ed.), *Nebraska symposium on motivation.* Lincoln, Nebraska: Univer. of Nebraska Press, 1964.

Schachter, S. & Singer, J. E. Cognitive, social and physiological determinants of emotional state. *Psychological Review,* 1962, **69,** 379–399.

Schwitzgebel, R. *Streetcorner research: An experimental approach to the juvenile delinquent.* Cambridge, Mass.: Harvard Univer. Press, 1965.

Schwitzgebel, R. & Kolb, D. Inducing behavior change in adolescent delinquents. *Behavior Research and Therapy,* 1964, **1,** 297–304.

Sears, R. R., Maccoby, B., & Levin, N. *Patterns of child rearing.* New York: Harper, 1957.

Shopler, J. & Thompson, V. The role of attribution process in mediating amount of reciprocity for a favor. *Journal of Personality and Social Psychology,* 1968, **10,** 243–250.

Slack, C. W. Experimenter-subject psychotherapy: A new method of introducing intensive office treatment in unreachable cases. *Mental Hygiene,* 1960, **44,** 238–256.

Slavson, R. R. *An introduction to group therapy.* New York: Commonwealth Fund, 1943.

Slavson, S. R. *Reclaiming the delinquent.* New York: The Free Press, 1965.

Staub, E. The reduction of a specific fear by information combined with exposure to the feared stimulus. *Proceedings, 76th Annual Convention, American Psychological Association,* 1968.

Staub, E. A child in distress: The influence of age and number of witnesses on children's attempts to help. *Journal of Personality and Social Psychology,* 1970a, **14,** 130–140.

Staub, E. Assertive training, role playing and self control. In D. Upper and D. Goodenough (Eds.), *Behavior therapy in the institutional setting. Proceedings of the First Annual Brockton Symposium on Behavior Therapy.* Roche Laboratories, Nutley, New Jersey, 1970b.

Staub, E. The use of role playing and induction in children's learning of helping and sharing behavior. *Child Development,* in press a.

Staub, E. Helping a person in distress: The influence of implicit and explicit "rules" of conduct on children and adults. *Journal of Personality and Social Psychology,* in press b.

Staub, E. & Conn, L. K. Aggression. In C. G. Costello (Ed.) *Symptoms of Psychopathology.* New York: Wiley, 1970.

Staub, E. & Sherk, L. The relationship between need approval and children's sharing behavior. *Child Development,* 1970, **41,** 243–253.

Staub, E., Tursky, B., & Schwartz, G. Self control and predictibility: Their effect on reactions to aversive stimulation. *Journal of Personality and Social Psychology,* in press.

Stone, L. J. & Hokanson, J. E. Arousal reduction via self-punitive behavior. *Journal of Personality and Social Psychology,* 1969, **12,** 72–79.

Stotland, E. & Blumenthal, A. The reduction of anxiety as a result of the expectation of making a choice. *Canadian Journal of Psychology,* 1964, **18,** 139–145.

Taylor, S. P. Aggressive behavior and physiological arousal as a function of provocation and the tendency to inhibit aggression. *Journal of Personality,* 1967, **35,** 297–311.

Thibault, J. W. & Coules, J. The role of communication in the reduction of interpersonal hostility. *Journal of Abnormal and Social Psychology,* 1952, **47,** 770–777.

Valins, S. Emotionality and information concerning internal reactions. *Journal of Personality and Social Psychology,* 1967, **6,** 458–464.

White, R. W. *The abnormal personality: A textbook.* New York: Ronald Press, 1964.

Wolpe, J. *Psychotherapy by reciprocal inhibition.* Stanford, Calif.: Stanford Univer. Press, 1958.

Wolpe, J. & Lazarus, A. A. *Behavior therapy techniques: A guide to the treatment of neuroses.* New York: Pergamon Press, 1966.

CHAPTER V

THE ROLE OF INHIBITION IN THE ASSESSMENT AND UNDERSTANDING OF VIOLENCE[1]

EDWIN I. MEGARGEE

FLORIDA STATE UNIVERSITY

Dr. Singer's invitation to come here and talk with you about our research on the assessment and dynamics of violence comes at a particularly appropriate time. Because our ancient forebearers happened to have five claws on each foot, we have been conditioned to think in terms of units of ten, and 1969 marks the tenth year in our program of research. Therefore it is a good time to look back over what we have done, and, more important, what we have not done, to add up the books and see what sort of balance, if any, we can carry forward into the next decade.

I must confess, however, that it is rather pretentious to call this work a "program of research." The word "program" implies a planned, systematic process, with studies following one another in a well-organized, orderly development. It wasn't like that at all. At the beginning I had no idea where this research was going to lead us, and along the way studies were performed because they appeared to be interesting at the time or because an opportunity was available to be exploited. After the fact, it is always possible to look back and perceive a pattern in the work, so I like to pretend to people that this all represented the gradual unfolding of some grand design. However, while this is the public image that I try

[1]The preparation of this paper and some of the research reported therein was supported in part by Grant MH15623-01 of the National Institute of Mental Health. Other phases of the reported research were supported by grants from the Hogg Foundation for Mental Health and the University of Texas Research Institute.

to foster, my private impression is much different. They say that an air-line pilot's job consists of long periods of tedium punctuated by moments of stark terror. The impression I get looking back over these ten years is of long periods of stupidity punctuated by one or two brief moments of insight. It seems remarkable now how blind I could have been then, and it is little comfort to reflect on the fact that ten years from now I will probably say the same thing about what we are doing at present.

My interest in aggression and violence began in 1959 when I was at the University of California at Berkeley. I was a bit ahead of my time in this regard, because this was before California pioneered the develop-ment of superior on-campus facilities for the study of violence. At that time it was necessary to go off campus and work with the convicted crim-inal instead of the ubiquitous college sophomore if one wanted to study violent behavior. In any case I worked part time at the Alameda County Probation Department. My primary research interest was in assessment using psychological tests, and in this clinical setting a major referral problem was the prediction of assaultive behavior in applicants for pro-bation. While the public has always been unhappy about being assaulted, they take a particularly dim view of being assaulted by the probationer who has been convicted of a crime but sent back to the streets because some "bleeding heart" psychologist told the judge that he was harmless.

In November of 1959 a case was referred to me that illustrated per-fectly the difficulties involved in making such predictions. The man in question, "Billy Jones," was a meek, mild-mannered, deferential person who had been convicted of assault with a deadly weapon. For several years he had been humiliated by another individual, "Sam Williams," who frequented the tavern where Billy did most of his drinking. Despite numerous goads and humiliations, Billy had maintained his equanimity and tried to be friends. However on the night of November 3rd he had apparently had enough. After being insulted by Sam for 45 minutes, Billy finally pulled a gun and shot him twice in the abdomen. When Sam ran, Billy followed him, cornered him on a porch, and shot him again. When Sam got up off the porch, staggered into the street, and collapsed, my persistent client walked over, put the muzzle of his gun against Sam's neck and shot him once more.

After considerable reflection it seemed clear to me that we were dealing with a case of overt aggressive behavior. An interesting thing was that the victim in this situation was a bully who some years before had also been convicted of assault with a deadly weapon as the result of an inci-dent in which he had, without provocation, attacked someone so enthusi-astically that he left him blind in one eye. On a subsequent occasion Sam had driven his automobile down a sidewalk in an effort to run down some people with whom he was having a difference of opinion. Here then were two individuals, both convicted of the same offense, but with quite different psychodynamics. Sam was an uninhibited sociopath and Billy an overcontrolled and excessively inhibited neurotic.

I would like to be able to report to you that upon examining this case I said "Aha!" and conceived the "program" of research that has lead me to this podium. Unfortunately this seed fell on fairly barren ground so at the time I simply scratched my head and went on about my business.

My business at that time was doing research on the validity of different psychological tests for the prediction (or rather the postdiction) of assaultive behavior. I was engaged in a sort of comparative shopping expedition in which I compared the discriminating ability of various tests so that I could select the best ones. Several such studies were performed, each focusing on a different test. The basic design was to select four groups of men and compare their scores on the instrument in question. Three of these groups would consist of juvenile or adult criminals. One criminal group would have been convicted of "extremely assaultive" offenses such as assault with a deadly weapon, mayhem, or murder. A second group would have been convicted of "moderately assaultive" offenses such as battery. While still violent, "moderately assaultive" behavior was less likely to kill or maim the victim. The third group would have been convicted of nonviolent offenses such as auto theft. The fourth would consist of a noncriminal sample of comparable age and socioeconomic status.

In the course of this research, which was carried out over a period of several years, a number of different psychometric instruments were evaluated. The first study, done in collaboration with Gerald Mendelsohn, examined the regular MMPI clinical scales as well as 12 new scales and indices that purported to assess hostility or control (Megargee & Mendelsohn, 1962). They included Panton's Adjustment to Prison scale, Shultz's Hostility Control and Overt Hostility scales, Cook and Medley's Hostility scale, Harris and Lingoes' Inhibition of Aggression scale, Gough's Impulsivity scale, Siegel's Manifest Hostility scale, Block's Ego Overcontrol, Neurotic Undercontrol and Bimodal Control scales, as well as Welsh and Sullivan's Active Hostility Index and Beall and Panton's Frustration Tolerance Index.

Although a number of these scales were able to discriminate the three criminal groups from the noncriminal group, none of the old or new scales could differentiate the assaultive from the nonassaultive criminals. Since this was the very discrimination that we were required to make in a probation setting, the results were quite discouraging. We were particularly discouraged to note that some scales apparently worked backwards, with the violent criminals being assessed as *less* hostile and *more* controlled than the nonviolent criminals and normals.

In an effort to explain this reversal, we hypothesized:

. . . that the extremely assaultive person is often a fairly mild-mannered, long suffering individual who buries his resentment under rigid but brittle controls. Under certain circumstances he may lash out and release all his aggression in one, often disastrous, act. Afterwards he reverts to his usual overcontrolled defenses. Thus he may be more of a menace than the verbally aggressive, "chip-on-the-shoulder" type who releases his aggression in small doses (Megargee & Mendelsohn, 1962, p. 437).

In retrospect this proved to be one of those brief flashes of insight; however, not being bright enough to realize this, I just continued with the assessment research.

The next step in this research was an attempt to construct our own MMPI assaultiveness scale. Using the MMPI protocols of the same subjects that had been tested in the cross-validation study, we manufactured half a dozen experimental scales, one of which was very promising when applied back to the original derivation data. When used with the optimal cutting score, it detected all the extremely assaultive and moderately assaultive subjects while misclassifying only 4 of the 25 nonviolent criminals. This yielded a validity coefficient of .86. The item content was strangely passive for an assaultiveness scale ("I like poetry," True; "When I get bored I like to stir up some excitement," False).[2] Nevertheless we selected this scale for cross-validation on a new sample. We suffered from a shortage of violent subjects at this point (remember this was back in 1961) so for the first and only time we abandoned our usual procedure of having separate groups of extremely assaultive and moderately assaultive criminals and simply compared a new sample of nonviolent criminals with a mixed bag of violent criminals. The promising scale washed out completely. The means, medians, modes, and ranges of the two samples were identical. I chucked the data in the bottom drawer of my desk and went back to searching for a good test of violent tendencies.

Next we tried the Rorschach test scored according to Murstein's Rorschach Hostility Index. No significant differences were obtained (Megargee & Mendelsohn, 1963). Studies of the Rosenzwig Picture-Frustration Study (Megargee, 1964b) and the California Psychological Inventory (Megargee, 1966b) showed no differences on the Extrapunitiveness or the Socialization scales respectively. A study of Fisher and

Cleveland's Barrier Score on the Holtzman Inkblot technique was some-what more encouraging since a significant positive correlation was ob-tained between Barrier scores on the HIT and ratings of aggressiveness made on a sample of 74 juvenile delinquents by their dormitory counci-lors. However the magnitude of the correlation was only +.23 which hardly indicated that it would be of much use in individual prediction (Megargee, 1965b).

The most interesting of the studies in this series was the last (Megargee & Cook, 1967). By this time, after six or seven years of knocking my head against the validational wall, it had begun to dawn on me that the problem was not that of selecting which of the many good scales available was best for my purpose, but instead that of determining if *any* scales dis-criminated differences in violence within criminal populations — or (on really bad days) whether *any* scale related to *any* behavioral criterion of aggression.

The literature was not encouraging. I had recently reviewed the assess-ment literature rather extensively in connection with editing a book (Me-gargee, 1966a) and it had become depressingly obvious that although some investigators obtained significant *positive* correlations between tests of hostility and behavioral measures of aggression, other investi-gators obtained significant *negative* correlations. Studies reporting sig-nificant findings were in the minority however, since most investigations reported zero-order relationships. It seemed likely that some of these inconsistencies in the literature stemmed from the fact that so many different test measures of aggression had been proposed and such a vari-ety of criteria had been used. With so many different operational defini-tions floating around, naturally the findings would differ.

Therefore in one last orgiastic validational study we took the TAT and Holtzman Inkblot Technique protocols of extremely assaultive, moderately assaultive, verbally aggressive, and nonaggressive delin-quents and scored them on *five* TAT aggression scales and *five* inkblot hostility scales that had been proposed by various authors. These scores were then related to *eleven* different behavioral criteria of aggression, including the nature of the offense, school conduct and attendance rec-ords, observations by custodial personnel of verbal and physical aggres-sion while in detention, and ratings of the amount of physical and verbal aggressiveness against peers and authorities reported by the delinquents in structured interviews.

The results were most interesting. The data showed quite different patterns of relationships depending on the particular scales and criteria used. Several of the TAT scales, for example, showed significant direct relationships with school conduct ratings. The more "need aggression" in the TAT scores, the worse the school conduct rating. However the TAT did not relate significantly to any of the other behavioral criteria.

The inkblot data were even more puzzling. Several of the inkblot hostility scales had significant *direct* relationships with the amount of physical aggression against peers and adults reported in interviews. One also had a *direct* relationship with school conduct. However the same scales had significant *inverse* relationships with the amount of physical aggression actually observed in detention. Apparently, then, the higher the inkblot hostility score, the more likely a chap was to get in trouble at school and to report a lot of aggression in an interview with a Probation Department psychologist, but the less likely he was to engage in overt aggression while in detention. While it was possible to construct *ex post facto* explanations of this pattern, none were very convincing.

Our masochism even extended to the point of doing a factor analysis. As you might expect, four neat orthogonal factors emerged – one for the inkblot hostility scales, one for the TAT aggression scales, one for the measures of observed aggression, and one for the ratings of self-reported aggression. As I noted earlier this was the last of our validational studies. I doubt if I need to explain why it was the last.

During the course of these investigations it had begun to occur to me that there was probably something wrong with the way we were going about assessing an individual's potential for violent behavior. There are four basic factors that must be considered in determining the likelihood for an act of violence (Megargee, 1969a, 1969c, 1970, pp. 97–153):

1. The first is the motivation to engage in aggressive behavior labeled variously as "hostility," "anger," "instigation to aggression," "need aggression," and so forth. Professor Buss in his presentation posed a most valuable distinction between "angry aggression" and "instrumental aggression." Both sources of motivation must be considered. Studies of homicides show that a large proportion occur within families and probably stem from anger. However the instrumental aggression of the Mafia "soldier" who makes a "hit" to fulfill a "contract" should not be overlooked.

2. The second basic factor is inhibitory mechanisms within the personality that are opposed to overt aggressive behavior. These go by different labels such as "super ego," "conscience," and the like depending on one's frame of reference.

3. The third factor is stimulus or situational variables in the external environment that may either facilitate or impede aggressive behavior. A lynch mob is an example of situational facilitation while a teacher

entering a classroom in which a raucous eraser fight is taking place is a good illustration of an inhibitory stimulus.

4. The fourth factor is the strength of competing responses that are incompatible with aggressive behavior. Even if all the conditions for an aggressive act are present — that is the combined strength of instigation to aggression and any facilitating stimuli outweigh the internal inhibitions and inhibitory stimuli — even in this situation it only means that an overt aggressive response is *possible*. Before it actually takes place this response must compete with other possible responses that may satisfy other needs. If the habit strength or drive strength of these alternative responses are stronger than that of the aggressive response, then they still may be selected instead.

Different researchers have focused on different components of the aggressive response. Some such as Brown and Elliott (1965) have focused on the competing responses, demonstrating how rewarding nonaggressive behavior decreases aggression. Psychologists such as Berkowitz and Le Page (1967) and Wheeler and Caggiula (1966) have studied stimulus factors in the laboratory while workers from a variety of disciplines have investigated stimulus factors, such as the behavior of the victim, in the field (MacDonald, 1967; Toch, 1966, 1969; Wolfgang, 1957). The most extensive research, inspired in large measure by the contributions of the frustration-aggression theorists (Dollard, Doob, Miller, Mowrer, & Sears, 1939), has been concerned with the factors influencing instigation to aggression. There has been somewhat less empirical attention paid to inhibitions against aggression, particularly extreme aggression, although correctional authorities, who are intimately involved with preventing violence, have by and large relied on programs designed to foster inhibitions, usually through the administration of punishment.

Of these four factors, the clinical psychologist who would try to predict aggressive behavior was usually limited to the assessment of instigation and inhibition in his client. This is his first major handicap. Most psychological tests focused on the first of these two factors, instigation, and neglected the second. Thus we had many scales of aggression and hostility, but few of inhibitions against aggression. These limitations helped make the prediction of violence and aggression difficult.

The most serious handicap, however, was an oversimplified picture of the violent man. The prevailing stereotype was that the assaultive person is characterized by such inadequate inhibitions or controls against aggressive behavior that almost any instigation to aggression would lead to acting out. For example, Berkowitz (1962, pp. 317–318) in his chapter on "Aggression in Crime, Homicides and Suicides" wrote:

Nevertheless, people who kill can be described with a relatively small number of concepts. They have not been exposed to exactly the same conditions but *all have suffered extreme (for them) frustrations.* Further, although their personalities vary in important respects, *their reactions to the intense thwartings can be understood in terms of* (1) *the perceived source of the frustration* and (2) *the strength of their inhibitions against overt hostility.* The formula discussed here is essentially a simple one. The person who kills generally does so because he has been frustrated.

Therefore according to Berkowitz the primary determinant of violence is frustration which has the effect of increasing instigation.

However, upon reflection, there would appear to be some drawbacks to the notion that the violent person is invariably someone with "all id and no lid." While this description certainly fit Sam Williams, it hardly applied to Billy Jones. If anything, Billy suffered from *excessive* inhibitions. If he had been less inhibited, perhaps he would have punched Sam in the nose long before so the situation might not have escalated to the point where shooting seemed his only solution. Perhaps in some people violence stems from *excessive* inhibitions. Perhaps in addition to the typical *under*controlled violent person there is also an *over*controlled type.

Given this brief and uncharacteristic lapse from stupidity, I set about to determine what evidence there might be to support this dichotomy. In addition to case studies of individuals like Billy Jones, there was the curious pattern of reversals we had noted in our first MMPI studies that had prompted similar speculations. Others had also commented on this possibility. Buss (1961, p. 203) had noted: "The individual (almost exclusively male) who is quiet and verbally unaggressive, but assaultive and perhaps murderous, is a rare type, but he exists." Thus informal observations from several sources suggested that the typology might be valid, but no reliable or reasonably rigorous quantitative data existed. Therefore a study to test the existence of the hypothesized typology was undertaken.

The major problem was to design the study in such a way that it would not be circular. Since it was obvious that our dependent variable would consist of various measures of aggressiveness and control, we needed some external, unrelated independent variable. If we surveyed the case records of violent individuals and selected those who seemed to be of the Overcontrolled type and compared them on various measures of aggressiveness or control with violent individuals who appeared to be of the Undercontrolled type, any positive results would be trivial. They would simply mean that the subjects we said were more controlled were in fact more controlled. Somehow we had to obtain an independent variable that was truly independent and not simply a parallel form of our dependent variable. We arrived at this independent variable by a rather circuitous route that some people have subsequently misinterpreted.

The typology indicates that the differences between the Overcontrolled and the Undercontrolled types is in the amount of inhibition against aggressive behavior. As the terms imply, the Overcontrolled violent person, if he exists, has considerably more inhibitions against aggression than the Undercontrolled person. If this is the case, then for the Overcontrolled person to commit an act of aggression it would be necessary for his level of instigation to aggression to be extraordinarily high, because instigation must exceed inhibition if an aggressive act takes place. On the other hand, individuals of the Undercontrolled type need not have much instigation to aggression before acting out in an aggressive fashion because little instigation is required to exceed their minimal aggressive inhibitions.

It was next necessary to make an assumption for which there was little, if any, evidence and which was somewhat at variance with prevailing conceptions of the dynamics of aggression. This assumption was that the degree of violence of the aggressive act is proportional to the degree of instigation to aggression. This appears straightforward enough, but it conflicted somewhat with many authorities such as Bandura and Walters (1959) who maintained that the degree of violence of the aggressive act was proportional to the net strength of instigation minus inhibition.

If our assumption that the degree of violence is proportional to the degree of instigation was correct, then it would follow that a group of people who had committed extremely assaultive acts such as homicide or assault with a deadly weapon would be likely to include some people of the Overcontrolled type and some of the Undercontrolled type. However, and here is the crucial difference, a group of people who had engaged in moderately aggressive behavior, such as fist fights, should consist almost exclusively of the Undercontrolled type. In other words, the Chronically Overcontrolled person, because of the extreme amount of instigation to aggression required to overcome his high inhibitions, would be likely to engage almost exclusively in extreme acts of violence if, indeed, he should ever aggress at all. The Undercontrolled type on the other hand would be capable of a full range of aggressive responses ranging from verbal rebukes and mild physical aggression up through and including extreme acts of violence such as homicide.

If this typology and the subsequent chain of logic is correct, this leads to a rather paradoxical prediction: an extremely violent group should be measured as being *more* controlled and *less* violent, *as a group,* than would groups of moderately aggressive or nonviolent criminals. Why? Because if we are correct the extremely violent group should be composed of *both* types of individuals, while the less aggressive samples would be composed *only* of the Undercontrolled type. The presence of the Overcontrolled subjects in an extremely violent group should alter the mean of that group relative to the others. On the other hand, if there was no Chronically Overcontrolled type, then an extremely assaultive group should be measured as *most* aggressive and *least* controlled.

I have explained the rationale leading up to this prediction in some detail because it has frequently been misinterpreted. Because we tested the typology by comparing extremely assaultive and moderately assaultive groups, it is easy to infer erroneously that I am proposing that *all* or even *most* murderers are overcontrolled. For example, in a critique of an early account of this work (Megargee, 1965a), Dr. Lee Robins of Washington University wrote that I was not ". . . simply trying to show that meek people sometimes commit murder, but rather that murderers are *by and large* meeker than those who commit less serious assaultive offenses (Robins, 1965)." In my reply I attempted to correct this impression as follows:

Dr. Robins states that in my article I was "not simply attempting to show that meek people sometimes commit murder" but in fact that is precisely what I was trying to do. No one with any experience in criminal psychology would deny that many, if not most, extremely assaultive crimes are committed by undercontrolled people. In the article I was not saying that John Dillinger is incapable of homicide; I was instead pointing out that Casper Milquetoast is also capable of murder. However, while Dillinger might also commit other lesser offenses such as strongarm robbery or assault, aggressiveness with Casper seems to be an all-or-none phenomenon so that while he might commit a murder or assault with a deadly weapon he is not likely to be found participating in a rumble with his local gang (Megargee, 1965c, p. 45).

In order to evaluate the hypothesis that an extremely assaultive group would be more controlled and less aggressive as a group, four groups of male juvenile delinquents were selected for study. In the first two groups were all the boys who had been detained for serious assaultive crimes in the Alameda County, California, Juvenile Hall during the ten-month period from July 1, 1962 to May 1, 1963. These crimes were rated for amount of aggressiveness on a ten-point Aggression Scale. This scale was then dichotomized and the nine Ss who had scored in the upper range from six to ten were defined as the "Extremely Assaultive" Group. This group included two cases of homicide, an attempted murder, five assaults with deadly weapon, and one particularly brutal beating. The remaining 21 subjects who had scored below six were defined as being "Moderately Assaultive." This group consisted primarily of cases of battery and gang fights.

Two contrast groups were also selected for study. The first consisted of boys detained because of defiance, unmanageability, and unruliness at home. This "Incorrigible" Group, consisted of 20 boys and was included since it was felt that they were likely to be high on verbal aggressiveness. The second contrast group consisted of 26 Property Offenders detained after thefts or burglaries. Neither of the two contrast groups included any boys who had known records for assaultive crimes.

During the first ten days of detention, the boys were observed by their unit counselors who filled out behavior check lists, rating scales and adjective check lists describing each boy. They were also examined by Probation Department psychologists who administered structured interviews based on those devised by Bandura and Walters (1959) and a standard battery of tests including an abbreviated WAIS, the California Psychological Inventory, the Rosenzweig Picture-Frustration Study, the TAT, and the Holtzman Inkblot Technique.

A total of 28 specific predictions were made concerning the various dependent variables. All tested aspects of the general hypothesis that the Extremely Assaultive (EA) group would be lower on measures of aggressiveness and higher on measures of control than the other groups in general and the Moderately Assaultive group in particular. (In the case of measures of verbal aggressiveness it was hypothesized that the Extremely Violent Group would be lower than the Incorrigible Group in particular.)

Of the 28 hypotheses tested, 22 were in the predicted direction, with EA least aggressive and most controlled. Fourteen received some measure of statistical support with p values ranging from .003 to .08.

To survey briefly some of the findings, it was found that the Extremely Assaultive Group had the highest percentage of first offenders. They also had the best school conduct and school attendance records. (It is noteworthy that the only two boys in the entire sample who had "outstanding" attendance records were the two boys who committed homicide.) In terms of the behavior observed in the unit, on every one of the measures used the Extremely Assaultive sample was least aggressive and most cooperative and controlled. The p values were generally lowest on these direct observations of behavior.

The psychological tests and structured interview yielded poorer results. On the structured interview, the EA boys reported the least physical aggression against authorities but not against peers. The more obvious psychological tests such as the TAT and Rosenzweig P-F Study showed no appreciable differences. The subtler tests such as the largely empirical California Psychological Inventory (CPI) and the Holtzman Inkblot Technique (HIT) proved to be better measures. On the CPI, the Extremely Assaultive group was highest on 13 of the 18 scales including those scales reflecting responsibility, self control, and academic achievement. On the HIT, the Extremely Assaultive group had, as had been predicted, the lowest color score, the lowest number of uncontrolled color responses, the highest movement score, and the highest movement-color balance.

Given the rather gross nature of both the independent and dependent variables, it was encouraging that the total pattern of the data was in the predicted direction. The results could in no way be regarded as definitive proof of the typology, but they certainly supported it while giving no support to the contrary notion that *all* violent individuals are of the Uncontrolled type.

Since this study was published (Megargee, 1966b) additional data that support the typology have been gathered by investigators in other laboratories. The first such study is a report on "The Differences Between Assaultive and Non-assaultive Juvenile Offenders in the California Youth Authority" by Martin Molof (Molof, 1967). Molof obtained extensive case history and behavioral data on 4,344 boys committed to the California Youth Authority in 1963. He divided his sample into three groups: (1) AHR: those convicted of assault, homicide or forcible rape; (2) B: those convicted of battery or simple assault; (3) NA: those convicted of nonviolent crimes. He then compared the groups on 55 dependent variables. Next he cross-validated his findings by performing the same operations on 2,000 boys referred in 1964.

Molof's AHR, B, and NA samples are roughly analogous to our extremely assaultive, moderately assaultive and nonviolent samples respectively. The comparisons most relevant to the typology are AHR versus B and AHR versus NA. In each case we would expect the AHR group to be better socialized.

This proved to be the case. Molof found a number of significant differences between these groups that proved to be reliable on cross-validation. In almost every comparison the direction of the differences showed the AHR group to have a more favorable family background and a history suggesting better socialization. In his discussion, Molof noted the similarities between the two studies and used the Overcontrolled-Undercontrolled typology to help explain his results.

Molof's population of delinquents committed to the California Youth Authority was fairly similar to the samples of juvenile delinquents that we had studied. Greater generality has been provided by a series of three studies performed by R. Blackburn, Senior Clinical Psychologist at Broadmoore Hospital, Crowthorne, Berkshire, England. While Molof's study referred to our findings in an effort to explain patterns that he had noted in his data, Blackburn's studies have all been specifically designed to test the typology using samples of violent offenders committed to a British psychiatric hospital.

In his first study, Blackburn (1968b) compared 38 extremely assaultive and 25 moderately assaultive psychiatric offenders on a number of MMPI scales and selected case history items. He reported:

> The Extremely Assaultive (patients) were significantly more overcontrolled, introverted and conforming and less hostile than the Moderately Assaultives. The Extremely Assaultive group contained significantly fewer with a criminal record or a diagnosis of psychopathic disorder than the Moderately assaultives, and in the majority of cases the offenses of the Extremely Assaultives involved individuals with whom they were acquainted in contrast to the Moderately Assaultives. The results support Megargee's hypothesis (Blackburn, 1968b, p. 827).

In his next study Blackburn compared the incidence of extreme or homicidal aggression in paranoid and non-paranoid schizophrenic offenders. On the basis of the typology he hypothesized, "Since extreme (i.e., homicidal) aggression appears to occur in individuals who are not characteristically aggressive (Megargee, 1966b), it was predicted that such offenses would be more frequent among the non-paranoid schizophrenics (Blackburn, 1968a, p. 1301)."

This study differed from those reviewed thus far in that the degree of violence was used as the dependent rather than the independent variable. The logic of the prediction rested on the assumption that paranoid schizophrenics are extroverted and thus relatively undercontrolled while non-paranoid schizophrenics are more introverted and hence relatively overcontrolled. If this is the case, then, given a sample of assaultive schizophrenic offenders, the (undercontrolled) paranoid schizophrenics might have committed a variety of assaultive offenses while the (overcontrolled) non-paranoid schizophrenics would for the most part be guilty of extremely assaultive offenses because of the high instigation needed to overcome their inhibitions.

I must confess to some skepticism regarding this hypothesis, for I have some misgivings about equating paranoid schizophrenia with undercontrol and non-paranoid schizophrenia with overcontrol. In terms of psychiatric nosology, I have been thinking primarily of the distinctions between violent people who would be classified as sociopathic and neurotic, and I have not yet confronted or thought through the application of this typology to violent psychotic patients.

In any case, Blackburn tested his hypothesis that non-paranoid schizophrenics would be more violent than paranoid schizophrenics by examining the relative incidence of murder and attempted murder in one group of 24 non-paranoid and another of 24 paranoid schizophrenic offenders. He also examined the history of persistent aggressiveness in each group.

Blackburn found that ten of the non-paranoid offenders and five of the paranoids had a history of homicidal assaults. This was in the direction he had predicted but the significance level was only marginal (.05 $<$ $p_{\text{one tail}} < .10$).

Another analysis that Blackburn reported was a more direct test of the typology. He found ". . . a significant inverse relationship between extreme assaultiveness and persistent aggression ($r_{\text{tetrachoric}} = -.56$; $p < .05$), indicating a tendency for those patients who have committed offenses of a homicidal nature to have no previous history of aggression (Blackburn, 1968a, p. 1302)." Thus extreme violence was often found in well-controlled individuals and, conversely, the habitually aggressive or undercontrolled individuals tended not to commit the more extreme acts of violence.

In his most recent investigation, Blackburn (1969) did a cluster analysis of the MMPI scores of all 56 male murderers admitted to Broadmoore Hospital over a period of 28 months.[3] On the basis of this analysis he was able to sort these patients into four clusters or types. Two types appeared to be overcontrolled and two undercontrolled.

Type 1, the largest type, included 30% of the total sample. On the basis of their score patterns, Blackburn described this type as follows:

In general, this group appears to be overly conforming, strongly controlled and unaggressive. The pattern of scores indicates that they tend to deal with strong emotional states of anger or anxiety with a use of avoidance mechanisms of denial and repression. This is the largest group which emerged from the analysis, and their personality characteristics are clearly those of the overcontrolled offender as described by Megargee. Here they will be referred to as an *overcontrolled-repressor type,* (Blackburn, 1969, p. 5).

The other type that appeared overcontrolled, but with different dynamics, was Type 3. This type constituted 14% of the sample. Blackburn stated:

. . . the members of this group exercised strong impulse control, and are socially introverted. Depression appears to be their main complaint, although there is also a degree of anxiety and predominantly intropunitive hostility. The pattern is typically that described by some clinicians as dysthymic, and the group is accordingly called a depressed-inhibited type. It will be noted that like Type 1, this group is overcontrolled but their intropunitiveness, anxiety, depression and social avoidance point to quite different adjustment mechanisms (Blackburn, 1969, p. 6–7).

[3]This sample comprised about 25% of the surviving murderers in England and Wales during this period (Blackburn, personal communication, 1969).

Turning to the undercontrolled types, Blackburn's Type 2 comprised 23% of his sample. This type was the most disturbed of the four groups and the pattern of scores indicated that they were impulsive and prone to acting out, but also anxious and somewhat introverted. Blackburn concluded, "They have some of the characteristics of Megargee's undercontrolled type, but as will be seen, Type 4 seems to fit the description rather better. Tentatively this group is labeled as a *paranoid-aggressive* type (Blackburn, 1969, p. 6)."

Type 4 was the smallest of Blackburn's four clusters comprising only 13% of the total. According to Blackburn:

This group is . . . marked by an absence of subjective intra-psychic distress, but reveals interpersonal difficulties characteristically dealt with by the externalization of hostility. It corresponds closely with descriptions of the primary psychopath and can be labeled with some confidence as a *psychopathic* type. It can also be identified as the undercontrolled type described by Megargee (Blackburn, 1969, p. 7).

In his discussion Blackburn stated:

How far does this support Megargee's dual typology? As we have seen, Types 1 and 4 appear to correspond quite well to the overcontrolled and undercontrolled types, and these account for more than two-fifths of the total. However, Types 3 and 2 could also be described in these terms. The most economic conclusion would appear to be that Megargee's typology is supported in that Types 1 and 3 combined, and Types 2 and 4 together represent the broad categories of overcontrolled and undercontrolled offenders, respectively (Blackburn, 1969, p. 8).

Thus the data that have been collected by independent investigators working with quite different populations indicates that this typology has some validity. My guess is that working with a British psychiatric population probably increased the incidence of the overcontrolled type in Blackburn's studies. While I have no data that bear on this, I imagine a judge or jury would be more likely to see the overcontrolled person as being disturbed and commit him to a hospital whereas the undercontrolled person would be more likely to be regarded as a "common criminal" and incarcerated or executed. Also the greater incidence of family murders and murders followed by suicide suggests a higher proportion of overcontrolled violence in England than the United States.

Let us suppose for the moment then that we can regard as valid the hypothesis that there is more than one type of violent offender.[4] This

---

[4]While we have focused on demonstrating that there is an overcontrolled type in addition to the undercontrolled type, this should not be construed as indicating that there are *only* two types of violent offenders. Those who engage in instrumental violence might constitute another type, as might essentially "normal" people driven to violence by extraordinary provocation or stress. These speculations must be checked by further research.

of course has a number of important implications for differential treatment in correctional settings:

In the case of the Undercontrolled Aggressive type, the basic therapeutic task is to increase the inhibitions against aggressive acting out. Normally such inhibitions are acquired through identification with a well-socialized parent figure with consequent introjection of his values. However, in the case of the Undercontrolled Aggressive person this has not taken place. If he is treated early enough, it might be possible to foster the growth of such controls by providing a parent substitute in the form of a case worker, clergyman, "big brother," or probation officer. Often, however, this is not feasible, so an alternative program must be used. This usually consists of providing external controls with automatic rewards for approved behavior and punishments for disapproved behavior. In order to control the schedules of reinforcement and protect society during the learning process, institutionalization is generally indicated. Such an institution may be called a camp, a school, a jail, or a penitentiary, but the basic philosophy and the basic program are usually the same.

Unfortunately, such programs are less effective than might be desired. It is difficult, even in an institutional setting optimally to schedule rewards and punishments, with the result that most inmates are on a partial-reward schedule when it comes to the expression of aggression. Instead of learning to inhibit aggression, they are more likely to form a discrimination and inhibit aggression only when they are likely to be caught. Moreover, the frustrations of life in an institution, as well as the life of an ex-convict, are likely to increase the instigation to aggression enough to offset any increase in inhibitions.

The most appropriate treatment for the Chronically Overcontrolled assaultive person, on the other hand, would be some form of psychotherapy. The goal of such therapy would be to reduce excessive inhibitions so that the individual can learn to acknowledge and accept his feelings of hostility and learn ways of expressing them which would allow some measure of need satisfaction while still not posing too great a threat to society.

If the potentially assaultive overcontrolled person is detected prior to an aggressive outburst, such a treatment program can be instituted fairly easily. However, it can be a delicate therapeutic task to remove such inhibitions in a person with a great deal of repressed hostility without precipitating either a psychotic break or excessive acting out.

Postoffense treatment on the other hand must cope not only with the problem of guilt, but also with limitations imposed by judicial procedures. If an extremely assaultive offense has been committed, it is likely that the patient will have to be treated in some form of penal institution. As noted above, the program of such institutions is to reward control and conformity and to punish assertiveness or aggression. This means that the goals of the institutional program and the therapeutic program will be at complete odds with each other. The patient will have few chances to practice assertive and mildly aggressive responses in a setting in which they are apt to be rewarded.

If an attempt were made to match the treatment program to the needs of the different types of inmates within a given institution, chaos would result. Undercontrolled Aggressive people would be punished for doing the same sorts of things that Chronically Overcontrolled people were being encouraged to do. This would naturally be interpreted as injustice and favoritism. It would, therefore, be necessary to treat the two types of offenders separately, either at different institutions or by incarcerating the Undercontrolled offender while placing the Chronically Overcontrolled person on probation with outpatient therapy. However, since the Chronically Overcontrolled assaultive person is likely to have committed the more severe offense, it would be very difficult to obtain support either from the public or from legislative bodies for such a program (Megargee, 1966b, pp. 20–21).

To the extent that the data support the typology, they also support the dynamics attributed to the two types until a more adequate causal chain is proposed and tested. The basic mechanism proposed for the over-controlled type was temporal summation and re-arousal of residual un-expressed aggressive instigation. Such notions are quite consistent with the theories of Dollard *et al.* (1939) and Freud. However, Berkowitz (1964) in his recent writings has taken issue with the concept of residual aggressive instigation remaining active over long periods of time. While it may be that the literature on catharsis and the efforts to fit aggressive phenomena into a hydraulic model have overworked the notion of sum-mation of residual instigation, it would be difficult for me to account for sudden, unprovoked explosions of violence by formerly docile, over-controlled individuals without resorting to such explanatory concepts. This does not mean that every person who inhibits his aggressive tenden-cies is perforce a volcano of potential violence, but in *some* individuals, particularly those unable to use alternative mechanisms such as displace-ment or sublimation, this does appear to be the case.

The fact that the dynamics of violence can be quite different from the dynamics of milder forms of aggression that can be studied in the lab-oratory also demonstrates that it can be hazardous to generalize from experimental studies of mild aggression to the more extreme forms of aggression such as violence. Instead violence is a topic that should be studied in its own right despite the difficulties in designing rigorous in-vestigations.

However, we got involved in this program of research because we wanted to improve our ability to assess and predict violent behavior. What are the implications of these findings for the prediction of violence? The first implication is that clinicians should pay attention to inhibition as well as to instigation. One clue that emerged was that projective tests may be particularly helpful in this regard. Although the hostile content scales of the Holtzman Inkblot Technique did not prove too useful, the movement and color scores did discriminate the samples. Similarly we have found that in college women a *failure* to give an aggressive story to a TAT card that strongly suggests aggression, particularly when told to tell the most gory possible story, is characteristic of repressed and inhibited women (Megargee, 1967). Secondly, given the ability to assess inhibitions, whether with tests or with case history data, the clinician must not fall into the trap of assuming that high inhibitions automatically rule out assaultive behavior. Instead he must remain alert for the overtly controlled but inwardly alienated individual who may be potentially violent.

The typology also had implications for the design of validation studies on tests of aggression. In the first report of this typology in 1964, I wrote:

Another implication concerns the use of aggressive subjects in the validation of psycho-logical tests. It is clear that assaultive subjects should not be indiscriminantly used as a criterion group for scales of hostility and control. At the very least, the subjects should be divided into moderate and extreme aggressive groups. If the extreme group gets a low score on a scale of hostility or a high score on a scale of control, it does not necessarily mean that the test is invalid; it may only mean that there was a high proportion of over-controlled subjects in the extremely assaultive criterion group. The investigator is safer using a criterion group of moderately assaultive subjects since it is less likely such a group contains many overcontrolled people.

Investigators should also beware of pooling data from the two types of offenders to-gether in a study of test validation. If this is done, no differences in central tendency might be found between the aggressive group and a control group since the overcontrolled and undercontrolled subjects tended to cancel one another out. The investigator might wrongly infer test invalidity (Megargee, 1964a).

Shortly after writing those words I had another of those infrequent lapses from stupidity. I recalled that while we had followed this procedure in validating everyone else's hostility scales, we had deviated from it in cross-validating our own scale. Because of the shortage of subjects, we had only used a single heterogeneous sample of violent criminals in the criterion group. Perhaps the scale might have had validity for one assaul-tive type but not for the other. Therefore I retrieved the scale from the bottom drawer and, going back over the cross-validation data, divided the violent sample into extremely assaultive and moderately assaultive sub-groups. Additional subjects who had been evaluated in the years since the initial study were added. Lo and behold I found that the ex-tremely assaultive subjects got high scores on the scale but there was little difference between moderately assaultive and nonviolent criminals. It seemed as if the scale might be differentiating the overcontrolled as-saultive type.

A series of studies were devised to test this hypothesis. Correlational studies using college students as subjects showed that the scale correlated significantly with other test measures reflecting rigidity, excessive con-trol, and repression of conflicts. Significant negative correlations were obtained with scales measuring rebelliousness, authority conflict, and manifest hostility. We also found that college women, whom we expected to be more inhibited in their expression of physical aggression, obtained significantly higher scores than college men. Failure to find a significant correlation with Edwards Social Desirability scale ($r = .12$, n.s.) provided some evidence for discriminant validity. Turning to criminal samples, a study of assaultive and homicidal Texas State Prison inmates showed that the men we had classified as "overcontrolled" on the basis of case history data in the prison files obtained significantly higher scores than a matched sample classified as undercontrolled (Megargee, Cook, & Mendelsohn, 1967.)

On the basis of these data, we published the scale, dubbing it the *O-H* or Overcontrolled Hostility scale. Since then, the most convincing evidence of its construct validity has come from a study of members of a fundamentalist religious sect who chose to go to prison rather than accept civilian service as required of conscientious objectors under the Selective Service Act of 1948. Reasoning that members of such a group must have extraordinarily high controls against the expression of physical aggression, their *O-H* scores were compared with those of other inmates of a Federal prison. Not only were the conscientious objectors' *O-H* scores significantly higher, but also 60% of them were found to have extreme scores (i.e., above a *T* score of 70) while only 10% of the other inmates had such elevated scores (Megargee, 1969b).

The mean scores obtained by the various samples that we have tested with the *O-H* scale over the years are shown in Table I. The data fall into a rather neat progression. The lowest mean raw scores, below 13, were obtained from male students and government trainees without extraordinary hostility or control. Mean scores in the middle range from about 13 to 15 were obtained by samples of criminals, who were presumably above average in hostility but not control, and from normal women, who were probably above average in control but not in aggressiveness. Scores in the upper range, above 16, were associated with extreme control and/or violence on the part of criminal samples.

To my knowledge, no validity studies of the *O-H* scale by other investigators have been published. Some data have been reported to me in personal communications by Blackburn and by Dr. Gary Fisher of the University of California at Los Angeles. Blackburn compared extremely assaultive and moderately assaultive psychiatric offenders, while Fisher compared the *O-H* scores of California prison inmates he had classified as "overcontrolled violent," "undercontrolled violent," and "nonviolent." The results of these two studies were disappointing. Although the "extremely assaultive" sample had the higher *O-H* score in Blackburn's study, and the "overcontrolled violent" had the highest in Fisher's, the differences in both cases failed to attain statistical significance. It is possible to find excuses for these failures to validate. For example in Fisher's study there was a serious racial unbalance among his groups and followup work by Howard Haven (1969) has confirmed Fisher's observations that Negroes obtain significantly higher *O-H* scores than whites.

TABLE I

MEAN *O-H* SCALE SCORES OF SAMPLES DIFFERING IN HOSTILITY AND CONTROL

		O-H raw score		
Sample	Source	N	Mean	S.D.
Extremely assaultive probation applicants	Alameda County (Calif.) Probation Dept. (ACPD)	14	18.43	4.22
Fundamentalist conscientious objectors	Federal Correctional Institution, Tallahassee, Florida (FCI)	10	18.40	2.76
Overcontrolled assaultive prison inmates	Texas State Prison (TSP)	21	16.24	2.69
Moderately assaultive probation applicants	ACPD	28	15.07	3.91
Federal prisoners (Consecutive admissions)	FCI	678	14.56	3.26
Undercontrolled assaultive prison inmates	TSP	24	14.00	2.98
Undergraduate women	University of Texas (UT)	126	14.00	3.16
Female government trainees	UT	30	13.93	2.82
Nonviolent probation applicants	ACPD	44	13.39	4.01
Male government trainees	UT	22	12.77	3.57
Undergraduate men	UT	50	12.36	2.83
Undergraduate men	UT	100	12.21	2.83

More recently, Dr. William C. White, Jr. has found that prison inmates with high *O-H* scores give significantly fewer extrapunitive and significantly more impunitive responses on the Rosenzweig P-F Study than do inmates with low *O-H* scores. In the presence of an aggressive model, both high and low *O-H* Ss increased their number of extrapunitive responses significantly, but the significant difference between the types was maintained. A nonaggressive model had no effect, however. White suggested that systematic application of the principles of imitative learning to the treatment of overcontrolled individuals might prove therapeutic but held out little hope for the efficiency of such therapy for alleviating the problems of the undercontrolled type (White, 1970).

Charles Wheeler is engaged in investigating whether inmates with high and low *O-H* scores differ in their thresholds for the recognition of tachistoscopically presented violent and nonviolent drawings. Preliminary analysis of the data indicate no such differences. If so, it would suggest that this behavior-based typology does not extend to differences in the perceptual sphere, at least in antisocial populations.

On a somewhat different level, I have become quite interested in the outstanding research on the psychophysiological correlates of aggression being done by Professor Jack Hokanson of Florida State University (Hokanson, 1970). We have recently established a laboratory at the Federal Correctional Institution in Tallahassee and are beginning to explore some of the possible bridges between our different approaches to the study of aggression.

While thus far we have been engaged in research on violence and aggression, the findings of the studies I have reported suggest that we would do well to spend some time studying nonviolent people and situations as well. Violent confrontations in our cities and on our campuses have attracted the attention of many scholars from a variety of disciplines. However, in focusing on the encounters that have led to violence, many investigators have apparently overlooked the fact that as much, if not more, could be learned through the study of potentially violent situations in which violence was somehow avoided. By comparing violence with nonviolence, it is possible to arrive at a better understanding of which factors are necessary or sufficient in the genesis of violence and, more important, of the inhibitory variables that may prevent violence in a conflict situation. On an informal basis we have done some research on nonviolent campus confrontations by interviewing students, both conservative and radical, faculty, administrators, and police. This has given us some new perspectives for our major research thrust and I hope that other investigators will also start studying nonviolence.

This then is where we stand at the end of our first decade of research, and some of our notions about the directions we might take in our second decade. What will actually occur during the forthcoming decade is, of course, anybody's guess. I am afraid our "program" of research will probably be just as happenstance and fortuitous in the years to come as it has been in the past. Hopefully, there will be a little more insight and a little less stupidity, but that remains to be seen. If you are kind enough to invite me back to New York in 1979, assuming there still *is* a New York in 1979, I will be glad to report to you on how well we have done.

REFERENCES

Bandura, A. & Walters, R. H. *Adolescent aggression.* New York: Ronald Press, 1959. Excerpts reprinted in E. I. Megargee & J. E. Hokanson (Eds.), *The dynamics of aggression: Individual, group and international analyses.* New York: Harper & Row, 1970.

Berkowitz, L. *Aggression: A social psychological analysis.* New York: McGraw-Hill, 1962.
Berkowitz, L. Aggressive cues in aggressive behavior and hostility catharsis. *Psychological Review,* 1964, **71**, 104-122.
Berkowitz, L. & LePage, A. Weapons as aggression-eliciting stimuli. *Journal of Personality and Social Psychology,* 1967, **7**, 202-207. Reprinted in E. I. Megargee & J. E. Hokanson (Eds.), *The dynamics of aggression: Individual, group and international analyses.* New York: Harper & Row, 1970.
Blackburn, R. Emotionality, extraversion and aggression in paranoid and nonparanoid schizophrenic offenders. *British Journal of Psychiatry,* 1968a, **115**, 1301-1302.
Blackburn, R. Personality in relation to extreme aggression in psychiatric offenders. *British Journal of Psychiatry,* 1968b, **114**, 821-828.
Blackburn, R. Personality patterns in homicide: A typological analysis of abnormal offenders. Paper presented at the Fifth International Meeting of Forensic Sciences, Toronto, Canada, June, 1969.
Brown, P. E. & Elliott, R. Control of aggression in a nursery school class. *Journal of Experimental Child Psychology,* 1965, **2**, 103-107. Reprinted in E. I. Megargee & J. E. Hokanson (Eds.), *The dynamics of aggression: Individual, group and international analyses.* New York: Harper & Row, 1970.
Buss, A. *The psychology of aggression.* New York: Wiley, 1961.
Dollard, J., Doob, L. W., Miller, N. E., Mowrer, O. H , & Sears, R. R. *Frustration and aggression.* New Haven: Yale Univer. Press, 1939. Excerpts reprinted in E. I. Megargee & J. E. Hokanson (Eds.), *The dynamics of aggression: Individual, group and international analyses.* New York: Harper & Row, 1970.
Haven, H. Racial differences on the MMPI *O-H* scale. *FCI Research Reports,* 1969, **1**(6), 1-18. Federal Correctional Institution, Tallahasee, Florida, 32304.
Hokansen, J. E. Psychophysiological evaluation of the catharsis hypothesis. In E. I. Megargee & J. E. Hokanson (Eds.), *The dynamics of aggression: Individual, group and international analyses.* New York: Harper & Row, 1970.
MacDonald, J. M. Homicidal threats. *American Journal of Psychiatry,* 1967, **124**(4), 61-68.
Megargee, E. I. *Undercontrol and overcontrol in assaultive and homicidal adolescents.* (Doctoral dissertation, University of California, Berkeley). Ann Arbor, Michigan: University Microfilms, 1964a, No. 64-9923.
Megargee, E. I. The utility of the Rosenzweig Picture-Frustration Study in detecting assaultiveness among juvenile delinquents. Paper read at Southwestern Psychological Association, San Antonio, Texas, April 1964b.
Megargee, E. I. Assault with intent to kill. *Trans-Action,* 1965a, **2**(6), 27-31.
Megargee, E. I. The relation between barrier scores and aggressive behavior. *Journal of Abnormal Psychology,* 1965b, **70**, 307-311.
Megargee, E. I. A reply to Robins. *Trans-Action,* 1965c, **3**(1), 45.
Megargee, E. I. (Ed.). *Research in clinical assessment.* New York: Harper & Row, 1966a.
Megargee, E. I. Undercontrolled and overcontrolled personality types in extreme antisocial aggression. *Psychological Monographs,* 1966b, **80**, (3, Whole No. 611). Excerpts reprinted in E. I. Megargee & J. E. Hokanson (Eds.), *The dynamics of aggression: Individual, group and international analyses.* New York: Harper & Row, 1970.
Megargee, E. I. Hostility on the TAT as a function of defensive inhibition and stimulus situation. *Journal of Projective Techniques and Personality Assessment,* 1967, **31**(4), 73-79.
Megargee, E. I. *The assessment of violence with psychological tests.* Report prepared for the National Commission on the Causes and Prevention of Violence, Task Force III: Individual Acts of Violence. Washington: National Commission on the Causes and Prevention of Violence, 1969a.

Megargee, E. I. Conscientious objectors' scores on the MMPI *O-H* (Overcontrolled Hostility) scale. *Proceedings of the 77th Annual Convention of the American Psychological Association*. Washington: APA, 1969b, 507–508.

Megargee, E. I. The psychology of violence: A critical review of the theories of violence. In D. J. Mulvihill and M. M. Tumin (Eds.), *Crimes of violence: A staff report to the National Commission on the Causes and Prevention of Violence*. N.C.C.P.V. Staff Report Series, Vol. 13. Washington, D.C.: U.S. Government Printing Office, 1969c, 1037–1115.

Megargee, E. I. The prediction of violence with psychological tests. In C. D. Spielberger (Ed.), *Current Topics in Clinical and Community Psychology*, Vol. 2. New York: Academic Press, 1970.

Megargee, E. I. & Cook, P. E. The relation of TAT and inkblot aggressive content scales with each other and with criteria of overt aggressiveness in delinquents. *Journal of Projective Techniques and Personality Assessment*, 1967, **31**, 48–60.

Megargee, E. I., Cook, P. E., & Mendelsohn, G. A. Development and evaluation of an MMPI scale of assaultiveness in overcontrolled individuals. *Journal of Abnormal Psychology*, 1967, **72**, 519–528.

Megargee, E. I. & Mendelsohn, G. A. A cross-validation of twelve MMPI indices of hostility and control. *Journal of Abnormal and Social Psychology*, 1962, **65**, 431–438. Reprinted in E. I. Megargee (Ed.), *Research in clinical assessment*. New York: Harper & Row, 1966.

Megargee, E. I. & Mendelsohn, G. A. Assessment and dynamics of murderous aggression: A progress report. Paper presented at the meeting of the California Psychological Association, San Francisco, December, 1963.

Molof, M. J. *Differences between assaultive and nonassaultive juvenile offenders in the California Youth Authority*. Research report no. 51, Division of Research, State of California, Department of the Youth Authority, February, 1967.

Robins, L. N. Psychology of the killer. *Trans-Action*, 1965, **3**(1), 55–56.

Toch, H. *The social psychology of violence*. Division 8 invited address, American Psychological Association Meeting, New York, September 1966. Reprinted in E. I. Megargee & J. E. Hokanson (Eds.), *The dynamics of aggression: Individual, group and international analyses*. New York: Harper & Row, 1970.

Toch, H. *Violent men*. Chicago: Aldine, 1969.

Wheeler, L. & Caggiula, A. R. The contagion of aggression. *Journal of Experimental Social Psychology*, 1966, **2**, 1–10.

White, W. C. Selective modeling in youthful offenders with high and low *O-H* (Overcontrolled-hostility) personality types. Unpublished doctoral dissertation, Florida State University, 1970.

Wolfgang, M. E. Victim-precipitated criminal homicide. *Journal of Criminal Law, Criminology, and Police Science*, 1957, **48**, 1–11.

CHAPTER VI

THE STUDY AND MODIFICATION OF INTRA-FAMILIAL VIOLENCE[1]

MORTON BARD

THE CITY COLLEGE,
THE CITY UNIVERSITY OF NEW YORK

> *"And Cain talked with Abel, his brother: and it came to pass, when they were in the field, that Cain rose up against Abel his brother, and slew him (Genesis 4:8)."*

In the year 1965, seven brothers were slain by their brothers in New York City. But, also, two sisters were killed by their sisters, while eleven sons and thirteen daughters were murdered by their mothers; and five sons and one daughter, by their fathers. Forty wives were dispatched by their husbands and seventeen husbands by their wives. In all, close family relationships accounted for 35% of all homicides in that year. Indeed, in fewer than 20% of all homicides were the victim and perpetrator complete strangers (N.Y.C. Police Dept., 1966). About 40% of aggravated assaults and rapes (constituting most of the serious crimes against the person) take place within the victim's home (Ennis, 1967). These statistics are close to the national average in both urban and rural areas. Cross-national studies yield similar findings throughout western society.

[1]The project described herein is supported in part by the Office of Law Enforcement Assistance, United States Department of Justice, Training Grant No. 157, with the co-operation and support of the New York City Police Department and The City College of The City University of New York.

To put it succinctly, as Malinowski (1948) did, "aggression like charity begins at home (p. 286)," As our society debates the specter of mass violence, how surprisingly little more than the scriptural account of Cain and Abel have we to draw upon in understanding the origins of human aggression?

Down through the years aggression has occupied the attention of count-less psychologists, sociologists, and anthropologists, and, more recently, the biologically oriented ethologists. The aggression debate has grown more heated . . . always seeming to rest in the same polarized position where: (1) aggression is seen as the directly instinctual residue of evolu-tionary development and (2) aggression is regarded as being a directly learned or culturally conditioned response. The simple fact is that neither extreme position appears to apply to *human* aggression. In each case, the extremists choose to ignore multi-disciplinary evidence that human aggression is a highly complex phenomenon, involving *at least* elements of both positions.

Perhaps it would be useful to summarize briefly a selected number of the approaches among the different disciplines. The ethologists have assumed the most unambigious and self-confident position. Both Lorenz (1966) and Ardrey (1966), reasoning from observations of animal be-havior, have attempted to establish that aggression is an invariable, genetically determined, and highly specific response pattern. If learning is involved at all, they maintain, it is in the development of socially adaptive outlets for the discharge of instinctually-rooted aggressive impulses. While simplistically appealing, their position suffers from the failure to account for the enormous range of stimuli which can evoke aggressive responses in man or to account for, as Mead (1967) has suggested, the symbolic capacity of man to discriminate among a range of aggressive responses. Nevertheless, the position of the ethologists is clear—man is innately aggressive and his responses are purely and simply evolu-tionary extensions of his biological past.

Most prominent among the psychological theories are those of Freud and the schools of psychoanalysis, as well as those of a reawakened and popular behaviorist approach. The advocates of modern behaviorism generally emphasize the more specific aspects of aggression—they con-cern themselves entirely with determining aggressive habit strength as a highly specific learned response.

The psychoanalytic schools, on the other hand, have experienced some of their greatest disharmonies on the theoretical issue of aggression. Freud's ideas on the subject underwent constant change (Freud, 1948). At first, when totally absorbed with libido theory, he relegated aggression to a minor role as a largely instinctual consequence of the stages of psycho-sexual development. However, later, when he became concerned with the question of the "ego instincts," particularly with that of self-preservation, aggression was his major emphasis. He then theorized that aggressive urges were reactive rather than biologically instinctive. It was this position that was to become central in the frustration-aggression hypothesis of Dollard and his associates (Dollard *et al.*, 1939). Freud's final theory, however, was that of the "death-instinct" and was both a pessimistic and more inevitable view of the instinctive roots of aggression, and he remained in the end much more faithful to his essentially biological approach to behavior.

However, psychologists, in addition to theorizing about aggression, have devoted themselves to the scientific study of the phenomenon: most typically in the laboratory. Through ingenious experimental methods, a considerable literature has emerged; much of it, while rooted in scientific method, suffers the constraints of "control" and hence of "artificiality." As Megargee has noted, "generally the psychological experiments on aggression are disappointing . . . laboratory studies on aggression have largely been confined to unruly student behavior, hostile reactions to frustrating psychologists, and the willingness of students to give each other electric shocks (Megargee, 1966, pp. 29–30)."

The sociologists and anthropologists, on the other hand, have somehow managed to avoid the nature-nurture controversy in theory construction and in study. Not confined to rigorous and often artificial laboratory conditions in order to test their theories, sociologists and anthropologists have achieved a much greater consensus through intensive study of social process and cross-cultural observation: to them, the origins of aggression are more convincingly social and cultural. Of all disciplines, it is the field of social conflict which may have most significantly contributed to our understanding of aggression. In fact, the turn-of-the-century social theorist George Simmel (1955) showed himself to be remarkable congruent with the "reactive" period of Freud's speculations on the issue of human aggression.

Indeed, the theories of psychologist Freud and sociologist Simmel were in agreement with those of anthropologist Malinowski (1948, p. 286) and finally, surprisingly, with ethologist Lorenz (1966). For the purposes of this discussion, most relevant is Simmel's proposition that antagonism is a central feature of intimate social relations; that the closer and more intimate an association, the greater likelihood of aggression and violence. It should be noted that, while Simmel and Freud referred to aggressive *feelings* in the social context, it was the anthropologist Malinowski (1948, p. 286) who pointed out that aggressive *behavior* also occurs more readily in close social relations. Even Lorenz's observations of animal interaction led him to say that "intraspecific aggression can certainly exist without its counterpart, love, but conversely there is no love without aggression (Lorenz, 1966, p. 217)." The theories of all four, then, can be said to coalesce in the proposition: *the intensity of aggressive interaction is related to the closeness of relationships.*

Unfortunately, it is probable that no single theory will ever explain the wide variety of human aggressive behaviors. However, as social scientists we are obliged to continue our explorations and to extend our understanding of human behavior within its social and psychological matrix. Most academicians and most professionals are isolated from the fields of social action and, when they do venture into the community, they study safe and well-established social systems. There is a real reluctance to become involved in new sub-systems . . . usually rationalized by the deification of "pure" rather than "applied" research. Fairweather (1967) recently indicted academic psychologists as being particularly devoted to "pure" research in the mistaken belief that emulation of the methods of the physical sciences will make for greater respectability. But as Sanford (1965) has pointed out, "the psychologists' naive conception of science has led them to adopt the more superficial characteristics of the physical sciences." "This," he maintains, "has made it difficult for them to study genuine human problems. . . ."

The greatest impetus for the study of "genuine human problems" undoubtedly occurred with the report by the Joint Commission on Mental Health and Illness (1961). The Commission brought into focus the nation's overwhelming mental health problem, the manpower shortages in the field, the appalling disregard of preventive approaches, and the inadequacy of services available to the large "silent" segments of our society. The report and subsequent legislated financial support stimulated critical self-appraisal among social scientists in general and among mental health professionals in particular. "Community mental health" and "community psychology" were to become bywords largely related to the Community Mental Health Act of 1963. Early efforts to meet the intent of the Act saw traditional approaches cloaked in the vestments of novelty; the uncomfortable realization grew that the mental health professions were imprisoned by their traditional pasts in attempting to satisfy the terms of the Act. If anything, frustrating attempts at innovation revealed that perhaps other disciplines such as sociology and anthropology were more suited by tradition and training to respond to the need for imaginative community programs than were psychologists and psychiatrists.

The approach to be described here should be viewed in this evolutionary context. It rests on the conviction that preventive intervention as a service strategy enhances the community's availability as a research laboratory in ways which cannot be realized by hospital or clinic-based service programs; that existing community institutions which characteristically deal with "genuine human problems" can be effectively utilized to modify behavior while at the same time affording unprecedented study opportunities (Bard, 1969a).

In large urban centers, rapid social change, alienation, increasing population density, and ever more complex economic competition conspire to subject the family and the individual to exacting pressures. For the disadvantaged in urban society, the personal effects may be extreme. Frustration, despair, and hopelessness can make for a volatile aggressive mixture largely kept inert by a system of social regulation which is the very embodiment of control. The police may be regarded simply as a domestic army which keeps civilian order, or they may be regarded as individuals involved in highly complex functions that extend far beyond mere repression. Cummings (1968) recently pointed out that, "although the policeman stood for control, much of his role inevitably involved support (p. 175)" and that more than one-half of the appeals to the police involve requests for assistance with personal and interpersonal problems. On the other hand, the police are also the only social institution specifically charged with managing real or threatened violence. Their intimate knowledge of violence and aggression is unparalleled by any others concerned with human behavior. Indeed, a policeman's ability to understand and deal with aggressive potentials often has critical survival value for him . . . a factor certainly absent in the pure setting of the experimental laboratory. That policemen often fail in their efforts to judge aggressive potentials is attested to by the fact that 22% of the policemen killed in the line of duty are slain while intervening in "disturbances" among people, most frequently in families (FBI Law Enforcement Bulletin, 1963).

The opportunity to develop a service program utilizing general police officers as psychological intervention agents offered the prospect of achieving the goals of both crime prevention and preventive mental health. In addition, such an approach held promise or revealing insights into aspects of human aggression and violence as it occurs in naturalistic settings. Also inherent in such an approach was the possibility of providing doctoral students in clinical psychology with an unusual consultative training experience; to have students exposed to atypical human problem situations, the kind precluded by traditional training in clinics and hospitals (Singer & Bard, 1969).

In recent years, there has been a growing recognition of the extent to which the family shapes the personalities of children and of the complexity by which that shaping occurs. The importance of the family environment in the genesis of behavior pathology is well documented. The results of these investigations suggest that early identification of an intervention in families where parents live in a perpetual state of hateful and sadistic involvement may have significant preventive mental health implications for their children. Most disordered families are diagnosed and treated only after breakdown has occurred and only after seeking help. Families who seek help are generally well educated and sophisticated in mental health matters; they come from the middle and upper classes and usually have the resources and awareness requisite to seeking help. Undoubtedly there are large numbers of families in difficulty whose class and educational limitations prevent their identification by usual mental health case-finding methods. The families who lack knowledge and sophistication in matters pertaining to mental health resources may be those most likely to involve the police when family crisis approaches breakdown (Bard, 1969b).

Consistent with the foregoing, a program in police family crisis intervention was designed to provide a unique service to a West Harlem community of about 85,000 bordering on The City College campus (Bard & Berkowitz, 1967). The residents are mostly working class and black, with a sprinkling of Latin Americans (8%) and whites (2%); a socially stabile, residential community.

The project consisted of three stages: Preparatory Phase, for selection of police personnel and their training; an Operational Phase, in which the Family Crisis Unit functioned with regular consultative support by the staff of The Psychological Center of The City College; and an Evaluative Phase for analysis of data.

PREPARATORY PHASE

During the first month of the project, 18 patrolmen were selected from among 45 volunteers. No effort was made to induce participation except by the offer of three college credits to be granted by the John Jay College of Criminal Justice of The City University. Selection was based on brief interviews to determine motivation, sensitivity, and stability. Applicants were required to have a minimum of three years' service and a maximum of ten. Nine white and nine black officers were selected for eventual biracial pairing.

For an entire month following selection, the men were released from all duties to engage in an intensive training program which included lectures, "self-understanding" workshops, field trips, discussion groups, and a unique opportunity to "learn by doing." Three brief plays depicting family crisis situations were specially written and performed by professional actors. Each play was performed three consecutive times with interventions by a pair of policemen in each instance. Each pair of policemen was unaware of the events which preceded their entrance. The plays had no scripted conclusions, the actors having been instructed to improvise to the behavior of the officers when they entered the scene. The value of the experience was to enable the members of the unit to see how the same set of circumstances could have entirely different outcomes, dependent upon the nature of their intervention. The technique proved particularly meaningful to the officers. The practice interventions were subjected to extensive critique and review by all members of the unit. Particular emphasis in training was placed upon sensitizing the men to their own values and attitudes about human behavior in general and about disrupted families in particular.

OPERATIONAL PHASE

At the conclusion of training, the Family Crisis Unit began its operations. For a 22-month period one precinct radio car was designated as the family car, to be dispatched on all family disturbance complaints regardless of the sector of their occurrence in the precinct. In other words, departing from usual practice, the family car could leave its own patrol sector even if the disturbance was within the jurisdiction of another sector car. A special duty chart permitted 24-hour-a-day coverage by members of the unit. A file of family disturbance reports was kept in the car for ready reference on the way to a dispute. This practice enabled the officers to know of previous interventions, if any, and of their outcomes. During the 22-month study period, the policemen of a neighboring precinct have been completing family disturbance reports in all instances of domestic disturbance. We are hopeful that these data will be useful in evaluating the project.

An added feature of operations was the regularly scheduled consultation for each member of the unit. Once each week the eighteen men appeared on campus in groups of six for individual consultation and debriefing with advanced graduate students in clinical psychology. In addition, each six-man group met with a professional group leader for the purpose of on-going discussion of a broad range of issues relevant to family crisis intervention. Naturally, both experiences enhanced data collection, making possible additional, more in-depth information than could be provided by family disturbance reports alone.

EVALUATIVE PHASE

The project has just entered its evaluative phase, after two years. The unit continues to function as a regular feature of the 30th Precinct's service to the community. However, while the men no longer have regularly scheduled consultations, The Psychological Center staff maintains "on call" availability for any member of the Family Crisis Unit.

The project is over and the task of data analysis is in its earliest stages (Bard, 1970a). It is expected that the data will be subjected to multi-correlation analysis, providing us with deeper insights into intra-familial violence. In addition, data analysis will provide the basis for methodologic refinements of the relatively crude methods employed in this project. Perhaps it is wise to regard the present effort as a reconnaissance, "where the most we can expect is to isolate useful questions and promising avenues of exploration rather than to aim for definitive answers (Parad & Caplan, 1963, p. 316)."

During the course of the project's 22-month operational phase, the members of the Family Crisis Intervention Unit serviced 962 families on 1375 separate occasions. At the moment, this largely unanalyzed mass of data only suggests the wisdom of Tolstoy's observation in *Anna Karenina* that "happy families resemble one another; each unhappy family is unhappy in its own way." Eventually, however, we should be able to define the nature of at least the kind of unhappiness that requires police intervention.

In the 22 months of operation by the Family Unit, we have been impressed by the fact that there has not been a homicide in any family previously known to the unit. While family homicides in the precinct increased overall, in each case there had been no prior police intervention. Further analysis will be necessary to understand the significance of this finding, but at least one possibility suggests itself. Gilula and Daniels' (1969) recent distinction between aggression and violence may suggest an explanation. They define aggression as an entire spectrum of assertive, intrusive and attacking behaviors, including a range of overt and covert attacks. They regard violence, on the other hand, as the distinct intent to do physical damage . . . intense, uncontrolled, excessive, sudden, and seemingly purposeless. It may be that calls to the police occur in the context of a range of aggressive acts; the violence occurs with such sudden and unpredictable fury that it occurs before police intervention can be sought.

It may be also that "class-linked" aggressive patterns need to be more clearly understood. There may well be a distinction, for example, between the aggression of lower class life, which is regarded as "normal," and violence, which is regarded as "abnormal."[2] It is well known that child-rearing practices of the middle and upper classes proscribe overt aggression as unacceptable behavior. Unlike the lower class, "don't hit" is a primary parental prohibition. Class differences of this order would lead to the hypothesis that, while police may be called less frequently for domestic disputes in middle and upper class communities, when they are, the behaviors are likely to be more violently serious. That is, since even minimal aggressive expression is denied to the middle and upper classes, when aggression is expressed, it is likely to be "excessive, uncontrolled, and sudden." We hope in the future to test this hypothesis through the operation of police family intervention units in middle and upper class areas.

We have been particularly impressed by the remarkable absence of injury to the 18 men engaged in this highest hazard program. It is estimated that 40% of injuries sustained by police occur while they are intervening in family disputes. In fact, most policemen regard a family dispute as among the most noxious and dangerous of all assignments. The 18-man unit, exposed for more than would ordinarily be the case to this dangerous event, sustained only one minor injury to one man during the course of the project. This remarkable absence of injury to a group of officers exposed to highly volatile aggressive situations strongly suggests the importance of the role played by the victim in the exacerbation of violence. Only recently, a new field of "victimology" has emerged in which the focus has begun to shift so that it is placed at least equally on the victim as well as perpertrator. Sarbin (1967) recently pointed out that danger connotes a relationship and that assaultive or violent behavior described as dangerous "can be understood as the predictable outcome of certain antecedent and concurrent conditions (p. 286)." Sarbin believes that degradation procedures within role-relationships which transform an individual's social identity to the status of a "non-person" is evocative of dangerous behavior. Since a policeman's work is such that he is always

[2]There is a suggestion of this in Davis' classic paper on child rearing within class and ethnic structures in American society: "The lower classes not uncommonly teach their children and adolescents to strike out with fist or knife and to be certain to hit first. Both girls and boys at adolescence may curse their father to his face or even attack him with fists, sticks, or axes in free-for-all family encounters. Husbands and wives sometimes stage pitched battles in the home; wives have their husbands arrested; and husbands when locked out try to break in or burn down their own houses. Such fights with fists or weapons and the whipping of wives occur sooner or later in most lower-class families. ... physical aggression is as much a normal, socially approved, and socially inculcated type of behavior as it is in frontier communities." (Davis, W. A. Child rearing in the class structure of American society, In M. B. Sussman (Ed.), *Sourcebook of marriage and the family.* Boston: Houghton, Mifflin, 1963, pp. 225–231.)

ready to classify the conduct of others as potentially dangerous, he may engage in degrading kinds of power displays which provoke the expected "wild beast" response. The officers in our project, through their sensitivity training, awareness of the language of behavior, and security in their mediation skills, may have learned to avoid fear-inspired premature power displays, thus avoided depriving their potentially violent clients of their social identity and hence avoided potentiating violence directed at *themselves*.

Another possible explanation may be based on the medical concept of iatrogenesis: physicians have long recognized that an authority with the power of life and death has the capacity to induce profound and unexpected changes in the course of diagnosis or treatment. The term refers simply to a disorder resulting from the actions of the physician during his ministrations. In other words, the very actions undertaken to relieve a disorder may in themselves create still further disorder.

While the physician is an authority with the power of life and death in dealing with *physical* disorder, the policeman is a life and death authority in instances of *social* disorder. The implications in this analogy, if valid, suggest the necessity for a re-examination of some of the basic assumptions of law enforcement.

The experiment in family crisis intervention shows promise of demonstrating that policemen provided with skills appropriate to the complexities of today's social existence succeed in minimizing violence which might otherwise be exacerbated by their well-meant but inept performance. Consider for a moment the bizarre paradox in our urban ghettos that, while the police are hated, feared and envied, they are the ghetto resident's primary resource in times of sickness, injury or trouble. For the economically disenfranchised, long disillusioned by unfulfilled promises of help and service, the police officer represents the ordinarily unattainable: a reliable source of help, instantly available *for any human problem*. If, however, the helpseeker's expectations are met by simplistic behaviors of repression consistent with a bygone era of law enforcement, resultant frustration, bitterness, and resentment may easily escalate to a violent outcome.

It is increasingly clear that most of a policeman's daily activity in today's society centers upon interpersonal service; indeed, it has been estimated that as much as 90% of his working time may entail such functions. Yet, little of the police officer's training prepares him to render these services with skill and compassion. In general, police training programs and police organizational structures are based upon questionable assumptions in the world of today. The notion that a policeman is simply a watchman over property or the strong repressor of the law breaker is just no longer realistic. Indeed, such ideas are just as outmoded as is the cherished fantasy of the legendary sheriff of frontier days, whose most valued posture was tough imperviousness to feelings and tight-lipped readiness to neutralize conflict by a quick draw in the middle of Main Street.

One can only speculate on the effects that such highly valued aspects of folk culture have had in shaping present-day police behavior. After all, films and television have furnished countless youngsters with simple formula solutions to the struggle between good and evil; outcomes which rest ultimately upon the triumph of good through the power of the six-shooter. Even casual observation of most American peace officers will testify to the modeling effectiveness of this steady diet of Hollywood "folk art." Just as young baseball players emulate the expressive movements of admired senior ballplayers, so do young policemen engage in a language of behavior which communicates the self-image of the determined, pistol-ready suppressor of evil.

If correct, such a limited law enforcement perspective, when supported by outmoded police organizational structures, has volatile potentials. It seriously limits the police officer's repertoire of response patterns and increases the likelihood of iatrogenic violence. Fantasy-based power displays, inappropriately applied in situations which call for a different kind of police response, are in themselves evocative of violence. Social conditions such as an exploding population, increased social mobility, and changes in family patterns have given the police responsibilities which require sensitive, reality-based skills unforeseen as recently as twenty years ago. To persist in training police for roles that are no longer viable is to contribute still further to social unrest and to encourage iatrogenic violence (Bard, 1970b).

Very recently, we completed a partial analysis of 300 interventions (i.e., 21% of the total). It is interesting to note that of this preliminary sample, 32% of the complainants reported physical violence, while 16% reported the threat of violence. It is of further interest to note, however, that although violence is a factor in almost one-half of the complaints, on arrival at the scene, the police are most frequently (30%) requested to arbitrate, mediate, or advise the disputants. In this connection, the specially trained officers have acquitted themselves well. In the comparison precinct, when police make referrals in family disputes, it is to the Family Court 95% of the time. No referrals are made to social and mental health agencies. In the experimental precinct, 45% of the referrals are made to Family Court and 55% to twenty different social and mental health agencies. In addition, there were about 22% fewer arrests in the experimental precinct than in the comparison precinct in relation to the number of family interventions. The lower rate of arrests in the experimental precinct is suggestive of the greater use of referral resources and of mediation. One can only speculate on the financial saving in reducing the burden on the courts by reducing the referral of inappropriate cases and by reducing the number of arrests. It is well known that upon reaching the courts, and long after the heated dispute has cooled, most complaints of this type are dropped anyway. Sophisticated police intervention can provide immediate mediation service but can also serve as a preliminary screening mechanism for final resolution of family disharmony.

The following case will illustrate the approach of two family unit patrolmen in one case involving threatened violence:

> On arrival at a small apartment, the officers were informed by an older woman that her married daughter had become enraged, had begun throwing dishes, threatened suicide by jumping out a window, and threatened the complainant and her own 12-year-old child with violence. The officers quickly calmed the agitated woman and learned that she had been depressed since her divorce six months earlier and on that particular day had returned from a frustrating visit to the bank, where she was unable to get her alimony check processed in less than 2 weeks. After decompressing the situation and eliciting the information, the officers took Mrs. C. to the bank, where they were able to arrange to have her checks processed in three days from then on.
>
> Suspecting that Mrs. C.'s emotional difficulties extended beyond her financial difficulties, they suggested a psychiatric consultation and they then escorted her to the Medical Center. A psychiatrist found her to be profoundly depressed, suicidal, and homicidal and recommended immediate hospitalization. The patient readily accepted the suggestion and was accompanied to Bellevue by the officers.
>
> In their report, the officers stated that it was their impression that Mrs. C. was profoundly depressed and that it had been precipitated by the divorce. They felt the incident at the bank reflected her inability to accept the reality of the divorce.

As in this case, many of the reports of violence are accompanied by the expectation that the police will remedy the grievance in the role of dispassionate third party. In fewer than 8% of the preliminary sample was an initial request made to have the other person arrested. Clearly, then, appeals to the police are in the nature of requests for authority and objectivity in the resolution of conflict—not for enforcement of law. It would appear that, while aggression may be socially and culturally sanctioned, there may be self-regulated limitations to the permissibility of violence.

Our preliminary analysis of 300 cases indicates that the family dispute is largely a matter of marital dispute. In 80% of the cases, the disputants were married (48% legally, 24% common law) or were separated (8%). Violent confrontations between adolescents and a parent accounted for 15% of the cases. In a surprising number of these cases it is our impression that parents appeal to the police to act as a more effective authority in disciplining or controlling an adolescent. A case in point:

> Mr. S. called the police with the following complaint: "My daughter stayed out late and was drinking. I want you to talk to her — I can't do anything with her." The responding officers determined the following: the 17-year-old daughter went out, drank, and did not return until 11:30. The father struck her and then called the police. Father stated that this eldest of his 10 children is rebellious, will not help in the house, and generally is the most difficult of all the children. The daughter appeared to the officers to be intoxicated. The other daughters in the family described their father as overly strict and unwilling to let any of them leave the house in the evening.
>
> The officers devoted considerable time to counseling the family. In the end, agreement was achieved by all concerned, including the daughter in question, to visit a local social agency for further counseling.

By the way, children were present in 41% of the interventions. If this is typical, one can only speculate on the modeling effects of parental aggression on such children — not to speak of the effects of a variety of police behaviors on the perceptions of children in such situations. One of our students has become interested in learning about the effects of observing parental violence upon perceptual processes and fantasy in these children.

It is difficult to know the kind of impact the program has had on the community as a whole. There are indirect signs that its presence has been felt. For one thing, the number of calls for family disturbance intervention has steadily declined over the two-year period, while the number of calls in the comparison precinct has remained constant. One possible explanation is that successful resolution or referral of initial cases has cut down the chronic or repeat cases. Yet, at the same time, there have been referrals made to the police unit by families who have been served and, hence, some increase might have been expected. The neighborhood grapevine has it that there are some "special family cops" who are O.K. In fact, the men have noted that, when their car rolls into a street (its number is apparently known), people fail to "freeze" as they would when just any police car appears. Also, after initial skepticism, other policemen in the area have grown to respect the work of the unit and to be grateful for its existence.

In no small measure, whatever the success the program has had is traceable to the fact that the professional identity of the officers has been preserved. They are not specialists in that they perform family crisis intervention to the exclusion of all other police functions. On the contrary, they are continuously engaged in regular police patrol but are available to provide family intervention when needed. In this instance, we have avoided role identity confusion — an often vexing problem when individuals are expected to provide services congenial with mental health goals. The policemen in the family unit have little doubt that they are policemen — they do not regard themselves as psychologists or social workers, nor do they perform as such. They restore the peace and maintain order, but it is "how" they do it that is the measure of their success.

We expect to learn a great deal about an aspect of social conflict resolution about which little is known. The nine teams of patrolmen in the unit have, in almost two years of operation, developed team styles of intervention. While we do not have detailed insight as yet, we do have certain impressions. There are some approaches which appear to be universal — for example, to separate the disputants, neutralize the potential violence, and then for each officer to engage in a dialogue with one of the disputants with as much privacy as possible. It is at this point that stylistic differences begin to show themselves. For instance, in one team of officers each characteristically then switches to the other disputant for a private chat and finally all four engage in a group discussion. Each takes a disputant as a client and then, with the two disputants watching, often in amazement, the two officers heatedly argue the case. This technique appears to sufficiently objectify the situation for disputants to permit meaningful discussion to follow.

One of the more satisfying dimensions of the project has been the opportunity to constructively utilize the unique qualities of policemen. The collaboration of police officers and social scientists to gain greater understanding of human behavior has proven itself to be quite tenable. Policemen have sharply-honed powers of observation; a skill with adaptive survival value for them. The successful employment of this skill in the service of the community and in the service of science has been only one of the exciting facets of this action research program.

We believe that this pioneering experimental social innovation involving a sub-system usually avoided by psychologists will encourage further research within existing community institutions. Even the present effort, which was more concerned with content than with elegance of form, will prove to be a forerunner of more sophisticated community psychology action research.

Our approach can be described as a relevent method for the study of human aggression and violence in its social and psychological matrix. It is action research — concerned with the world of real people, living as real people live. Clearly, if we are to understand the origins of violence and aggression, we must study the basic family unit, for there is undeniable evidence that violence is a family affair. Our method provided a novel research framework while at the same time it brought together the unlikeliest of bedfellows—law enforcement and mental health. But in both, the emphasis was on the prevention of crime and upon early and effective intervention and hence prevention of emotional disorder. But, above all, effective community psychology action research should be designed to effect change and innovation in existing social institutions while at the same time offering otherwise unavailable opportunities for research leading to the increase in our knowledge of man's behavior.

REFERENCES

Ardrey, R. *The territorial imperative*. New York: Atheneum, 1966.

Bard, M. Extending psychology's impact through existing community institutions. *American Psychologist,* **24,** 1969a, 610–612.

Bard, M. Family intervention police teams as a community mental health resource. *Journal of Criminal Law, Criminology and Police Science, 60,* 1969b, 247–250.

Bard, M. *Training police as specialists in family crisis intervention: Final report.* Washington, D.C.: U.S. Government Printing Office, 1970a.

Bard, M. Alternatives to traditional law enforcement. In F. F. Karten, S. W. Cook, & J. S. Lacey (Eds.), *Psychology and the problems of Society.* Washington, D.C.: American Psychological Association, 1970b, 128–132.

Bard, M. & Berkowitz, B. Training police as specialists in family crisis intervention: A community psychology action program. *Community Mental Health Journal, 3,* 1967, 315–317.

Cummings, E. *Systems of social regulation.* New York: Atherton Press, 1968.

Davis, W. A. Child rearing in the class structure of American society. In M. B. Sussman (Ed.), *Sourcebook of marriage and the family.* Boston: Houghton, Mifflin, 1963.

Dollard, J. *et al. Frustration and Aggression.* New Haven: Yale Univer. Press, 1939.

Ennis, P. H. Crime, victims and the police. *Transaction,* June, 1967, 36–44.

Fairweather, G. W. *Methods for Experimental Social Innovation.* New York: John Wiley & Sons, 1967.

FBI Law Enforcement Bulletin, January, 1963, 27.

Freud, S. *Group psychology and the analysis of the ego.* London: The Hogarth Press, 1948.

Gilula, M. F. & Daniels, G. Violence and man's struggle to adapt. *Science,* 1969, **164,** 396–405.

Joint Commission on Mental Health and Illness. Final Report: *Action for Mental Health.* New York: Basic Books, 1961.

Lorenz, K. *On Aggression.* New York: Harcourt, Brace & World, 1966.

Malinowski, B. An anthropological analysis of war. *Magic, Science and Religion.* Glencoe, Ill.: Free Press, 1948.

Mead, M. Alternatives to war. (In The anthropology of armed conflict and aggression.) *Natural History,* Dec., 1967, 65–69.

Megargee, E. I. Assault with intent to kill. *Transaction,* Sept./Oct. 1966, 28–31.

New York City Police Department. Press Release No. 30, March 31, 1966.

Parad, H. J. & Caplan, G. A framework for studying families in crisis. In M. B. Sussmen, (Ed.), *Source book in marriage and the family.* (2nd ed.) Boston: Houghton & Mifflin Co., 1963.

Sanford, N. Will psychologists study human problems. *American Psychologist,* 1965, **20,** 192–202.

Sarbin, T. The dangerous individual an outcome of social identity transformation. *British Journal of Criminology,* July, 1967, 285–295.

Simmel, George. *Conflict and the web of group affiliations.* Glencoe, Ill.: Free Press, 1955.

Singer, J. L. & Bard, M. Community consultation in the doctoral education of clinical psychologists. *The Clinical Psychologist,* Winter, 1969, 79–83.

AUTHOR INDEX

Numbers in italics refer to the pages on which the complete references are listed.

SUBJECT INDEX

171